PROUD AND LONELY

Proud and Lonely is a new history of science fiction and its fans in Australia. It tells the story of its arrival in Australia in the 1920s, and the start here of a sub-culture of fans of the genre.

Dr Leigh Edmonds shows how science fiction was seen as a low form of literature and didn't get public acceptance until at least the 1970s. Because of the frequent ridicule, fans of the genre kept quiet about their interest in public.

But in private they sought out other fans, locally and overseas. They corresponded, started clubs and published amateur magazines about the genre.

In fact they created a fascinating sub-culture that was a microcosmos of Australian life from the 1930s to the 1960s.

Dr Edmonds' history makes a significant contribution to the study of the field, and it will be of value to people interested in cultural and literary studies.

Proud and Lonely is part one of a two-part history exploring how science fiction fandom developed in Australia, from its beginnings in the 1930s to the first World Science Fiction Convention held in Australia, in 1975.

This book deals with the early period up to 1961, when government regulations prevented most science fiction from being imported into Australia, and the seeds were sown of a gathering energy that would raise Australia's profile in the global science fiction community.

Also by Leigh Edmonds:

A Permanent Reminder: A history of the RAAF Association Aviation Heritage Museum of Western Australia

The Vital Link: A history of Main Roads Western Australia 1926-1996

Cathedrals of Power: A short history of the power-generating infrastructure in Western Australia 1912-1999.

Living By Water: A history of Barwon Water and its predecessors

H M Prison Beechworth: The End of an Era 1856-2004

A Colourful Life: A Memoir of Ferencz Schwartz/Fred Agar OAM

Bringing Home The Bacon: A History of the Harris Family's Castlemaine Bacon Company 1905-2005

The Vital Link: The Transition Years 1996-2006

A Good School: Haileybury's post-war years

Working for all Australians 1910-2010: A brief history of the Australian Taxation Office

Australia Takes Wing 1919-1938: The History of Civil Aviation in Australia Volume I

Colonel Haileybury's Little Army: A history of the Haileybury Cadet Unit 1930-1975

Stability in Flight 1939-1973: The History of Civil Aviation in Australia Volume II

Western Airways: Flying in Western Australia 1919-1941

PROUD AND LONELY

A History of
Science Fiction Fandom
in Australia 1936 to 1975

Part One: 1936 to 1961

Leigh Edmonds

NORSTRILIA PRESS

NORSTRILIA PRESS
www.norstriliapress.com
11 Robe Street, St Kilda, Victoria 3182, Australia

Copyright © Leigh Edmonds 2024.

This work is copyright. Apart from any use as permitted under the Copyright Act 1968, no part may be reproduced, copied, scanned, stored in a retrieval system, recorded, or transmitted, in any form or by any means, without the prior written permission of the publisher.

Book and cover design by David Grigg.
Edited by Alan Stewart
Index by Bruce Gillespie

Typeset in Crimson Pro, Roaster Original, and American Typewriter.

Paperback ISBN: 978-0-6453696-8-7
eBook ISBN: 978-0-6453696-9-4

'It is a Proud and Lonely Thing to Be a Fan.'
(Attributed to Rick Sneary by Bob Tucker)

CONTENTS

Foreword	1
Introduction	3
1926–1940	11
1939–1940	25
1941–1945	40
1946–1952, Sydney	61
1952–1953, Sydney	80
1950–1953, Melbourne	99
1953–1954, Sydney	121
1954–1960, Sydney	133
1953–1957	152
1953–1956, Melbourne	164
1957–1961, Melbourne	178
Fork in the Track	187
Chronology	199
Sources	207
Index	210

FOREWORD

The opening of Abraham Merritt's story *The Metal Monster* has always stayed in my mind in explaining the wonder of science fiction.

> In this great crucible of life we call the world—in the vaster one we call the universe—the mysteries lie close packed, uncountable as grains of sand on ocean's shores. They thread gigantic, the star-flung spaces; they creep, atomic, beneath the microscope's peering eye. They walk beside us, unseen and unheard, calling out to us, asking why we are deaf to their crying, blind to their wonder.
> Sometimes the veils drop from a man's eyes, and he sees—and speaks of his vision...

Such a person is the scientist and the science fiction fan. The scientist seeks truth in the reality of the universe, the science fiction fan seeks 'truth' in the works, often wildly unscientific, of science fiction.

One group of seekers formed in Sydney in the 1940s, and in Melbourne in the early 1950s a small group of such wonder seeking readers was brought together by Race Mathews.

This is our story.

— **Dick Jenssen**
(Founder member of the Melbourne SF Club)

INTRODUCTION

In September 2010 I found myself wandering around the vast halls of the Melbourne Convention Centre at Aussiecon 4, the 68th World Science Fiction Convention. At the time I was in the process of moving house, I was nearing the end of a major three year history project, and it had been maybe twenty years since I'd read any science fiction. While I'd enjoyed the science fiction I'd seen on television, I had little interest in the genre.

Instead, I had gone off and become a history professional and was now more familiar and comfortable with history conferences and seminars. But I'd been to the previous three Worldcons held in Australia and it would be a shame not to attend the fourth.

Occasionally I asked myself why I was there when I no longer had any active involvement in what was going on. I had only one task, the official opening ceremony, but apart from that I was free to wander around as I pleased with my thoughts. I marveled at the size and scope of the convention, remembering back to the first convention I'd attended in a little room upstairs in the Melbourne SF Club in 1966 and the first Worldcon in Australia we'd run at the Southern Cross hotel in 1975. I had belonged then but I didn't belong now. I resigned myself to occupying my time going to program items (something a trufan of my generation would never do) but, as it turned out, I didn't get to many.

The Melbourne Convention Centre reminded me of a railway station. Off the main concourse were rows of meeting rooms of various sizes with illuminated signs at the entrance telling what program item was being held inside. All you had to do was find a program item that interested you, find the appropriate room number and get on board with the topic of that session. To get to them, however, you had to walk down the long concourse which was teeming with people and it seemed that I kept on bumping into people I knew but hadn't seen for ten or twenty years. 'Hello, how are you?' 'Haven't seen you for how many years?' 'What are you up to?' And away we went. The only thing the Convention Centre needed was a decent bar to make the convention the full fannish convention experience.

One of the people I met was the tall, energetic and enthusiastic Chris Nelson. A librarian, I had first met him in Perth where I had studied and worked, and then life had taken him off to the Pacific Islands and other exotic places that he wrote about in his fanzine, *Mumblings from Munchkinland*. Among other things, he had also been delving into the history of Australian science fiction fandom, contacted and talked to some of Australia's first fans and written about them.

Chris said, 'You're a historian. You need to write the history of Australian fandom.' I shook my head, 'No, I don't!' I had in my head ideas for half a dozen histories that needed writing and a history of Australian fandom was not one of them. 'Think about it,' he said.

I didn't think I was thinking about it but my subconscious was apparently mulling it over but not telling me about it. Then I was on the escalator at the end of the concourse going up to the huckster's room when I saw Chris coming down. 'What am I going to tell him', I thought. And then, suddenly, the whole idea came to my mind; the shape the history would take, how it could be done, the concluding point and rationale for the whole thing, it was all there. Later, when I saw Chris again I said I'd do it, but I had other priorities and things that had to be done first, so it would take time.

It's taken thirteen years and the project is not yet complete. When I've finished with it, this history will conclude at Aussiecon, Australia's first Worldcon held in 1975. The main reason for this is that after Aussiecon fan activity in Australia became so large and diverse that it would be too difficult to distill from everything that happened the stories that I thought needed telling and the areas of human activity I want to explore in this history.

Of course nothing goes quite as expected, and so it was with my original plan for this project. Being innocent of most of what had happened in Australian fandom I thought I would be able to complete this history in a few months and knock it off in about 50 000 words. Silly me! The historical evidence is very extensive, the story more intricate than I had expected and the theory underlying an understanding of what happened more complex than I had foreseen. As a result, this is part one of the history that I had planned. It extends from the first records of science fiction fandom in Australia to the end of the 1950s when the first phase of fandom here came to an end. It also runs to half again the length that I had originally thought would cover the entire period. I've already gathered a lot of evidence for the second part but will need to do more research before I can start work on writing it. But I *really* hope it won't take another thirteen years to bring this project to its conclusion.

If you were to ask me what kind of historian I am, I'd tell you I'm a historian of technology. Not in the technophilia sense of the history of machines but in the sense of the systems in which the machines are created, maintained and used by people. History should be about what people do, what they are like and what motivates them. In this history science fiction is the machine that motivates and drives people, but it is the relationships between the people, their motivations and their personalities that explains why this story unfolds as it does.

Science fiction and history have a great deal in common because the past is as unknowable to us as the future. History cannot be a statement of fact about what happened in the past because we might *know of* the past but we can't *know* it in the same way that we know the present because we live here and now and not there and then. No, history is stories told about what happened in the past to help us understand who we are and how we came to be here. It is cobbled together and interpreted from memories — fallible as they are — and scraps of information that have survived from the past into the present that are constructed into stories to make sense of the past to us in the present.

Science fiction is the same. It is the extrapolation of present day preoccupations, experiences and knowledge into settings in the future that tell us who we are by exploring who we might become and how we might find our ways to those futures. Both history and science fiction are written from imagination, taking evidence, experience and knowledge from the present and extrapolating them into the past and into the future. And just as there are countless stories about what the future might become there are also many different stories about what happened in the past and what it was like to live there. This history is the story I have written from my study and interpretation of the evidence I have found from the past. Consequently, if you were to attempt to tell a story about the same people and places you could write a quite different story.

Australia is a land of stories. It is good to think about the past and the future here as stories because that is how Australia's first inhabitants knew this land. For over 60,000 years they understood their land through the stories they told about it so that the ways they acted and lived their lives made sense in their present. A mere two and a bit centuries ago Westerners invaded this land and imposed upon it different ways of knowing, believing that what they did and how they did it was explained by the stories they told themselves, about their history and their future. This dominant culture imposed itself upon the older culture and discounted its stories about the land as myth, fantasy and nonsense.

About a century ago a new kind of story telling came to this land. It had more in common with the stories told by this land's original peoples than the stories told by the dominant Western culture. Like the old stories, the new stories were called myths, fantasy and nonsense, and indeed they were by some of the standards of the dominant culture. But just as the old stories had been relevant to the land of their time, and remained relevant to the remnants of that culture, the new stories were relevant to the world as it was then becoming. So, please think about two things as you read this history.

First, that the land which the people of this story walked upon had first belonged to a story telling people and been taken from them. Second, that the people of this story were, in their own way, struggling to establish the new form of story telling in this land and that they consequently suffered under the beliefs and attitudes of the dominant culture. This story is thus, in part, about how the pioneers of this new story telling lived within that dominant culture and created their own culture and community under that dominating worldview, in this land.

I've done a lot of reading so I could write this history, only some of it the source material. A lot of my reading has been in the areas around a history of science fiction, a bit of literary history, a bit of cultural history and theory and other interesting areas. For a year or so I became interested in the academic field of fandom studies, a subbranch of cultural studies. Almost all of it is the study of various fandoms which investigates and analyzes their social and cultural developments, mostly in the period following that of this history using tools of cultural and social theory, and making up some new ones, rather than the historical approach I have taken in this work. This history has not been written as an academic discourse on the topic of science fiction fandom in Australia so I have removed most of the traditional referencing from it, leaving most of that which relates directly, or almost directly, to quotes from the historical sources. You can find a listing of all the sources I've used in writing this history in the Sources section at the rear of this book.

Through my interest in fandom studies I ended up contributing a chapter to a book on Australian fandom studies called *Aussie Fans*.[1] Mine is the first chapter called 'Fanac in Isolation', and summarizes the development of science fiction fandom in Australia in the period also covered by this history. When the review of my chapter came back from the peer reviewer it said I had not given any theoretic explanation for what I had written. I had sort of taken it for granted but I then had to write it out, so I did and glued it to the beginning of that chapter. Since that chapter and this history deal with the same theoretical questions, and they are not stated plainly in the text of this history, here they are.

Perhaps most fundamental is Geoffrey Blainey's seminal work of Australian economic history, *The Tyranny of Distance; How Distance Shaped Australia's History* which argues that Australia's geographical remoteness (due to the long distances between Australia and its colonial forebears in Europe and the United States) has been central to shaping the country's history and identity. This suggests that the development of science fiction fandom in Australia suffered from the same kind of isolation that the

---

[1] *Aussie Fans: Uniquely placed in Global Popular Culture*, eds Celai Lam & Jackie Raphael, University of Iowa Press, 2019.

country more generally experienced and that, as with the development of Australian culture more generally, and its economy more particularly, the small size of the nation's population (6.78 million in 1936 and 13.89 million in 1975), and the distance between population centres, significantly constrained the development of fandom in Australia.

Second is the history of culture in Australia, perhaps most accessible in John Rickard's *Australia: A Cultural History*. Australia's dominant culture was Western, drawn almost exclusively from the British Isles until the middle of the Twentieth Century and therefore expressing itself in the same fashion as it was in the home country with the same cultural and class biases. Innovations in American culture began only to intrude significantly upon this culture in the 1930s through its movies, music and literature. The literature of modern science fiction came to Australia in the shape of American pulp magazines that were imported in relatively small quantities and generally regarded as an inferior form of literature. The early Australian fans of science fiction were therefore small in number, isolated from the dominant Australian culture and also from pulp science fiction's roots in America.

The third theoretical underpinning is an idea from historical geography which goes under several titles including 'space adjusting technologies' and 'time-space compression'. Very interesting work could be done on how the rapid advancement of space adjusting technologies in the years following the 1970s led to significant changes in the nature of Australian science fiction fandom as the speed and quality of transport and communication improved, although that is mostly outside the scope of this part of the history. One point to consider in relation to this idea is that the first Worldcon to be held in Australia was in 1975, only four years after the high passenger capacity Boeing 747 entered service on the trans-Pacific air route in September 1971. This began reducing air fares to a level which made intercontinental air travel accessible to most people so that fans in North America could afford to attend a convention in Australia for the first time.

The first and third theoretical underpinnings are, I think, important in distinguishing the development of science fiction fandom in Australia during this period from fandoms in other English speaking cultures in the unspoken assumptions we and they held. Back at Aussiecon, having decided that I would eventually write this history, having my oral history recording equipment with me and knowing that the American fan Andy Porter, who had been a catalyst to developments in Australia fandom, was at the convention I went to interview him for this project. During the interview I asked him a question which would have, in asking an Australian fan of his generation, led to a long answer about the places where they found that sold science fiction, the second hand shops they scoured in search of it and the clubs and contacts they formed so they could find more of it. In short, a long quest after their prized reading material that I later heard from the early Australian fans I interviewed. On hearing my question Andy looked at me strangely and replied simply, 'From the local drugstore'. Thus have the geographic and cultural differences between our two cultures shaped the assumptions on which our different fandoms have been based and operated with different priorities in the same historical period.

I had hoped to write this history in a more personality based, or 'fannish', style. However, the nature of the historical evidence has not made this possible. During the period that this part of the history explores most Australian fans, with a couple of notable exceptions, appear to have taken their involvement in science fiction and its fandom very seriously. This was probably because they knew the public disregard and disdain for science fiction and believed they should present it in a serious and sensible form to make it more acceptable to the community in which they lived so frivolity and personal reflection were frowned upon. The result, for me as a historian, is that I am not able to look behind the masks those early Australian fans presented to the world. I can imagine a play in which the characters of Veney, Castellari, Molesworth, Evan, Stone and all the other Sydney Futurians turn to the audience, lift their masks and give voice to their feelings, but they have hidden them from me so I cannot bring them to life as people for you. Which is one of the limitations and challenges of history.

The primary sources for this first part of the history of Australian science fiction fandom are the fanzines from the period held in various archives and personal collections located in Australia and overseas. Unlike most cultural subcultures, science fiction fandom, with its tradition of fanzine publication, has left us a very rich source of historical evidence. Unfortunately, and unlike later phases of Australian fandom, the masks those early fans presented means I can tell you very little about them as people so this history, which is written from their source documents, is more impersonal than I would have liked. Fortunately, I was able to interview four of the main fans from the period of the formation of fandom in Melbourne: Race Mathews, Dick Jenssen, Lee Harding and Merv Binns, so the chapter about their involvement in fandom has more personal insights and a more personal feeling. The only Sydney fan from this period I was able to interview was Doug Nicholson who gave me some important anecdotes and insights from his memories and experiences of his involvement in Sydney fandom. All the rest comes from the fanzines of the period and Vol Molesworth's *A history of Australian science fiction Fandom* which is, I think, a biased and almost impenetrable work, but not untruthful.[2]

---

[2] Vol Molesworth, *A history of Australian science fiction Fandom*, 1935-1963, (first published in full in The Mentor and separately by Ron Clarke in 1980, reprinted 1994-95 and reprinted by Graham Stone, 2009).

I found this story could be told most clearly by expressing it thematically rather than chronologically, organized on the larger scale by the places in which events took place. This made sense because there was very little continuing contact between the fannish communities in Australia before the 1960s. On the smaller scale I have also told the story by grouping together fannish activities such as publishing fanzines, running clubs and conventions even though they all occurred concurrently in real life and affected each other. In order to convey some of the sense of the mingling of all these activities over time I have provided a chronology at the end of the story to give you a feeling for how everything fitted together in the experience of the fans of that time.

Having explained myself and my methods to you, and told you why you are reading this, I'd like to finish by thanking and acknowledging a few of the people who have helped with this history and made it possible. First of course, and with an ironic grin, thanks to Chris Nelson for giving me this task. Next, great thanks to Robin Johnson and the late Valma Brown for their support and encouragement. It would have been impossible to write this history without the research I was able to carry out in a number of libraries around Australia with the generous and useful assistance of the people who work there. These libraries were the Special Collections of Murdoch University, the Special Collections of the Monash University Library, Rare Books & Special Collections of the University of Sydney, Rare Books at the State Library of Victoria and the Special Collection of the National Library of Australia. A few sources of historic evidence also came from private fannish collections.

My debt of gratitude also goes to those who took the time to talk to me about their experiences in fandom and their thoughts about them, Lee Harding, Merv Binns, Dick Jenssen, Race Mathews, Doug Nicholson and Bill Wright. My sincere thanks also to Alan Stewart, David Grigg, Bruce Gillespie and Rob Gerrand for their invaluable help in publishing this history. As for everyone else of the fannish crew you are, as the platitude goes, too numerous to mention. And as the other platitude goes, you know who you are. My sincere thanks anyhow.

And now, after having completed the formalities, welcome to the first part of this story. I expect the pleasure of speaking to you again after the intermission to tell you how the story ends.

—**Leigh Edmonds**
January 2024

P.S. There are a few 'fannish' terms and concepts used without explanation in this history. Rather than me stopping to explain them, why don't you go to the repository of all fannish knowledge, Fancyclopedia III, for explanations. It's on the interweb at *https://fancyclopedia.org/Fancyclopedia_3*.

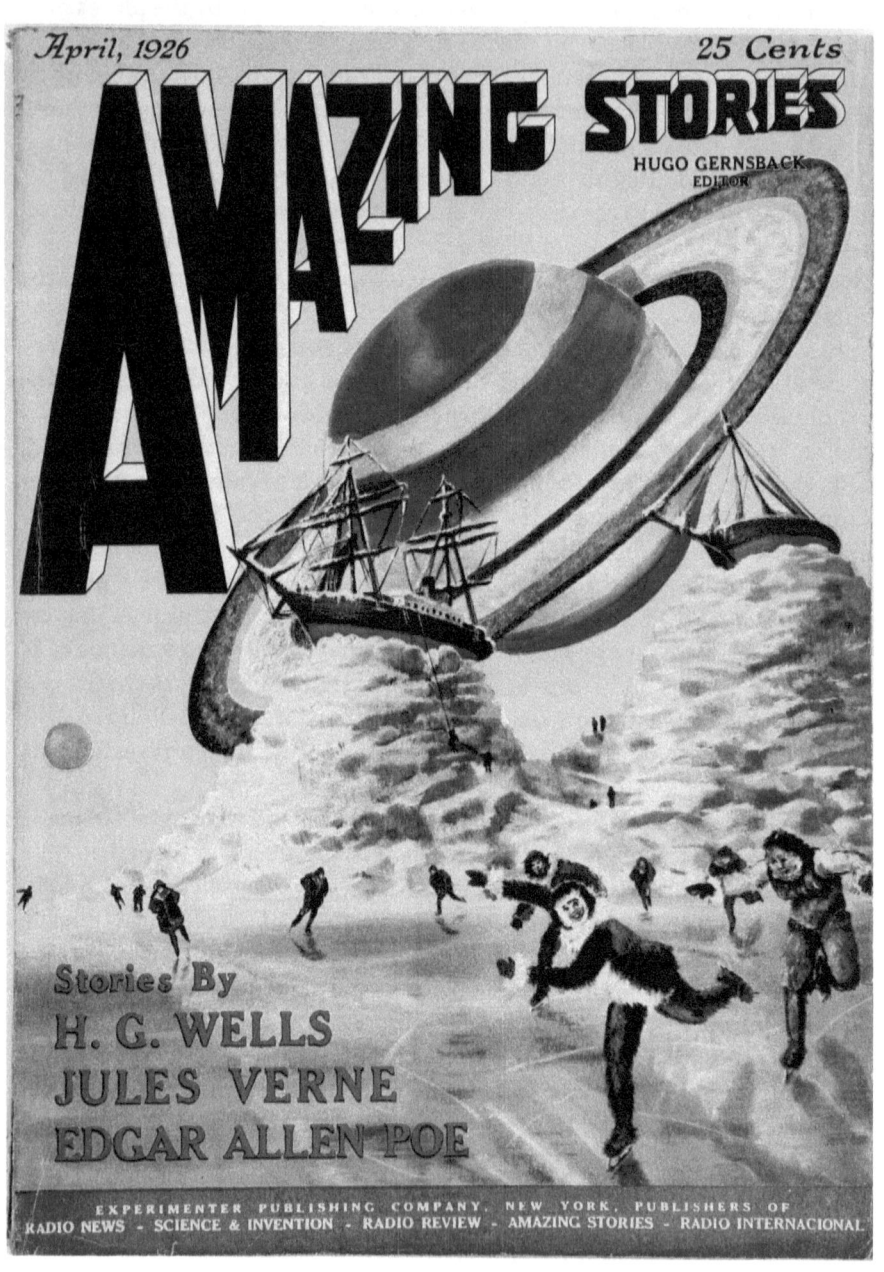

The first issue of *Amazing Stories,* April 1926

CHAPTER 1
1926-1940

Many years later George Turner recalled seeing, in 1927, the first issue of *Amazing Stories* on display in a wire rack on the McGills kiosk in Elizabeth Street, Melbourne. It was, he wrote, a gaudy and irresistibly attractive treasure trove and an addiction was born in that joyous glance.[1] Many others, in Australia and the rest of the English speaking world, became similarly intoxicated.

Amazing Stories was the first American pulp magazine dedicated to publishing science fiction. This genre of fiction already existed and was widely known through the work of Jules Verne, H G Wells and many other authors, but the genius of the magazine's editor, Hugo Gernsback, was in packaging the genre in a gaudy cover and publishing it in the popular American pulp magazine market where it found a dedicated readership.

Many youngsters had already acquired a taste for the scientific romances of Verne and Wells and the sometimes fantasy and fantastic stories published in the British boys magazines such as *The Rover, Boys Own, Modern Boy* and *Chums*. They might also have seen comic strips published in newspapers such as Speed Gordon[2] and Buck Rogers, but they were only a prelude to the impact the first pulp science fiction magazines had on these youngsters.

Gernsback's new magazine entered a tough market already populated by many other magazines containing stories about crime, romance, western adventures, sport and more. What separated his magazine from the rest was its stories about the future and the place of science in that future. This captured the imagination of a particular group of readers; young, male, largely middle-class and relatively well educated for that time. It appealed to a sense of adventure but also the possibilities of what lay in a future where science mattered and made adventure and exploration possible.

These tales set *Amazing Stories* apart from other pulp magazines. Like them the writing was generally considered inferior to 'higher' forms of writing with its poor expression, characterisation and storytelling. However, other pulp fiction genres were set in a real world that most readers could

---

[1] George Turner in *The New Millenial Harbinger* 5.
[2] 'Flash Gordon' retitled because of a meaning of the word 'flash' in Australia.

relate to and understood. Science fiction went beyond the bounds of reality into a world of fantasy and fantastic imagination which opened it to criticism and ridicule as escapist and inferior to significant literature. So when young Bert Castellari paid his regular visits to George Nash's little bookshop and magazine stall in Randwick, Nash would ask if he'd come to buy more 'bughouse books'. This attitude pushed the readers of pulp science fiction into a ghetto which led to the rapid creation of a sub-culture of dedicated science fiction readers and collectors.[3]

Moral attitudes also played a part in this public attitude towards science fiction in Australia. In 1938 a public campaign against 'sordid literature' began in Perth and led to the call for 'decent-minded citizens' to protest against 'imported filth and dirt'. Soon the Commonwealth government amended its Customs Act to prohibit importation of any goods deemed obscene, indecent, blasphemous or seditious. By August 1938 forty-nine magazines were listed as officially banned, a mix of detective, exploitation, horror and 'true story' pulps, including *Weird Tales*.

Amazing Stories followed the lead of other pulp magazines and began including a letter column for its readers in its January 1927 issue. In it readers could comment on the stories in the magazine and other things related to science fiction, creating a sense of community around the magazine. Some of the published letters included names and addresses which allowed readers to contact each other personally, either by writing letters or visiting each other if they lived close by.

Amazing Stories success encouraged publication of more science fiction pulp magazines with titles including *Wonder Stories*, *Astounding Stories* and *Startling Stories*. Their letter and news columns grew as the community around the science fiction magazines also grew. At the same time the common disdain and criticism of science fiction created a close-knit group which developed a self-awareness not found in the communities around other genre pulp magazines. Members of this community began calling themselves 'science fiction fans', which soon contracted to simply to 'fans' and their community called itself simply 'fandom'.

Fandom quickly grew into a sub-culture with traditions and a language that expressed its culture and customs. They created words that gave their subculture a special sense of defensive exclusivity such as 'prozine' for the professional science fiction magazines and 'fanmag' — later replaced by the more euphonious 'fanzine' — for the magazines they began to publish and circulate within fandom.

---

[3] There are a few stories about early encounters with science fiction. For example, Bert Castellari in *Mumblings from Munchkinland* 15, Chris Nelson's article about Graham Stone in *Mumblings from Munchkinland* 34, Alan Roberts in *Mumblings from Munchkinland* 17, Arthur Haddon in *Mumblings from Munchkinland* 31, Eric Russell in *Woomera* 1 and Alan Connell in *Cosmos* 3.

stories are on record; the jury of discussers has read them; and I, hereby, challenge Miss Robb to point out to that jury page references to a few of the places in which consistency is most blatantly conspicuous by its absence. Verisimilitude is purely relative; its presence or absence cannot be pointed out in any one exact paragraph, as can violations of consistency. It is my contention, however, that the "Skylarks" sound more plausible with Seaton as he is than they would have sounded had Seaton been drawn as Miss Robb wants him. I may, of course, be wrong—you, the jury, will have to decide that.

Fifthly—Miss Robb is "holst by her own petard" in calling to her aid the book, "Cruelty to Words." Just where in that book, my dear Olive, and how authoritatively, does it bar colloquial language in *conversation*, as an adjunct to character drawing? Also, just where, in my published stories, have I violated tenets of good composition in any of the fashions so ponderously exemplified by Mr. Weekley?

Sixthly:—I do not ascribe my singular conjugal felicity (and believe me, ace, you chirped it then, even if you did think you were kidding somebody) to my use or abuse of languge, nor to anything else about myself. If Jeannie were not Jeannie, said felicity would very probably be anything else but. Indeed, it may even be that her toleration of my "merely crude" love-terms is only another manifestation of an unusually magnanimous nature.

Edward E. Smith, Ph.D.,
Hillsdale, Mich.

(Because Dr. Smith can so ably defend himself, we will make no comment, except to agree with his suggestion that all missiles in this battle be sent us.—EDITOR.)

A LETTER GIVING US THE ACCUMULATED WRATH OF YEARS FROM A CORRESPONDENT WHO WRITES TO US FOR THE FIRST TIME

Editor, AMAZING STORIES:

Here's another voice amongst the crowd of people that have read A.S. from the first, and who are only now beginning to write to the Editor. This being my first letter, you may prepare to receive all the accumulated wrath of years, dealt out in tons and hundredweights. No, don't worry—I prepared a whole drawer full of brickbats, but I've mislaid them.

A.S. has had rather an adventurous existence, with ups and downs in plenty, but now the middle way has been found at last, and improvement is steady. In the beginning you used to reprint the older stories, and jolly good they were. "The Land that Time Forgot," "A Columbus of Space," and "Station X," and "Treasures of Tantalus," were great yarns. ("The Moon Pool" was rather a fraud after all I expected of it), but the authors of those days were afraid to venture too far into scientific marvels (though Burroughs and Cummings did wonders), and so their productions cannot compare with the masterpieces of now. Still, I vote for a reprint now and then, or rather, I uphold the idea broached by Messrs. Miller and Jenson, to issue either a set of scientifiction classics or a reprint annual. There are dozens of available yarns: Burroughs, Merritt, Cummings, R. M. Farley, etc., have written dozens of yarns you have never published. Which reminds me—try and get in on Edgar Rice Burroughs' tales before the "Blue Book" snaffles them, as is the case; he is, in a different way, as good as E. R. Smith.

Much as I revere Mr. Smith, I consider that he ought to come a grovel in the dirt as penance for the disgusting way he ended the "Skylark" yarns, just as we were settling down to await another dozen or so of them. Then he ought to grovel again for killing off Du Quesne. Though his villainies were many, I liked "Blackie." But three yells for "Spacehounds of IPC," *Superbe et magnifique*, as the Froggies say. Campbell writes a lot more science than Dr. Smith, but he will not reach the plane of that gentleman until he learns to write a story with a plot in it, instead of a rather feebly connected series of events. Talking of authors, I must throw in some praise for Stanton Coblentz (is he Coblentz the astronomer?), Miles J. Breuer, Jack Williamson, David H. Keller, Abner J. Gelula and L. A. Eshbach.

Breuer's sole claim to fame lies in "Paradise and Iron," a real classic, but the rest of his yarns were tripe. Jack Williamson used to be bad, but "The Stone from the Green Star" far outdoes Merritt in some of the descriptive passages. The conceptions were beautiful. Keller is always surprising one. Gelula's "Automaton" was an excellent example of a thin plot well treated. Harl Vincent is a most curious personage; sometimes he writes little gems, such as "Invisible Ships" and "Too Many Boards," and sometimes, he dares to pen such utter antiquated, unintelligent infantile rot as "Tanks Under the Sun." He could leave out the American "dialect" in his conversations and not lose by it. I don't think that even Americans always talk like his characters. Yes—I admit that, being Australian, I am prejudiced, but I think you will agree with me.

I am glad you got rid of Paul. His face funguzed Professors make me have hysterics. Wesso is the uncrowned king of the artists.

In your November, 1931, issue, Mr. Fisher says in his letter, that the light of the sun would have to go a roundabout way to be reaching us now, and he does not believe that by looking in an opposite direction we could see it. According to the space curvature theory of Einstein, this is quite possible, for the light would merely travel round the spacial sphere and return to its starting point. This, unfortunately, cannot be verified, because it has been calculated that the circumference of the said sphere is so great that when the light reached us after its journey, it would be too feeble to enable us to see its source.

Nevertheless, it is a generally accepted idea nowadays, that light does eventually return to its starting point after having traversed all space.

On the question of time travel, this is too illogical in its results to be possible. For one thing, we could travel into the past and change history. For instance, some one might go and kill Lord Nelson just before the Battle of Trafalgar, or arm Napoleon's troops with bombs and cordite and give him a few steel battleships. In that case, all history would have been changed, and the modern times would be entirely different. No, we can't meddle with the past. Ditto for the future. With a time machine, one could find out that one was to be killed the next day, and merely hop over into the day after next, and so be living after one is dead. Too bad. The idea lately seems to be that time is a sort of river, and the present is a boat floating in the stream, and the clever inventor makes the boat travel a little faster, but we do not travel appreciably forward. Poor traveler sets control for a thousand years hence, and is dead of old age before he gets there. Nix on time traveling.

My little note groweth long, and the editor modeth in boredom. Well, another couple of pages and I'll be finished.

I must expect to be crushed under with criticism on those last two paragraphs about space-curvature and time-travel. Somebody will pick holes in my ideas. I must apologize if they are too scientifically incorrect, but at the age of 15 one has not yet gained his Ph.D., etc. Still, at the age of 15 one does have an opinion on how rotten some stories are, and I think that I can do better than some of these written by "occasional" authors who write one tale and then forever hold their peace.

Here's to AMAZING STORIES, the best of all the science fiction magazines. It makes one cheerful to think of it.

George R. Turner,
67 Highbury Grove, Prahran 51,
Victoria, Australia.

(We are getting a great many letters from Australia, for our magazine has very friendly readers in the Antipodes half way round the world from us. Your letter from your distant country is so full that it hardly needs an answer. We are much interested in your comparison between Dr. Smith and Mr. Campbell. Mr. Coblentz, who is acquiring quite a standing in literature, is not the astronomer. Miles J. Breuer, David H. Keller are both physicians of very high standing. We are hoping to see "Automaton," by Mr. Gelula, on the screen soon. The Universal Pictures Corporation, is producing it now, but has not announced its release date yet. Dr. Breuer's "yarns" have been admired by all. It is absurd to designate them as you do. When you visit us some time in the future, you will find that American cultivated people and even the more common ranks really use very little slang. We absolutely agree with you that time travel seems absurd, but it is a good basis for a story, and we cannot be too sure of any absurdity.—EDITOR.)

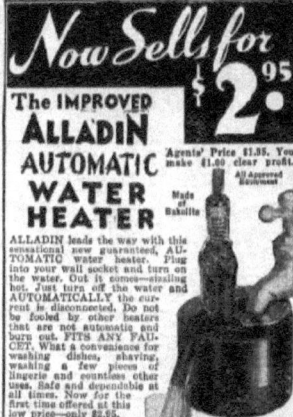

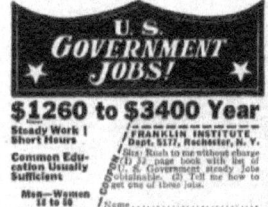

Fan groups began to form in the largest cities but most fans read and enjoyed their science fiction in physical isolation. However, they began creating a widespread community that had started in the prozine letter columns but also used the postal system for communication. During the 1930s the sub-culture of fandom created fanzines and conventions to strengthen the bonds of the community. This community grew in strength and maturity in the United States through the 1930s with a smaller but similar community in Britain.

Some Australians were also keen to join this subculture and wrote to the prozine letter columns with their ideas and opinions. However, their isolation on the other side of the world did not encourage them because it took at least a month for new prozine issues to arrive in Australia, just as long for a letter sent from Australia to arrive in America and longer again to be published. This made it very difficult for Australians to take an active and up-to-date part in the conversations generated in the prozine letter columns. Despite this the letter columns were an important part of the prozines to many Australian readers and when Australian authorities cut sexy advertisements out of issues of *Wonder Stories* readers complained because that also cut out some of the letters.

Before World War 2 over eighty letters from Australian readers had appeared in the prozine letter columns.[4] Most of them were written by enthusiastic teenagers. When John Gregor's first letter was published in 1935 he was 14 years old, as was Bill Veney when one of his letters was published in 1938. Norma Williams was 18 when her letter was published in the same issue of *Amazing Stories* as Bill Veney's. Williams, like many other letter writers, said she would like to get in touch with overseas 'pen pals' and many probably did. In a later letter Gregor mentioned he had received copies of *Amazing* from his pen pals after his first letter had been published. After a letter from Marshall McLennan was published in *Astounding* in 1935 he received many letters and some requests for information about science fiction in Australia. He corresponded with overseas fans including Americans Sam Moskowitz and Harry Warner Jnr and Walter Gillings in Britain. He was mentioned in Gillings' *Scientifiction* fanzine in 1937 and had short notes

---

[4] We know the details of Australian and New Zealand appearances in the letter columns and fan columns of the prozines thanks to the work of Chris Nelson who has published lists of those appearances in his fanzine, *Mumblings from Munchkinland* from issues 28 to 33. He gives details of each contribution and its location so that each letter or mention can be found readily. Many of the writers are now unknown but those whose names will appear later in this story include Bert Castellari, Bert Chandler, Alan Connell, Roger Dard, John Deverne, Noel Dwyer, David Evans, Ron Graham, John Gregor, Ralph Harding, Warwick Hockley, Marshall McLennan, Rex Meyer, Vol Molesworth, Charles Mustchin, Eric Russell, Don Tuck, George Turner, Bill Veney and Norma Williams. Three of them, Ron Graham, Ralph Harding and George Turner reported having been captivated by the first issue of *Amazing Stories*.

> tics, microscopy, art and psychology. . . . William Veney, 11a Lawson Street, Paddington, Sydney, NSW, Australia, would like to exchange letters with AMAZING STORIES readers, foreign and Australian. He's 14. . . . Norma Williams, 18 and single, would like to have pen-pals in North and South America and England. She is interested in stamps, reading, chess, microscopes, (she owns a 450X), and various other subjects. Write her at 35 Cook Road, Paddington, Sydney, NSW, Australia. (If you don't know William Veney, Norma, this is a coincidence!)

Bill Veney and Norma Williams' notices in *Amazing Stories* October 1938, p. 138.

about some Australian science fiction activity published in James Taurasi's *Fantasy News* in 1938 and 1939.

Australian science fiction enthusiasts may also have contacted each other using addresses found in the letter columns, but we have no record of it. Records of fandom in Australia began in the pages of *Wonder Stories* around 1935.

After Hugo Gernsback lost control of *Amazing Stories* he launched another prozine which was quickly titled *Wonder Stories*. To promote science fiction, fandom and his new magazine Gernsback launched the Science Fiction League in 1934 and published news about it in *Wonder Stories*. Part of the League's organisation was a series of chapters formed in various cities, in reality fan clubs comprising members of the League.

The May 1935 issue of *Wonder Stories* contained a proposal by William E Hewitt to form a chapter of the League in Sydney. The September issue reported that an informal meeting had been held and the December issue announced that the Sydney Science Fiction League, Chapter 27, had been chartered on 15 August 1935. Wallace Osland was its Director, two other members were William Hewitt and Thomas Mallett, and another was expected to join soon. By February 1936 the Sydney Chapter of the League had six members including Charles LaCoata. They held fort-

> **THE SYDNEY CHAPTER**
>
> This is to announce that on August 15, 1935, the SYDNEY SCIENCE FICTION LEAGUE, Chapter Number Twenty-Seven, was formed and organized by Wallace J. J. Osland, the Director, and given Charter. This is the first foreign Chapter of the LEAGUE outside of the British Isles. Charter members include the following (member number follows name): William E. Hewitt (599), Thomas Mark Mallett (834), and Wallace J. J. Osland (782).
> So far, three unofficial meetings have been held by this Chapter before it was Chartered. Being so far away, it takes a long time to exchange communications with Headquarters. A Mr. Jury was present at the third meeting and will join the parent body as soon as he can. A leaflet will be prepared to advertise the LEAGUE around Sydney—this will be discussed further at their next meeting. The Chapter reports that the Australian authorities had cut out parts of their copies of WONDER STORIES—the sexy advertisements—and they have complained about this because it spoiled some of the readers' letters. However, Headquarters is glad that this will not have to continue, as no more sex ads are published in the magazine.
> Our Australian members in and around Sydney will be glad to get together with these active fans, we know, so we ask them simply to send their names to Wallace J. J. Osland, Director, SYDNEY SCIENCE FICTION LEAGUE, 26 Union St., Paddington, Sydney, New South Wales, Australia.

Notice of the Sydney Chapter of the Sydney Science Fiction League.
Wonder Stories, December 1935, p.757

nightly meetings in members' homes and discussed subjects such as 'science versus religion'. One member of the group owned a printing press and published a small pamphlet that was distributed around Sydney to attract

(LtoR) Eric Russell, Bill Veney and Bert Castellari in Sydney, 1939.
(Chris Nelson, *Mumblings from Munchkinland* 14)

members.[5]

The Sydney chapter of the League met through most of 1936 but interest declined and only LaCoata and Hewitt remained in touch, for a while. Molesworth later suggested that the problems of living in Depression Sydney were more pressing than talking about the future or, perhaps as Hewitt later told Veney, the other members simply lost interest. There were suggestions for the formation of chapters of the League in Brisbane, Toowoomba, Melbourne and Adelaide but nothing eventuated and the Science Fiction League had ceased to exist in Australia by the end of 1936.

Another beginning occurred in 1937 when five boys at the Randwick Intermediate High School discovered they shared a liking for science fiction. Two of them, Bill Veney and Bert Castellari, were also on the staff of the class magazine and decided to start a magazine of their own, which they called 'Spacehounds'. It was handwritten and there was only one copy that was passed around to interested readers. They only intended it to be an outlet for their writing and illustrating efforts but, within a couple of weeks, it had developed a following and took three or four days to return to its editors. By the seventh or eighth issue it had also found its way into the teacher's staff room where Castellari was congratulated for his energy and Veney criticised for his spelling.

---

[5] In September 1941 Eric Russell purchased an old issue of *Amazing Stories* and found in it a very crudely printed semi-quarto slip of paper telling readers to contact a member of the Science Fiction League in Sydney if they were interested. But by then no science fiction enthusiasts lived at the given address.

Castellari and Veney published ten weekly issues and a 'quarterly' before they stopped because the annual examinations were approaching. 'Spacehounds' had shown them there might be an interest in that kind of publication so they resolved it would not be the end of their efforts. The following year, 1938, was their final year at school so they decided to postpone their publication efforts to concentrate on schoolwork. During the year Veney also met the brothers Eric and Ted Russell, both avid science fiction readers but, as Eric was also in his final school year, they agreed to postpone any activity until 1939.

Despite that decision, during 1938 Eric Russell suggested that they form an official club that they called the Junior Australian Science Fiction Correspondence Club (JASFCC). Veney was the General Secretary, Eric Russell the Secretary, Castellari the Assistant Secretary, and there were two more members, Meleski and Ted Russell. They planned a chain letter that members would pass around, each adding to it, but that didn't work because they all lived near each other so it was easier to talk in person.

The JASFCC became more active and began holding formal meetings in February 1939. They decided they would also publish a fan magazine and contact every other fan in Australia they could find. They were successful in contacting several interstate fans including, Marshall MacLennan in Victoria, John Deverne in South Australia, Don Tuck in Tasmania and Keith Moxon and Chas Mustchin in Queensland.

They planned a fan magazine called *Australian Fan News* in the early months of 1939. They didn't know how to print it but one of Veney's workmates, Frank Flaherty, offered to help with typing and duplicating. Castellari, Eric Russell and Veney assembled the contents of their fanzine but had no clear idea of what they wanted except the title. The resulting 12 page foolscap fanzine was a real disappointment to them and, although it was dated May 1939, they didn't post it until August. There was no second issue because Flaherty was transferred to a new job and the boys lost the use of both the typewriter and duplicator.

Although they were very discouraged by their first effort Eric Russell was keen to try again and began gathering material for a new fanzine. The group also

Cover of *Australian Fan News*, c. May 1939
(Fanac.org)

planned to set up a club library of magazines and an art gallery, but some members dropped out and the club's executive had lost heart by July 1939.

A similar club was also formed in Sydney at the beginning of 1939 by Vol (properly Voltaire) Molesworth and Ken Jefferys. They called it the Junior Science Club and aimed to attract youngsters interested in science. It had over a dozen members by the middle of the year and published two or three issues of the *JSC Bulletin*. However, the club suddenly disintegrated and was left moribund, like the JASFCC.

The two groups had competed for members for more than three months and Castellari and Molesworth, who both started work as copy boys at the *Sydney Sun* newspaper at the beginning of 1939, disliked each other. However, both groups had similar interest and had learned a little about running clubs. Molesworth also thought it possible to be interested in science and science fiction so he was prepared to participate in science fiction related activities.

Over the next few months the two groups merged with a common interest around science fiction. At the same time American fandom began to influence fans in Australia and encourage them to think about how they could join in. The first avenue was through correspondence with overseas fans and then through their own fanzines that they could send to America.

American fan Harry Warner Jnr saw Castellari's address and wrote to him and, early in 1939, sent Castellari a copy of his fanzine, *Spaceways*. Castellari and his friends had seen nothing like it and it electrified them with its solid and attractive format and intelligent conversation about science fiction. They had never imagined that an amateur publication could be so good and that turned their thoughts to how to emulate it, and *Australian Fan News* was their first attempt..

John Deverne in Adelaide also began receiving overseas fanzines which inspired him to respond with his own. He saw what a fanzine looked like but was isolated in Adelaide with nobody to write material for him, so he copied, without permission, about ninety percent of the content of his fanzine from the overseas fanzines he had received. The result was Australia's first fanzine, *Science Fiction Review*, which Deverne published in March 1939. It was small, sixteen page octavo, printed on a hektograph and bound in a black manilla cover. He printed less than twenty copies and sent them to overseas fans, with a couple of copies sent to Sydney where it did not impress the fans there very much. (Not long after publishing *Science Fiction Review* Deverne went silent and did not reappear until the 1950s, using a different name.)

Veney, Castellari and the Russell brothers had discussed what they wanted to do even before *Australian Fan News* had been posted . Eric Russell wanted to try a small fanzine that wouldn't cost too much or be too difficult to produce and Veney wanted to start a local science fiction club. They decided it would be best to do one thing at a time and, since Eric Russell had the clearest idea about what he wanted to do, they supported him first. The first issue of their fanzine was published in October 1939 and their new club met for the first time in November 1939. From the beginning the fanzines and clubs were closely intertwined but, to make the story clearer, let's begin by considering the fanzines.

Eric Russell published the first issue of *Ultra* in October 1939. It was a very modest fanzine comprising twelve pages of thin folded foolscap paper that was laboriously produced. To print it

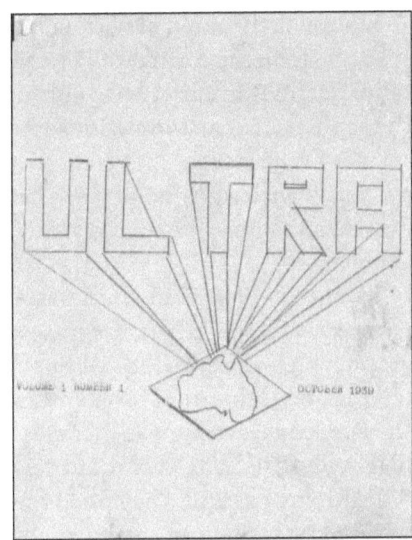

Ultra 1, Australia's first regular fanzine (Author's collection)

Eric and Ted Russell rented a typewriter and used carbon paper to make six increasingly faint impressions of each page. They did this three times, giving them 18 copies. It was small, neat and contained contributions from Castellari, Veney, 'A G Ghoul', 'The Rambler', Eric and Ted Russell and Harry Warner Jnr. It was produced on a shoestring and looked like it, but they were very proud of their achievement. It was something they could send to their overseas friends and producing it cost so little that they could afford a second issue.

Ultra showed the influence of American fandom and their knowledge of fannish events there. It commented on the current prozines, referred to the exclusions from the recent New York convention and parodied the First Staple War that had been fought in the letter columns of *Astounding* and *Wonder* several years earlier and become part of fannish folklore.

Ultra's second issue was published in December 1939 in the same labour intensive way, with similar contents. After that Ted Russell made a flatbed duplicator and following issues were produced on it in purple ink at first because black ink was too expensive. This allowed them to print more copies and make their fanzine look more like the American fanzines they received. It included art drawn onto stencil by Ralph Smith, a page of faan fiction written by Hoy Ping Pong (Bob Tucker) and longer pieces of fiction by Veney and Molesworth. It was an attractive little 14 page fanzine which Tucker described in *Le Zombie* as 'a honey'.[6]

---

[6] *Le Zombie* 25.

Molesworth joined in with *Luna*, the first issue published in December 1939 in a foolscap format of 12 pages. Second and third issues appeared in January and February 1940, both eight pages on quarto paper. They followed the same format as *Ultra* with some news, some commentary on the current science fiction scene, some fiction and a letter column. They were neatly produced with right-hand justification because fans thought that gave their fanzines a more professional look, even though it took a lot of effort to achieve.[7]

In January 1940 Veney and Castellari published the first issue of *Futurian Observer*, a fortnightly foolscap news fanzine. They used a flatbed mimeograph which was not difficult but took time, which they happily spent talking about things. If *Ultra* and *Luna* were modeled on Warner's *Spaceways*, the *Futurian Observer* was modeled on Tucker's *Le Zombie*. They said they planned to publish news about science fiction and fandom and some issues did, if there was any. They filled the rest of their two pages with comment on what was happening locally, some of it frank and unflattering to other local fans. In turn, readers were also free with their criticism of the fanzine's bad duplicating, spelling errors, typing errors, grammatical errors and general untidiness. Castellari replied that they gave priority to regularity over appearance. They printed between 50 and 100 copies of each issue but never had many paying subscribers and were happy to trade with other fanzines or send copies to people who were interested.

In April 1940 Molesworth announced he was going to stop publishing *Luna* because, he said, it had not received sufficient support and he didn't think Australian fandom was big enough to support three fanzines. Before long, however, he returned with a new fanzine called *Cosmos*. It began as a letterzine modelled very closely on *Voice of the Imagi-Nation* which was published in America by Forry Ackerman and Morojo.

Thirteen issues appeared between April 1940 and January 1941 but Molesworth was inconsistent so his fanzine went through several changes. At first he focused on letters but soon began including articles. Then he lost interest and, from the middle of June, Castellari and Veney published three single sheet issues. Apparently re-energised Molesworth returned to *Cosmos* in August, this time planning to publish regularly two pages of news and whatever else came to hand. However, by September, *Comos* had grown to twelve pages of well produced letters, fiction and articles. After that it continued irregularly until the 13th and final issue which was published at

---

[7] Right hand justification was achieved by typing the contents of the fanzine twice. After the first version had been typed the typist counted the number of unused spaces at the end of each line and then incorporated them into that line of text when it was retyped so that each line ended with the last letter at the same end of the line as every other line. This process made the page look more professional but also involved a lot more typing and was less spontaneous because every word had been planned in advance.

the end of January 1941. Molesworth suggested he was stopping publication for financial reasons but also announced a new fanzine, *Psychos*, which would be monthly with letters and essays. However it was never published.

A surprise to Sydney fans was *Austra Fantasy* published first in June 1940 by two Melbourne fans, Warwick Hockley and his friend Keith Taylor. It was small, carbon copied and primitive in comparison to Sydney fanzines. What it lacked in polish it made up for in enthusiasm with contents including fiction, verse and prozine and film reviews. The second issue appeared in September 1940. It was larger, hektographed and with contributions of fiction and articles from Sydney fans David Evans, Molesworth, Eric Russell, Veney, and a cover drawn by Ted Russell.

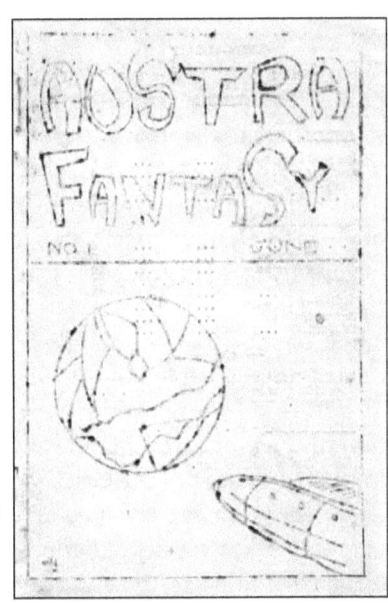

Austra Fantasy 1, the first fanzine published in Melbourne. (Fanac.org)

By the third issue Hockley and Taylor had bought a duplicator so it was much cleaner and attractive, with contributions from most well-known Sydney fans.

In mid 1940 a group of Sydney fans decided to combine their efforts to produce a fanzine that was better than *Ultra*.[8] When the first issue of *Zeus* was published in August 1940 it included an elaborate cover by Smith, an article by Don Tuck, some faan fiction by Molesworth and a couple of items written under pseudonyms.

The *Zeus* group split before the second issue was published so there were two second issues. One was published in November 1940 by Noel Dwyer, with the assistance of Ralph Smith, and the other was published in December by Ron Levy, with the help of Bert Castellari and his sister Roma Castellari. (For convenience fans at the time referred to the Dwyer version as *Pseudo Zeus*.) The Dwyer edition was hektographed with artist Ralph Smith illustrations on almost every page and a multi coloured cover. The third and final issue of *Pseudo Zeus* was published in February 1941.

The second issue of *Zeus* was sixteen quarto pages, mimeographed with a cover by Roma Castellari and contributions from Veney, Molesworth and Bruce Sawyer. The third issue, published in February 1941, was more adventurous and colourful with black, red and green inks used to give it a chaotic

---

[8] The group were Noel Dwyer, Ron Levey, Ralph Smith, Keith Hooper, Bill Veney and Bert Castellari. Hooper dropped out before the first issue was published.

but colourful appearance. It showed how much Sydney fans had learned about fanzine production in a year. There were two more issues of *Zeus*, one published later in 1941 and the final one in 1942.

Another small fanzine, *Hermes*, was published only once in August 1940. It was a single sheet styled as a supplement to *Ultra*.

At the beginning of November 1940 Warwich Hockley published the first of what he planned to be a tri-weekly fanzine called *Melbourne Bulletin*. It began with two pages, grew to four with the second issue and six pages the third issue early in 1941. It attracted contributions from most Sydney fans and it seemed that, despite their disagreements, Sydney fans were keen to contribute to the Melbourne fanzines.

Ultra and *Futurian Observer* continued on steadily. *Ultra* appeared on a roughly bi-monthly schedule and improved in quality as Russell gained experience. Issues contained usually mediocre artwork, a variety of fiction, articles on various subjects, reviews and editorial and reader comment. Through consistency, improving quality and contributions from most of Australia's fans, and occasionally an American, *Ultra* became the best fanzine being published in Australia.

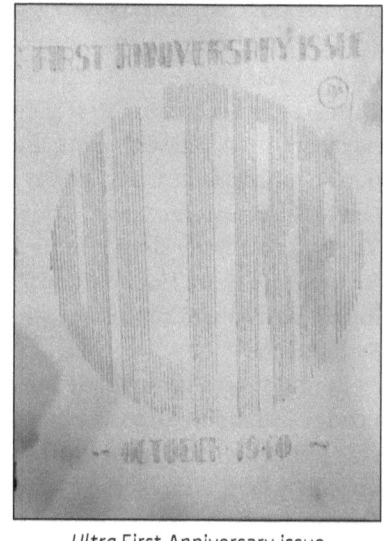

Ultra First Anniversary issue
(Rare Books & Special Collections, Sydney University)

Russell published *Ultra*'s 34 page first annish in late 1940. It was delayed by a month because of the cost of producing such a large fanzine and because, despite his plans, not all Australian fans had contributed (the gap was filled by two Americans including a Chicon report written by Tucker).[9] The printing was spotty in places and some of the hand drawn artwork was primitive, but it demonstrated a good level of experience and confidence.

Futurian Observer maintained its more or less fortnightly schedule through 1940. The single sheet contained whatever news the editors could find and, if there was little news, their views on fan activities in Sydney. They wrote what they thought in plain, vigorous and sometimes inflammatory language. The issue of 3rd November 1940, for example, comprised little more than a highly critical review of the Sydney club's first year. The issue of

---

[9] *Ultra* 2/1. The contributors were Don Tuck, Chas Mustchin, Keith Moxon, John Cunningham, Bob Tucker, Bert Castellari, Bob Veney, Colin Roden, Noel Dwyer, Davie Evans, Warwick Hockley, Ken Williams, Vol Molesworth, Bruce Sawyer, Keith Hooper, Keith Taylor and Ralph Smith.

17th November contained excerpts of Harry Warner's report on Chicon and a detailed and critical examination of why the club had failed to send any kind of representation to the convention, and who was to blame. The following issue, 1st December 1940, was devoted almost entirely to an attack on Eric Russell over some comments he had made in *Ultra*.

Australian fans had poured a great deal of energy into their fanzines; in finding printing equipment, learning how to use it and in writing and drawing for them. From October 1939 to about the end of 1940 less than a dozen fans, only a couple older than 17, had published around 55 issues of nine titles and 350 pages.[10] They expended this effort partly as an outlet for youthful enthusiasm and energy, partly to express their devotion to science fiction and partly to join worldwide fandom.

Through their fanzines and letter writing the young Sydney fans began to get noticed overseas. At first the American response in reviews in fan and prozines was condescending but it gradually improved as the quality of Australian fanzines improved.

Letters from Australian fans were sometimes published in *Voice of the Imagi-Nation*, including from Molesworth, Eric Russell and Alan Roberts, a fan from Brisbane whose witty and clever contributions criticising science fiction quickly earned him a reputation as a stirrer in American fandom. A Veney article about Australian fandom that appeared in Warner's *Spaceways* 9 drew some attention. Tucker's *Le Zombie* mentioned emerging Australian fandom several times with comments on Australian fanzines as they arrived, including a 'thumbs up, but drooping' for the second issue of *Luna*. Tucker also took some news and favorably reviewed the first issue of *Futurian Observer*. In the 29th issue Tucker gave thumbs up to *Cosmos* 1 and *Ultra* 4 and a 'Quite okay, too', to *Futurian Observers* 7 and 8.[11]

Australian fanzines recognised American fanzines by including reviews of the ones they received and booster ads for the ones they liked with *Le Zombie*, *Spaceways* and *Voice of the Imagi-Nation* being popular. Overseas fans occasionally appeared in Australian fanzines and Fred Pohl and Don Wollheim sent occasional news items that were included in Australian fanzines. Harry Warner wrote to Molesworth saying that *Luna* was starting to see publicity in America and Doc Swisher wrote that he liked *Luna* 3, had seen Veney's article in *Spaceways*, and wanted information about Australian fanzines.

Australian fanzines also had value as trade items for American fanzines and prozines. Molesworth traded *Luna* for seven American fanzines including *Le Zombie*, *Spaceways* and *Voice of the Imagi-Nation*. The editors of

---

[10] These numbers are a little rubbery because it appears that not all issues of all titles have survived to be counted now in 2023.

[11] *Le Zombie* 29.

Futurian Observer traded regularly with several overseas fanzines, sending copies to America on every mailship leaving from Sydney for North America.

About half of the content of most Australian fanzines was fiction — generally short and poorly written. Most Australian fans had some fiction published in their fanzines and keenest contributors were Molesworth and a new fan, David Evans, who hoped the door to professional publication would open through writing fiction for fanzines. Most agreed that writing fiction was good practice for later professional publication and they hoped to follow the lead of many New York Futurians who had established professional careers through involvement in fandom.

There was, however, no market for science fiction in Australia because of the country's small population and the public disdain for the genre. Fans like Ralph Smith and David Evans thought Sydney fans might generate enough enthusiasm for science fiction if they worked together so professional writing in Australia might become possible and an Australian prozine emerge.

The hopes of fans were raised in mid-1940 when a western fiction magazine, *Wild West* appeared on Australian bookstalls. It was of little or no interest to science fiction and fantasy followers but it was issued because of the exclusion of imported American Western fiction and it seemed possible to them that an Australian science fiction magazine might also be published. Sydney fans launched a campaign sending letters to the publishers suggesting an all-story magazine featuring at least one fantasy story each week. There was, however, no resulting magazine.

There was little enthusiasm for trying to sell their stories to the American prozines though Molesworth and Allan Connell said they had received American rejection slips. The distance from Sydney to New York, and the time and cost it took to bridge that divide, were too daunting. The only local market they had was Australian magazines, such as *Quiz* and *Man*, and newspapers that often published short fiction and serials. Several fans had some publishing success and David Evan, Alan Roberts, Vol Molesworth, Eric Russell, and possibly Colin Roden, were published later in the Sydney papers *The Sun* and *The Mirror*.

CHAPTER 2
1939-1940

While Eric and Ted Russell were working on their first fanzine Veney was planning to launch a science fiction club in Sydney. In October 1939 he, Castellari and Eric Russell decided it was time to start the new club and invited Molesworth, Meleski, Ted Russell and a newcomer, Ron Levy to attend the first meeting of the club at Veney's home on 5 November 1939. At that meeting they resolved to call their club the Futurian Society of Sydney.

The term 'Futurian' had been coined several years earlier by Michael Rosenblum in Britain and then been adopted by a group of fans in New York. Veney was corresponding with American fans including one of the New York Futurians, Don Wollheim, who suggested that he name the new Sydney club Futurian. Veney proposed it at the club's first meeting and it was adopted.

Calling themselves 'Futurians' was more than just a good way of avoiding having to call themselves science fiction fans at a time when the usual response to announcing that they read it was ridicule. It also expressed a view that science fiction should be more than just an enjoyable form of fiction, it was a political view that science could create a better life for everybody and, as Futurians, they could help foster that improvement by promoting science fiction which gave expression to the possibilities offered by science.

Some science fiction fans learned a little about science from the prozines and formed the belief that science was the key to the future. By reading science fiction they thought they were educating themselves in the possibilities of the future so, by calling themselves Futurians, young Sydney fans expressed a belief that science fiction was more than escapist literature. That by reading and promoting science fiction they were helping to create a better future, so supporting and promoting science fiction was a social responsibility. The term 'Futurian' combined that belief in the positive force of science to create a better future with a growing political awareness in some fans in reaction to world events including the Great Depression, the growth of fascism and the Spanish Civil War.

At first a Futurian was simply a person 'interested in the future' but the definition soon became more strident. Molesworth wrote that: 'A Futurian always had an interest in the changing world, did not busy himself in a pile of musty magazines, but looked forward to seeing something in those magazines — dreams come true. In a sense, to be Futurian is to be the possessor of an honoured distinction'.[1] A year later Veney wrote more enthusiastically: '...let us shout the ideals, the hidden truths of science fiction! It is what the world needs. Hope! A faith in a better tomorrow. And we fans are the ones to carry this message of the things to come.'[2]

Some, perhaps most, of Sydney's young fans were receptive to these ideas. Most were in their mid-teens by 1939 so their lives had been shaped by the environment of deprivation and scarcity of the Great Depression which constrained their lives and limited their expectations. Their circumstances made them socially aware and committed because they believed that science fiction was important in showing what was possible in the future. Science fiction offered an escape from the confining world around them but it also encouraged them to think that the future could be better, more liberating and exciting than their present.

This environment and their personal circumstances had made Veney and Castellari virtually socialists by 1939. Veney's father was a waterside worker with very strong left-wing politics and Castellari had seen the sheer poverty of many people he knew and saw the indescribable injustice and unfairness in the world. They also knew that there had been better times in the past and hoped they would come again.

In the severely depressed economy of the late 1930s there was little opportunity for them to go anywhere or do anything to achieve their dreams. Few could aspire to a higher education and they left school when they were fifteen to help support their families. For them life was not a matter of what they wanted to do, it was what circumstances forced them to do. The opportunities for careers did not exist so they expressed their aspirations in what they read and what they felt about it. Many years later Castellari commented:

> We were kids from nowhere and weren't getting much of an education by modern standards — barely enough to live with. But we were gripped by the possibilities of the world [and] the use of science and science fiction was an extension to some extent of what we believed.[3]

Unlike Veney and Castellari, Vol Molesworth came from the wealthier but conservative side of politics with a father who was as member of the United Australia Party in the New South Wales Legislative Council and had links to the New Guard (a quasi-fascist organisation of the early 1930s). He had a private school education which gave him a better command of the English

---

[1] Vol Molesworth, *A history of Australian science fiction fandom*, Chapter 1.

[2] Veney, *Austra Fantasy 6*.

[3] Interview with Bert Castellari, *Mumblings from Munchkinland 15*.

The entire membership of the Futurian Society of Sydney at their fourth meeting, 14 January 1940. Back row LtoR: Ralph Smith, Bill Veney, Eric Russell. Front row LtoR: Ted Russell, Bert Castellari and Vol Molesworth
(Chris Nelson, Mumblings from Munchkinland 30)

language, made him an experienced debater and gave him a great deal of self-confidence. He was a ball of energy who couldn't quite see why others were so slow, but he was also volatile and lacked the ability to complete projects without help.

The youth and immaturity of Society members was their greatest weakness because it made their general outlook and conduct adolescent. The only older science fiction fan they knew was Charles La Costa who had been a member of the Sydney SF League. He was primarily a collector with a large library which impressed Society members and which he allowed them to borrow from, but he did not become very involved in their activities.

At the Society's first meeting Veney talked about their high expectations and the belief that many more fans would join them. It was their hope, he said, that Futurian ideals would expand the Society into an Australia wide organisation. However, the reality of their club rarely matched these high aspirations. Science fiction might have been the door to the future but running a science fiction club amicably was beyond their abilities.

The Society held eighteen meetings in its first ten months. There had been five members at the first meeting and a total membership of thirteen by then with seven or eight attending meetings regularly.[4] Meetings were held at the

---

[4] The third issue of *The Sydney Futurian*, published in November 1947, gives as the founding members of the Society: Bill Veney, Bert Castellari, Eric Russell, Ted Russell and Vol Molesworth. It goes on to list, as members who joined in the following ten months, Ralph Smith, Ron Levy, Neville Friedlander, Keith Hooper, Noel Dwyer, Davie Evans, Bruce Sawyer, Colin Roden, Len Stubbs and Ken Williams. (*The Sydney Futurian* 3.) This list does

homes of the member's parents, fortnightly from May 1940, on the first Sunday and third Wednesday of the month with the Wednesday meetings planned to be at Veney's place. Refreshments were served after meetings, most likely by the boy's parents.

Society meetings were run to an agenda which included debate about Society business, discussion of the prozines, quiz competitions, round robin stories and other diversions including ESP and rocket experiments. There were formal presentations such as Roma Castellari and Ralph Smith speaking about various aspects of illustrating and wider ranging discussions on topics such as Atlantis and other lost continents and, at another meeting, the works of Stanley Weinbaum, which drifted into scientific arguments.

The formality of Society meetings was reinforced by the authoritarian and legalistic tendencies that Molesworth inherited from his father. The Society's constitution bound it to formal procedures which seem to have focused its activities inwards and caused friction between members by directing meetings towards debates in which excitable and earnest young men could test themselves against each other. One cause for friction was the provision of the constitution that members had to be elected into the Society. As a result for example, at the seventh meeting of the Society, Ken Jefferys was elected to membership without objection but Roma Castellari (Bert Castellari's sister) was elected only after several objections, probably because she was a girl at a time when girls were not supposed to be interested in things like science fiction. At another meeting Molesworth's proposal that a club library be established was 'hotly debated' and eventually carried by five votes to three.

Meetings became strained and acrimonious with heated debates, disagreements and disruptions. *Futurian Observer* wrote that the seventh meeting was the 'most strained and unsettled ever' due to the disruption of one member. Disruption was even worse at the following meeting and Veney, the Society's Director at the time, vowed that disruptions would be 'stamped out'. But the situation did not improve.[5]

In writing later about this period in the Society's history Molesworth lay the blame for the growing antagonism in the Society on the formation of factions around the editors of Sydney fanzines. Veney's actions towards the end of 1940 support this contention, but youthful competition and antagonism between different temperaments and interests also played a major part

---

not include Roma Castellari and Ken Jeffrey who were elected to membership during the Society's seventh meeting. The sources are not clear on exact names and numbers. Molesworth summarized that the Society had gained twelve new members during this period but that there were never more than thirteen members because four members had resigned during the period. (Molesworth, *A History of Australian science fiction fandom*, Chapter 1).

[5] *Futurian Observer* 7 and 8.

in the atmosphere surrounding the Futurian Society of Sydney during 1940.

A list of Australian fans published in *Ultra* in May 1940 included the names of sixteen Australian fans, nine of them living in Sydney.[6] Some of them had been discovered through the letter columns of the prozines but most of the people they contacted were not interested in participating in science fiction fandom. They shared an interest in science fiction with the Sydney youngsters but were more interested in collecting than activities such as clubs or publishing fanzines. One was Charles Mustchin who had built up a substantial collection at Coolangatta in Queensland. Others were Jack Radford and Frank Maggs in Adelaide and Howard Pollard and Ralph Harding in Perth. Harding had been collecting for many years, since he discovered the first issue of *Amazing Stories*. In Melbourne Marshall MacLennan had a very large collection he had built up after his first collection had been stolen in 1934. By mid-1940 he had about 200 fantasy books and all the magazines except two issues of *Amazing* and one issue of *Amazing Stories Quarterly*.[7] He was, however, older with a family and less time or inclination to become involved in fannish activities.

Top: Warwick Hockley
(Melbourne Bulletin 7)
Below: Keith Taylor
(Melbourne Bulletin 6)

The Sydney group also discovered a few who were younger and more like minded; Keith Moxon in Brisbane, Don Tuck in Hobart and Warwick Hockley and Keith Taylor in Melbourne.

Keith Moxon had plans to launch a club and access to a duplicator so he began thinking about publishing a magazine. By April 1940 his plans had grown to publication of a lithographed semi-professional magazine to be called *Imaginative Stories*. However, response to his proposal was poor so he cut it back to a mimeographed magazine and began soliciting material and subscriptions. After a while Sydney fans heard little from him and some

---

[6] *Ultra* 5. The names were Howard L Pollard in Western Australia, Jack Radford and Frank Maggs in Adelaide, Marshall Maclennan in Melbourne, Chas Mustchin and Keith Moxon in Queensland and Don Tuck in Tasmania. In Sydney they were Bill Veney, Bert Castallari, Roma Castellari, Eric Russell, Ted Russell, Vol Molesworth, Ralph Smith, Neville Freedlander and Ron Levy.

[7] *Austra Fantasy* 2.

became critical, but wrote little about it because they didn't want to let Americans know that everything in the Australian garden was not rosy. In September Sydney fans learned Moxon had contracted pneumonia and later heard he had suffered a relapse and been taken to a rest home for a few months. As he recovered Moxon announced he had contributions from the Sydney author Allan Connel and from David Evans, Vol Molesworth and others. However, he lost interest in the project and fandom and Sydney fans heard nothing more from him after early 1941.

Don Tuck in Hobart was corresponding with the Sydney group by February 1940. He tried to find other science fiction readers through his bookstall dealer and hoped to form a Futurian Society of Hobart. However, he was also studying at the university so his time for other activities was limited, though he kept up correspondence with fans around Australia and overseas.

Warwick Hockley and Keith Taylor in Melbourne only announced themselves to Sydney fans after the list in *Ultra* had been compiled. Unlike Moxon and Tuck, they became active and enthusiastic contributors to Australian fandom through their fanzines.

World War 2 had little direct effect on Australian fandom for the first two years. Fans experienced the fighting overseas only through newspapers and newsreels because enlistment for Australia's overseas military force had a lower age limit of 19 and the call up age for military training and the militia was between the ages of 18 and 35. Almost all Australian fans were younger than that but some expected to get call up notices for military training and enlistment in the militia during the year. However, whatever they thought about the war they made no mention of in their fanzines.

The young Australian fans began corresponding with British fans Rosenblume and Youd from early 1940 but the war threat to Britian was much more immediate and news the failure of Britain's two prozines and the failure to launch *New Worlds* made bleak reading in Australia. Most British fanzines folded so only the *Pseudo Futurian*, *SFR War Bulletin* and *Fantasy War Bulletin* kept arriving in Australia.[8]

The main effect of the war on Australian fans was on the mail, their lifeline to the rest of fandom. By June 1940 nine out of ten letters arriving in America from Australia had the little sticker 'opened by Censor' on them. Disruption of shipping services meant there were noticeable delays in receiving mail from America and when the *RMS Niagra* was sunk in June 1940 two issues of the *Futurian Observer* addressed to American fans went down with it.

The largest, longest and most dramatic impact on Australian science fiction fandom came indirectly.

---

[8] *Futurian Observer* 21.

No 8. April 21st, 1940. 2d.

SCIENCE FICTION MAGAZINES BANNED!

A grave situation has arisen. The Federal Government has issued a list of American pulp magazines which will be banned from this country. Included in this list are all stf magazines now entering the Commonwealth. ASTOUNDING, FFM, TWS, SS, etc., etc., all fall under this ban. The magazines will continue to appear in Australia for two months, owing to the fact that shipments are already on route. Not content with completely banning the magazines from the stands, the Government has decreed that new subscriptions cannot be commenced. Subscriptions that have already been placed will be allowed to carry on until their expiration.

The latest news on this matter, at the time of writing, comes from Victoria. There, the Federated Newsagents Association has asked the Government to reconsider its decision, stating that the dollar exchange is negligible. Probably the newsagents in other States will co-operate in this appeal and the chances of the ban being repealed may become more promising. Behind them also will be the reading public, who must sooner or later, raise objections to the curtail on this cheap form of literature. It must be borne in mind that already the newer magazines have been prevented from appearing on the stands, that is, ASTONISHING STORIES, SUPERSCIENCE STORIES, PLANET STORIES, etc. etc.

AUSTRALIAN FANDOM CARRIES ON:- Despite these distressing circumstances it is gratifying to know that the small, but active, band of fans intend to carry on their work of popularising science fiction. Hopes are high for the British reprint editions of eight magazines, so that at least we'll have some form of reading. Even if the British reprints fail to appear, American publishers have been considering putting the idea into operation out here.

Futurian OBSERVER will carry on, but it is doubtful whether we can fulfill the promise of four pages, for at least a while. Also Molesworth has quite unexpectedly issued Cosmos - a sixpager appearing tri-weekly.

Best news of all comes from Keith Moxon of Brisbane, who has issued a circular giving notice of Australia's first semi-professional magazine. It will be lithographed, containing from ten to twelve quarto size inages, and will be issued semi-yearly. Departments will include "Have Your Says Sir," a department in which readers throw their stones or toss their bouquets; a lecturette on some scientific matter; free use of an exchange department in which is stated your willingness to buy or sell or exchange science fiction magazines; a column devoted to the latest news on club activities; and, to top all, will print ---- with co-operation of readers ---- an everlasting debate. "Are We Any More Civilised Than We Were 200 Years Ago?" Only amateur writer's material will be used and only the very best of these. Scientific articles will also be supplied by amateurs. Cover, will be painted by a talented artist.

The name of this publication is to be HOMO. Watch it grow!

Further information on this magazine will be printed in our next issue, dated May 5th.

At the end of 1939 the United States government revised its prohibition on weapons exports and, through a technicality, allowed Britain and its allies to purchase weapons but not Germany and its allies. However, all weapons had to be paid for in cash. By the end of 1940 Britain had ordered over $1.2 billion worth of American aircraft alone and they had to be paid for when they were delivered.

British gold reserves paid for a lot but all unnecessary spending of British money in America had to be restricted to conserve scarce capital to pay for the war, including Australian purchases from the United States. Consequently, on 1 April 1940 the Australian government introduced prohibitions against the importation of a wide range of goods from non-sterling countries. They included many categories including some agricultural machinery, flooring and wallpaper, cutlery, motor cycles and 'certain classes of publications, of which details will be announced later'.[9] Among these publications were almost all American pulp magazines including the science fiction prozine. Newsagents protested, claiming the savings would be negligible, and fans wrote letters of protest to Sydney newspapers, but the embargo remained. Magazines that had been paid for before the embargo started could still be imported so it was not until about July 1940 that the final shipments of American magazines appeared on Australian newsstands.

Australian fans relied on the latest prozines for their steady diet of science fiction and the fan material that connected them with other mail-based fan communities. Before the embargo Molesworth had collected twenty-two science fiction prozine titles and purchased six prozines every third Wednesday. Now there was virtually nothing and it was the same for everyone. Some fans hoped the embargo would lead to the rejuvenation of Australian publishing and that a science fiction magazine might emerge, but that did not happen.

Technically, the embargo was not against the importation of American magazines, it was a prohibition on sending Australian money to the United States to buy them. This meant the importers who sold the magazines in Australia could no longer buy them and Australians could no longer subscribe to them. It also meant Australian fans could not subscribe to American fanzines or send money for other fan activities such as supporting the coming American convention in Denver by buying memberships.

Although Australians could not buy American magazines, that did not prohibit Americans from sending them to Australians as gifts, and American fans like Forry Ackerman sent many. Parcels of prozines from America that arrived in Sydney were welcomed, shared around and probably read by many. Australian fans could send their fanzines, or anything else that might be of interest to American collectors, in trade for American prozines so, in the

---

[9] *Argus* (Melbourne), Monday 1 April 1940, p.5.

minds of Australian fans. their fanzines became almost a form of currency that could be traded in America. Some Australian fans also wrote to the prozines in America asking for help and Don Tuck offered to trade mint stamps and postcards for prozines.

Despite the generosity these few prozines were a trickle in comparison to the rich flow before the embargo. That trickle also depended on the continuing generosity of American fans and that gradually diminished. To make matters worse, customs authorities in some Australian States were suspicions of the prozines that did arrive and Don Tuck in Tasmania was warned about receiving magazines from America in the post and, when they kept coming, they were confiscated.

To fill this vacuum fans started seriously going around bookshops and secondhand shops looking for old magazines to add to their collections or sell or trade with others. It is likely that some American prozines arrived in Australia as ballast on ships. In the years before the war, and in the early war years, ships from overseas carried paper as ballast, including pulp magazines. They were dumped on wharves as virtually worthless but usually taken away by book shops and distributors to be sold in their shops and on their newsstands.[10]

Sometimes the books and magazines that fans found could be bought for a few pence but the price of one shilling became common and some rare items sold for as much as two or three shillings as scarcity increased. Sometimes fans were lucky. Early in 1941 Castelarri and Levy came across a heap of old *Wonder Stories* and *Amazing* in a city book stall and bought about sixty of them. Later in the year an enormous number of post embargo magazines appeared in the Royal Arcade Bookstall and fans eagerly snapped them up for good prices. Graham Stone raised some of the money to buy these magazines by selling some of the less wanted material in his collection for two pence each, but when he went to buy them back they cost him six pence.

Around the time the embargo began news arrived that some American prozines were going to be reprinted in Britain and that they would be coming to Australia. These reprint editions, known as British Reprint Editions (BREs), would be limited to about 96 pages without the serials, some of the shorter stories, most of the interior illustrations and the American advertisements and fan material. BREs began arriving in Sydney in late October 1940, reprints of the American *Astounding* and *Unknown* from late 1939. At first only a few shops sold them so they were hard to find but by May 1941, *Astounding* and *Unknown* BREs were being sold from most newsstands

---

[10] There has been much vigorous debate about whether or not this actually happened. However, it was a commonly held belief in postwar Australian fandom so it cannot be discounted.

for between 7½d and 1/- each. Fans welcomed them but considered them inferior to the American prozines and only as a poor substitute.

The embargo on American prozines may have been one of the reasons why fandom in Sydney became so fractious in the second half of 1940. Sydney fans' love of science fiction was the common interest that bound them together but, with their supply much reduced, they had less in common to talk about so other things began to occupy their minds. They were young and passionate so they had to find something else to be enthusiastic about. That turned out to be themselves.

Castellari wrote in the first issue of *Futurian Observer* that the youth of Australian fans would be a problem. None of them was more than 17 when they started the Futurian Society of Sydney. They could be active and enthusiastic but, he said, they needed adult guidance if the Society was to be stable and successful. However, the only adult science fiction enthusiast they knew was Charles La Costa who had helped them get established but did not play an active role in their group.[11] The only other adult who joined them was David Evans who was around 31 years old when he became involved. However, the age difference between them would soon cause other problems.

With their energy and ideals the Society started with gusto. They made great plans about what they would do — libraries, fanzines and more — but their lack of maturity and experience led them to fail in all they planned. When they set themselves a goal they were unable to achieve they lost interest in it and set themselves a new goal. This created a growing sense of frustration and finger pointing at other members who were, they said, to blame for their failures. The result was a series of false starts with inactivity following activity and a feeling of success followed by failure which blighted the atmosphere of the club.

The lack of progress affected the motivation and interest of Society members no more so than Molesworth. At the beginning of March he announced he would stop publishing fanzines and that keeping his science fiction library was too expensive. In April he resigned from the Society for unexplained reasons but a month later he was back, reelected to the membership and again active.

Their first major failure occurred in March 1940 when Society members decided to create a club library of books and magazines and appointed Ron Levey as the Librarian. However, an executive committee decided to dissolve it before it had barely started, apparently because of lack of support.

In May David Evans suggested the Society should publish a club fanzine that would promote science fiction by uniting the activities of science fiction enthusiasts. They all agreed and said they would cease publishing their own

---

[11] *Futurian Observer* 1.

fanzines and participate in one club fanzine, except Eric Russell who said he would not stop publishing *Ultra* whatever the Futurians decided to do. In the excitement of the meeting Evans was elected to edit this new club fanzine. Two weeks later they had changed their minds and abandoned the idea.

In July, inspired by the discovery of fans in other Australian cities, an informal meeting of Sydney fans decided to launch a new organization, the Futurian Society of Australia to bring together all Australian fans in one group. It was not to be a club like the Society, its main role would be to create a register of Australian fans and perhaps publish an official bulletin of some kind. Veney was appointed president and Eric Russell as secretary and a committee was appointed to contact all interested fans in Australia. A list of Honorary Members was published; Bert Castellari, Charles La Coste, Marshall MacLennan, Charles Mustchin and H Pillock but very little more happened after that.

David Evans
(*Ultra* 2/4, April 1941)

In August they resolved to make a three minute sound recording of their voices to send to the Worldcon in Chicago that year. However, the recording was not made and the suggestion that a telegram might be sent, because it was too late for the recording, also failed to materialise.

This lack of achievement uncovered another problem. What did the Society exist for? A relatively new member, Neville Friedlander, resigned after the change of mind about a club fanzine because, he said, the Society should be an outlet for amateur authors and that a club magazine could have been a way of promoting science fiction in Sydney. Following his resignation a very rowdy meeting debated the Society's purpose. Ralph Smith said there should be more emphasis on scientific research. Friedlander had thought the society existed to support writing science fiction but Ron Levy said he had joined the Society to discuss science fiction, not to write it.

After an hour and a half of loud disagreements the meeting agreed that the source of their trouble was in giving too much attention to fanzines and not enough to discussing science fiction. They agreed that from then on the club would concern itself mainly with discussions, debates, lectures and other activities related to science fiction and that any discussion about fanzines would take place only before and after meetings. Eventually they decided that the Society's policy would be the discussion of science fiction and kindred topics. Talking about fanzines would be barred from meetings but, at the following meeting, the policy was changed so discussion of fanzines would be allowed at meetings, but only for one hour.

Publishing fanzines had become the major fan activity in Sydney and Molesworth thought the reason Society members had decided against a club fanzine was because those involved in publishing fanzines were jealous of the elevated positions that gave them in the small community. Agreeing to it would also have cut them off from their direct links with fans overseas.

That might have been part of the reason, but friction also came because they disagreed on what the club fanzine should be. Some supposed a club fanzine would be a combination of all their fanzines and be widely distributed while others thought it would be released only to members. Some thought it should be a news sheet devoted entirely to Society activities while others thought it should be run along professional lines and sold on bookstalls.

By the middle of 1940 the Society had split into factions focused around *Ultra*, *Futurian Observer* and Molesworth fanzines. The disagreements over a club fanzine and the Society's purpose exposed the divisions in the Society and Friedlander gave feuding in the club and the lack of unanimity by the members as another reason for his resignation. Evans criticised society members for their inconsistency and said that a club magazine would have stopped rivalry.

Geography also had an influence with fan groups in Ranwdick and Coogee who probably associated with each other outside the Society. There were also individual and group feuds, the most lively being between Veney and Eric Russell over Veney refusing to duplicate *Ultra* for what Russell considered a reasonable cost (although Molesworth later wrote that Veney and Russell remained firm personal friends).

The falling out between Sydney fans that had created two versions of *Zeus* was a symptom of the friction and changing alliances in Sydney fandom. It also demonstrated the importance they placed on producing good quality fanzines to impress fans in America. Perhaps the disagreement was as much about what they thought would be more appealing to American fans than simply a falling out among fans in Australia.

Friction between fans came out in the Sydney fanzines and Molesworth's *Cosmos* helped to inflame it. It became a forum where they could air their complaints and make their accusations. Much of it was conducted in mock humour but with bitterness just below the surface that magnified small grievances into major disagreements. Veney later said that *Cosmos* was the only fanzine of the time that successfully trod on everyone's toes.

Many of the letters in *Cosmos* were written in harsh, biting and critical language. Veney accused Molesworth of deliberately causing trouble and Evans wrote that *Cosmos*'s atmosphere created a puerile squabble that did not help Sydney fanzines or the Society. Veney and Castellari's writing in the *Futurian Observer* could be as blunt, harsh and hurtful as Molesworth and his correspondents. The animosity in their fanzines probably fueled disagreements at Society meetings which then became the fuel for more disputes in fanzines.

All this was made worse by the atmosphere at Society meetings which had been disorderly almost from the beginning. At the time *Futurian Observer* told the story of two Society members standing on Coogee Beach watching some barking and biting dogs. 'Look', said one to the other, 'a FSS meeting!'[12]

At a very disruptive meeting at the end of June Evans offered to 'referee' discussions and Veney, as Director, gave him authority to maintain order at the meetings. Nobody objected. Several following meetings passed peacefully under Evans control and he was elected Society Director at the first meeting in September. Evans made it clear he would run meetings as he pleased but members began to resent his control. He also raised again the proposal for a club magazine but the existing fanzine editors said they would not allow their fanzines to be taken over, so Evans said the society would publish its own.

The failure to achieve anything of significance and Evan's control of the Society meetings created a general sense of malaise which led three members, Ralph Smith, Keith Hooper and Noel Dwyer, and possibly more, to resign from the Society. At the meeting on 22 September lack of interest in the Society was so palpable that Castellari proposed it should be dissolved, but Veney suggested it should instead be suspended for a short period. The meeting agreed. Evans resigned as Director because he thought it would be better for the club, and for him, if he had nothing more to do with it. He was very disappointed, he had probably hoped that a Society magazine could be used to launch writing careers, for him and others in the Society.

Futurian Observer blamed the ages of all involved, particularly Evans. It wrote that the members' age ranged from 16 to 18 years, some going on for 19. They knew adult science fiction fans but they had not joined or taken part in Society activities. Evans had shown interest in them but where other adult fans had treated them more or less as equals, Evans had treated them as his inferiors and the young Society members has taken the wrong attitude towards him in return.[13] Veney also complained that, despite all the effort

---

[12] *Futurian Observer* 19.

[13] *Futurian Observer* 19.

that had been put into the Society, they had achieved nothing. Ideas of things to do had been proposed but had stopped due to the opposition or lack of support from Society members.[14]

The turmoil in the Society was only a dim reflection of events in the wider world around them. After nine months of relative peace during which the Society was founded Germany invaded France and the Low Countries. In May and June 1940, while the Sydney Futurians were arguing about their role and future, the Battle of France was lost. While Evans was enforcing peace at Society meetings and bringing it to the verge of extinction the Battle of Britain was being fought in the sky over England. Preoccupied, or perhaps not knowing what to write about these events, Australian fans wrote nothing about them in their fanzines, although they could not have been ignorant of or unaffected by them.

Even though the Society had been put into suspension its members still believed they had to be organised in some way and, again, gave up on one goal and set themselves another. Molesworth thought the suspension of the Society drew a line under what had happened previously and that Sydney fans were now experienced enough to do better with a new club.

Walking home from the meeting at which the Society had been suspended members of its opposing factions, Veney, Castellari, Levy, Molesworth and the Russell brothers decided to form a new club. They would be strict in electing new members who had to take an active part in club affairs and contribute at least one page to a new magazine they would produce. Their new club would be known as the Fantasy Club (which they quickly renamed the Science Fantasy Club) and Molesworth would be Director and Levy the Secretary.

Veney proposed to launch this new club at a meeting of selected Futurians in November 1940 but there is no evidence that the meeting ever took place. It is likely that most Sydney fans had lost heart and interest in fan activities but another factor was that one of the major forces in the Sydney group, Molesworth, became seriously ill with diabetes and went into hospital not long after that September meeting. He remained there for the rest of the year and kept up correspondence with overseas fans while there. Some of the Sydney group visited him and the Society's first anniversary was marked only when Veney and Castellari visited Molesworth and they talked over what had happened.

Ill health also affected other Australian fans at the end of 1940. Moxon in Brisbane was in hospital with pneumonia, Steve Taylor in Melbourne was in hospital with dyptheria, Mustchin in Coolangatta had been involved in a motorboat accident and Alan Roberts had been hit by a truck.

Like them fandom in Australia was in poor health at the end of 1940 but

---

[14] *Futurian Observer* 17.

Veney was not ready to let it rest there. He discussed the situation with several of what he called Sydney's 'progressive' fans and he and Castellari decided to try to resolve their problems at a conference where they could be discussed and resolved. The meeting, called the Sydney Science Fiction Conference, took place at Veney's place on the evening of Friday 6 November 1940.

Despite a general invitation to all fans only ten were present. Molesworth was not one because he was in hospital.[15] Veney began by briefly discussing the current situation as he saw it and then asked others to give their opinions. Growing out of this discussion was the general opinion that the Society should be revived, on a 'workable basis'. The discussion then turned to what 'a workable basis' was.

Veney had already prepared an eight point plan about how that basis might be achieved and it was vigorously debated for the following hour and a half, during which agreement was reached on most points. Two main issues remained, one was whether Society membership should be open or closed, as had been proposed for the Fantasy Club. Veney wanted the club to be closed but the majority preferred an open membership, so long as prospective members could meet the standards expected of them, which would be decided by a vote of the membership on proposed new members.

The other important issue was the role of fanzines in the Society. The meeting generally agreed that many of the Society's past problems had resulted from factionalism due to the existence of fanzines. The meeting decided that fanzine editors could be members of the Society so long as they refrained from printing any damaging material about the activities of other Society members or published letters from fans outside the club attacking members. They also decided that the club could issue an irregular club organ that could be easily converted into a defensive barrier against attack. Fan editors would also not be allowed to make detrimental statements about the Society while they remained members, unless they submitted the material for censorship by the club as a whole before printing it.

The meeting concluded around 10 pm when some of the members had to leave for home. Those who remained spent a much more enjoyable time chatting about science fiction and fandom.

---

[15] They were Charles La Coste, who chaired the meeting, Castellari, Cordner, Levy, Roden, Sawyer, Stone, Veney and the Russell brothers. *Futurian Observer* 21 and 21 *Extra*.

CHAPTER 3
1941-1945

By the beginning of 1941 the war was starting to have a greater impact on Australian fandom. In February the *Futurian Observer* published a roll-call of all known Australian fans and reported that the only one known to be on active service was George Turner. Nobody had heard from him after he left Australia with the second contingent of the 2ndAIF but he was thought to be somewhere in North Africa. Many others were approaching their eighteenth birthdays when they could be called up for three months military training and enlistment in the militia. The first Australian fan to go was Bruce Sawyer and others expecting to be called up during 1941 were Bill Veney, Noel Dwyer, Bert Castellari, Charles La Coste, Ralph Smith, Ken Williams, Alan Connell and Don Tuck.

As they got older Australia's young fans also began to grow up, at least a little. Castellari and Molesworth started work as copy boys at Sydney's *Sunday Sun* in January 1939, Veney started in a company that sold typewriters, and their interests also began to expand.

Girls were one of those new interests many of them shared. In the eighth issue of *Melbourne Bulletin* Noel Dwyer commented that all the fiction they had so far written in their fanzines excluded girls and asked if they should now include girls in their stories. 'We aren't children any more', he wrote. Hockley agreed, writing: 'We've go to start throwing off our juvenilistic traits'.[1]

Although they became interested in more than science fiction these young fans wrote almost nothing about it in their fanzines. Perhaps they thought it inappropriate to include such personal details in fanzines dedicated to the discussion and promotion of science fiction so only a couple of letters Hockley published in *Melbourne Bulletin* hint at a lively social life in Sydney fandom. Here is Noel Dwyer having a 'bonzer time' at a party where there were girls, and getting home at two in the morning. There is Bill Veney at a jitterbug party demonstrating that he was the best jitterbug in Australian fandom, Bert Castellari picking up a 'sort' (who looked just like Dale in *Flash Gordon*) on the corner of Pitt & Market Street, Bruce Sawyer looking for a girlfriend and Eric Russell, who was apparently tall, being embarrassed

---

[1] *Melbourne Bulletin* 8.

going on a blind date with a girl who was only four feet six. That's all their fanzines tell us about the social lives of this generation of Australian fans.²

Wartime conditions and censorship brought fandom to the attention of Australia's intelligence authorities and Hockley and Taylor were ordered to attend an interview at the Army's Intelligence Department. There they were presented with some letters, including one from Bob Tucker, and asked to explain the acronyms, cultural allusions and references that were commonly used in fannish correspondence of the time. Who was Hoy Ping Pong? What did 4e, LeL and Vom stand for? And what was the SPWSSTFM? An attached note said 'this letter contains so many abbreviations that it is impossible to understand it'. Hockley and Taylor had to explain what everything in the letters meant before they were released with the warning 'Never do such a thing again'.³

Bruce Sawyer
(*Ultra* First Annish)

Several new members joined the Sydney group including Graham Stone and Arthur Duncan. Stone had read about fandom in the prozines but not made contact until George Nash, owner of the book stall in Randwick that sold science fiction, told him of other boys who lived nearby who also read science fiction magazines. He wrote to them and received an enthusiastic reply from Castellari. He first encountered Sydney fandom at the Conference in November 1940 which left him dazed and mystified but he soon joined the Society and enjoyed compiling quiz competitions for their meetings that others found too hard.

Arthur Duncan met Graham Stone at school and they started combing the second hand bookshops together on Saturday mornings. He attended his first Society meeting in August 1941, started subscribing to fanzines and already had plans for his own fanzine, more a school magazine with an interest in science fiction than a fanzine, to be called *Venus*.⁴

---

² *Melbourne Bulletin* 5. There may be surviving personal correspondence in archives or personal collections somewhere that would reveal more. However, the work involved in locating and sifting through such evidence is outside the scope of this history and therefore I have not looked for any.

³ *Austra Fantasy* 5.

⁴ During the war Duncan discovered that his father had not legally adopted him and that his real name was Arthur Haddon, which is the name he used when he returned to fandom after the war.

Australian fans continued to pour their creativity into fanzines which also helped them keep in touch with fans overseas. However, publishing became progressively more difficult during 1941. One problem was the varying quality of stencils, paper and ink which made it difficult to maintain a high standard of reproduction. In one case the printing of an issue of *Ultra* was very poor because the ink was so expensive that Russell diluted it with kerosene, which then made it too thin. Hockley and Taylor learned there were two kinds of stencils, one that was best for typing and the other for drawing, but sometimes they had difficulty getting the ones they needed.

Access to typewriters and duplicators also caused problems. Most fans started by borrowing or hiring typewriters and duplicators but moved on, if they could, to owning their own. Some started with carbon copy or hektograph printing but soon moved on to mimeograph to improve the look of their fanzines. They could make a cheaper flatbed duplicator but it put more stress on stencils that limited print runs and often gave very poor results. If their equipment broke down they had to suspend publication until they could fix the problem themselves or afford to have it repaired.

Lack of money was another problem, so when Hockley and Taylor had to make a payment on their duplicator and buy stencils and paper, they had no money left for postage so an issue of their fanzine was delayed. Similarly, the cost of publishing the large *Ultra* annishes strained Eric Russell's resources so following issues had to be delayed. Maintaining energy and interest was also challenging and led to several changes in the editorship of Sydney fanzines and declining publication schedules of all Australian fanzines.

Ultra, Second Anniversary Issue
(Rare Books & Special Collections, Sydney University)

Most Australian fanzines looked relatively poor with content that was rarely above average but there were highlights as Australia's young fanzine editors improved their skills and techniques, creating a few excellent examples of the fanzine editor's art in 1941. Some fanzines like *Ultra, Zeus* and *Austra Fantasy* experimented with multi coloured pages produced by using two or three colour stencils and ink drums. The art published in Australian fanzines also became increasingly sophisticated and confident as the artists gained experience. Ralph Smith was the main contributor and drew many covers, while several others including Ted Russell and Bruce Sawyer had their work published occasionally.

Ultra and *Zeus* were the main Sydney fanzines with three issues of *Zeus*, but only one after March 1941, and six issues of *Ultra* published on a fairly regular bi-monthly schedule. Most issues comprised about twenty pages with the March issue of *Zeus* running to 38 pages and the second annish of *Ultra* running to 52 pages. *Zeus* concentrated on fiction, with Molesworth and Evans contributing stories to all three issues, letters of comment and full and detailed minutes of early FSS meetings. *Ultra*'s contents were a little more varied with a regular 'Ramblings in Science Fiction' column and a great deal of fiction with stories by Evans and Molesworth in most issues. The Second Annish, published in November 1941, was virtually a roll call of Australia's active fandom.[5]

Futurian Observer continued regular publication but the lack of regular news meant it adopted a 'print anything' policy to fill its pages. Veney lost interest, or may have been put off by the continuing feuding in Sydney, and resigned from the fanzine in February 1941. Ron Levy soon joined Castellari as co-editor but much of the early energy had gone from the fanzine and they appear to have kept publishing mainly so they had something to trade with fans overseas. It had become 'Fortnightly (sometimes)' by August and even then they printed copies only every third week or so and sent issues out in batches, most likely to meet the departure times of the mail boats sailing for North America.

Taking *Futurian Observer's* place as a regular newszine was the *Science & Fantasy Fan Reporter*, first published on 12 August 1941 and appearing weekly for the rest of the year. It began with three editors, Colin Roden, Eric Russell and Graham Stone, but Stone dropped out after the sixth issue because he was still at school and did not have the money to pay his share of the costs. Molesworth replaced Russell after the eleventh issue, but he dropped out after the 17th issue, leaving Roden the sole editor. It was a small, compact fanzine of no more than four pages which collected and published news about fans and fandom in Australia. It lacked the quarrelsome nature of *Futurian Observer* with only occasional editorial comment. Roden presented news about both fan and professional matters in such a way that even the most touchy Sydney fans couldn't take offense and its objective treatment and regular appearance gave a level of stability to Sydney fandom for a while.

Sydney fans made several attempts to launch new fanzines, with little success. After the enthusiasm generated by the Sydney Conference in November 1940 Molesworth planned to publish a new 'Luna-ised' *Cosmos* but the last issue of that fanzine was published in January 1941. He planned a

---

[5] *Ultra*'s second annish included articles by Tuck, Veney, Stone, Hockley and the Rambler, fiction by Molesworth, Evans, Dwyer and Smith, and poetry from Evans, Sawyer and Roden.

new fanzine called *Psycho* that did not see print but published the first issue of *Telefan* in March 1941. It was a lively four page fanzine in the style of *Cosmos*, but there was no second issue. Ted Russell published the first issue of *Future*, which was to be the journal of the FSS, but there was no second issue. Also enthused by the Conference Eric Russell published one issue of the *FFA Bulletin* in January 1941, a single brown quarto sheet duplicated on both sides, but not a second issue. At the beginning of April Molesworth published two issues of *Spaceward* for Futurian Federation of Australia but when Arthur Duncan tried to publish a third issue around September the results were so bad that he was too embarrassed to send it out.

Warwick Hockley and Keith Taylor in Melbourne continued to publish fanzines with little fuss, four issues of *Austra Fantasy* and ten of *Melbourne Bulletin*. Each one was an improvement on previous issues. The ninth issue of *Melbourne Bulletin*, for example, was printed in three colours using a combination of typing and drawing stencils to achieve a high quality of art reproduction which was enhanced with shading plates, templates and other techniques. The sixth issue of *Austra Fantasy*, which was published around the same time, demonstrates all the same techniques and was only less visually interesting because there were more pages of type, much of which was poorly printed (in the copy I've seen) which may have been due to the quality of stencils or ink rather than Hockley's publishing abilities. Australian fans produced nothing like these colourful and visually exciting late Hockley fanzines for many decades to come.

During the year *Austra Fantasy* grew to include larger contributions including short fiction, articles and letters. It was notionally quarterly and three issues were published in 1941, each of over 20 pages. Almost everybody who was anybody in Australian fandom contributed and it became an outlet for some of the arguments in Sydney fandom with fans there writing to Hockley complaining about other Sydney fans and explaining their attitudes. Bill Veney said *Austra Fantasy* became Australia's best fanzine with a mixture of fact, fiction and commentary, and Hockley's innovative use of colour and design.

In Hobart Don Tuck found three other science fiction readers, Bob Gaeppen, John Symmons and Lindsay Johnson and together they published *Profan*. They had the encouragement and advice of Hockley and published three issues between April and September 1941. At first they had planned to concentrate on writing about the prozines but, after the first issue and due to the embargo on importing American prozines, they broadened their interest so there was the usual mix of contents including short fact and fiction, letters of comment and Tuck's trademark author listings.

Profan rivalled the best fanzine produced in Australia during this period. It suffered from many of the common fanzine production problems including uneven printing and often uninspiring content, but it was also much tidier in appearance than most other Australian fanzines with, by the third issue, multi-coloured reproduction on several colours of quarto paper.

Some Australian fans still hoped to become professional authors and continued writing fiction for their fanzines as a hoped for prelude to a professional career. In March 1941 David Evans made arrangements with an Australian magazine to publish six science fiction or fantasy stories and invited manuscripts of about 2000 words, saying it was a professional experiment and accepted manuscripts would be paid for at current magazine rates. However, by June he had only received manuscripts from Moselworth, Veney and Roden and the project stalled.

Evans had six stories by October 1941, two he had written, two from Molesworth and one each from Veney and Roden. However, by then paper shortages and the introduction of licences for permission to publish magazines meant the project was reworked into a book published in magazine form. If it was successful a series of books would follow, appearing at regular intervals in the style of western magazines already being published locally. The first issue was planned for publication in early 1942, but the events of December 1941 ended that hope.

Through the course of 1941 Sydney fans gradually lost contact with other Australian fans. They kept in touch with Don Tuck in Hobart but he was also busy studying at university. They heard little from other collectors including Howard Pollard in Perth, who had one letter printed in *Cosmos*, and Marshall McLennan in Melbourne who had little interest in science fiction fandom outside collecting and whose increasing work pressure left him little spare time to follow his main interest.

The only active fans outside Sydney were Warwick Hockley and Keith Taylor in Melbourne. Keith Taylor was Hockley's good friend and shared his interest in science fiction but did not have access to either a typewriter or duplicator so his activity was limited to supporting Hockley. In early 1941 they jointly bought a mimeo and Taylor wrote that he was planning his own fanzine, but it did not eventuate. Like many young fans still at school Hockley's activity was limited by lack of money but after he started work as a laboratory assistant at the Vacuum Oil Company in March 1941 he found he had more money but less time and energy for fan activity.

Soon after his introduction to fandom Hockley said he hoped to establish a Futurian Society in Melbourne, but he was never able to find enough science fiction readers interested in fan activities to form it and he gave up on the idea towards the end of 1941. Around August 1941 he hit on the idea of promoting interest in science fiction and fandom by placing copies of his fanzines for sale at McGills Newsagency. However, by late in 1941 pressure of work, perhaps some despondency at not finding fellow fans in Melbourne, and the state of Sydney fandom, meant Sydney fans rarely heard from him. By December Hockley was in sole charge of an analytic laboratory and doing some research and other work, Taylor was also working, so they had all but disappeared from fandom.

Australian fans regarded themselves as the third branch of international fandom, after North America and Britain, and the fanzines and letters they sent to and received from overseas were vital in helping them feel part of a much wider community. Hockley dedicated the ninth issue of *Austra Fantasy* to two American fans who had been major supporters of the young Australian fans, Bob Tucker and Forry Ackerman. Tucker gave Australian fandom an occasional nod in the pages of *Le Zombie* with mentions and sometimes comments on their fanzines, describing the April 1941 issue of *Ultra* as 'a better Aussie product'.[6]

Their dependence on this kind of encouragement was shown when they read with distress the news that Tucker was taking a break from *Le Zombie* and, later, that he had been called up for military service. Ackerman and Morojo's *Voice of the Imagi-Nation* also supported and encouraged Australian fans through its letter column which contained news and gossip from the rest of the fannish world. Some Australian fans also wrote to Ackerman and their letters appeared occasionally in his fanzine including from Molesworth, Levy, Evans and Roberts. In July Ackerman sent a recording of the voices of some American fans to Sydney fans but the sound was so very faint it could barely be heard.

Australian fans were very interested in the American conventions and wanted to be a small part of them. After their failure to send any kind of representation to Chicon in 1940 the Society planned to send something to the Denver convention and Molesworth became the convention's Australian representative. However, disorganisation in the Society meant nothing happened and, while Hockley in Melbourne planned to send a telegram to the convention, he found it would cost 25/- (more than a quarter of his weekly salary) so he sent an airmail letter which arrived late (by this time there was an air mail service to North America every third week).

Australian fans looked to North America for leadership and inspiration. *Futurian Observer* wrote that American fandom was more mature and that they should help Australian fans with advice and assistance as they also matured. 'Who in America wanted to help Australia with his/her advice and who of those who want to give it can give us good advice?', Castellari wrote.[7]

Australian and British fans started corresponding in 1940. By then British fandom was severely handicapped by the state of the war and mails became unreliable and sometimes damaged or lost. Michael Rosenblume received

---

[6] *Le Zombie* 34, 37 & 45.

[7] *Futurian Observer* 38.

and distributed copies of *Austra Fantasy* and *Melbourne Bulletin*, and probably Sydney fanzines, and observed the state of fandom in Australia from what he read there. He wrote, in *Melbourne Bulletin* in August 1941, that British and Australian fandom had a great deal in common but also a great deal of difference. Australians didn't have the distractions of the British experience of air raids but British fans were on the whole much older and adult in thought, manner and behavior. He wrote: 'Austrafandom squanders far too much of its energy on internecine squabbles — which fact you print out in your letters'. He asked, 'How can you achieve anything if that is what happens?'[8]

Rosenblume's question went unanswered in Sydney where the peaceful co-operation promised by the conference in November 1940 did not last long.

Reinvigorated by hope and enthusiasm after the November Conference Veney and Molesworth began planning a convention to be held in Sydney on Easter Sunday, 1941, to be called Sydcon. They planned it would take place between 1 pm and 5 pm with a banquet in the evening. There would be displays of rare fanzines and books and a selection of stills from fantasy movies. The program would begin with a general introduction and discussion, followed by lectures and speeches given by well-known fans, an auction, a business session, and other attractions. 'Let Bygone by Bygone — Come to Sydcon!' their publicity said.[9] Veney and Molesworth published a circular promoting the convention and Molesworth also had promotional stickers printed,

Despite their plans things did not go well. The first meeting of the revived FSS on 21 January 1941 decided that all those who had been at the November Conference were elected members and a new member, Alan Cordner, was also elected. However, Molesworth had been in hospital during the Conference and therefore had to be reelected to FSS membership. A small membership committee (Veney, Castellari and Cordner) decided Molesworth did not have the necessary qualifications for membership so he was rejected and had to leave the meeting. (Molesworth later blamed this on an instant dislike he and Cordner had taken to each other when they first met.) A little later Castellari and Levy, both outraged at what had happened, also resigned.

Molesworth took his rejection badly and announced he was leaving fandom. He washed his hands of Sydcon and left the 500 stickers he had ordered for somebody else to pick up and pay 8/6 for. He said he was unlikely to publish any fanzines for the future and, if he did, it would be solely for trading with American and local fanzines, not to uplift and advance science fiction fandom.[10]

---

[8] *Melbourne Bulletin* 8.
[9] *Cosmos* 2/2.
[10] *Futurian Observer* 29.

By then the FSS had been reduced to a handful of members, perhaps six at best, but they planned to redevelop the club as a close knit and progressive organisation with a rotating chairmanship and small but interesting meetings that concentrated on an analytic study of various phases of science fiction. Meetings were held regularly every second Friday night. At a meeting in March Graham Stone gave a lecture on why *Wonder Stories* was better than the old *Amazing*. It created discussion so they decided there would be more lectures in future but this apparently rarely took place.

Veney, who was apparently unhappy with the direction the FSS had taken, resigned towards the end of April because, he said, he wanted to devote his time to his other interests including the YMCA, dancing, hockey and public speaking. He discussed the plans for Sydcon at a FSS meeting and they decided to drop the idea as being impractical and too difficult to organise in such a short time.

Despite his resignation from the Society Veney had not lost interest in science fiction and he later tried to attend a meeting with two friends, but was turned away because of a technicality in its rules. He and his friends, Jack Hannan and Darrell Cox, then formed the Sydney Science Fiction Association. With another member they held several informal meetings and resolved to discuss only science and science fiction and not take any part in fan activities. However, they soon lost interest and the group broke up amicably.

In place of the failed Sydcon the FSS organised a second conference in Sydney which was held on Easter Sunday, 13 April 1941. Eric Russell, who was behind it, sent out a postcard saying it would discuss the problems of Australian fandom including the Futurian Federation of Australia and the FSS. Twelve fans attended but Castellari could not because he was working. Later he asked Molesworth, 'How did the convention go? What was accomplished?' 'Nothing!' Molesworth replied, 'But we had a swell time.'[11]

The conference had been called with the serious intention of resolving the problems of Sydney fandom so the afternoon began with discussion of fan affairs, but achieved little. Castellari had written a two page speech about why he thought Sydcon had failed, it was read to the gathering and then disregarded. There was some talk of a national fan magazine, a national prozine library and a convention in Melbourne. Another suggestion was to have fan rallies not associated with existing clubs to discuss fandom that were simply 'spontaneous get-togethers' to maintain the threads of fandom.[12] The only real business decided was to rename the Futurian Associ-

---

[11] *Futurian Observer* 34. The fans there were Sawyer, Cordner, Evans, La Coste, Levy, Molesworth, Roden, Eric and Ted Russell, Stone, Veney and a fan from Newcastle, R Cudden

[12] *Ultra* 2/5.

Second Sydney SF Conference. LtoR R Cudden and son, Charles LaCoste, Ron Levy, Vol Molesworth, David Evans, Bill Veney, Bruce Sawyer, Graham Stone and Colin Roden
(*Ultra* 2/5 June 1941)

ation of Australia as the Futurian Federation of Australia and appoint Molesworth an office holder.

Despite the original intention to discuss Sydney fandom's troubles the conference eventually drifted into talking about anything that interested the fans there, anything but fan affairs. Eric Russell later wrote in *Ultra* that the occasion had been enjoyed by almost everyone and there had been many hilarious sidelights, but an opportunity to help towards a better Australian fandom had not been grasped.

After the Conference Castellari began to drift out of fandom, perhaps because of what had happened, or not happened, there. His work in the newspaper world, and association with people there, led him to begin reading more widely and to expand his world view.

There was, however, one significant outcome from the Conference. During it Cordner told Molesworth that he had been wrong in opposing

Second Sydney SF Conference. LtoR Charles LaCoste, Allan Cordner, Graham Stone, Vol Molesworth and Ted Russell
(*Ultra* 2/5, June 1941)

Molesworth's election to the FSS in January, that he would be resigning from the Society and that Molesworth should rejoin. Molesworth rejoined the Society at the meeting on 22 April and Cordner resigned a week later. Molesworth said he had been drifting out of fandom because he had a new job that took much more of his time and energy so he had no time to publish a large fanzine but when he rejoined the FSS it was with energy and enthusiasm so he soon took over control of the Society from Eric Russell who was only too willing to relinquish it.

Molesworth's strong personality and confident manner impressed some of the group but he could also be abrasive and, at times, cruel. He made fun of Stone for his fear of spiders and once told Veney he was 'the most intelligent idiot he'd ever met', and that was 'praising you up'.[13] Others could be just as abrasive and the one who used the pseudonym Emma Bizzybody wrote that some fans were conceited, some bigheaded, some just plain silly, some were publicity-seeking, some childish and some were 'just b—dy fools like Levy and Castellari'.[14] This abrasive nature caused tension in the group and created an environment ripe for argument and feuds. These aggressive attitudes were taken for granted and became an acceptable form of behaviour in the group.

Molesworth's propensity for legalities also soon emerged. He decided to overhaul the Society's past resolutions to determine the state of its constitution and, in May, tabled a list of 59 resolutions the club had carried in the past. They crossed out the ones that were outdated, leaving ten which were then approved. He also thought the Society should be put on a more secure financial footing so Roden was elected to the new position of Treasurer.

Under Molesworth's leadership the Society also continued its indecisions. They decided that there would be a club fanzine to be called *Future* and created the position of Editor for it. Over the next few meetings the members discussed ways of publishing it without success. Finally, in mid-July the position of Club Editor was dispensed with and science fiction quizzes and more discussion of stories were re-introduced.

As had happened the previous year the youth and immaturity of many group members caused problems. Charles La Costa commented that they were liable to too much inconsistency because they were young and, in his letter of resignation, Cordner wrote he was 'sick of mixing with a bunch of adolescents'.[15] In a letter to *Ultra* Hockley said that fandom needed to grow up and likened it to a big kindergarten.[16] When Dwyer resigned from the

---

[13] *Mumblings from Munchkinland* 13.

[14] *Futurian Observer* 38.

[15] *Futurian Observer* 35.

[16] *Ultra* 3/1. He went on to say that fandom did not exist to solve the problems of the world but he published his fanzines purely for the pleasure of its readers and editor.

Society later in the year he said it was not worthwhile and they should put their efforts into patriotic community work instead.[17]

The animosity and tension in the FSS was less evident in the pages of Sydney fanzines than previously because, it seems, there was a deliberate effort not to write much about it because of the reputation it gave Australian fandom to fandoms overseas. Molesworth commented, in a letter to *Voice of the Imagi-Nation*, that this also reduced the level of conflict in the group because it gave them less to argue about.[18]

The nervousness in Sydney fandom was further unsettled by a series of hoaxes perpetrated after the Second Conference. Molesworth and Stone blamed them on Castellari and Levy, or Castellari alone, but he thought the anonymous letter writer, Emma Bizzabody, was also the hoaxer. Nobody confessed and the hoaxes remain a small mystery.

In the first hoax Eric Russell received a telegram signed Hockley saying he had arrived in Sydney and would be attending the Conference. Next, a single sheet of paper from 'Australian Science Fiction News Limited' began arriving in fans' mail boxes around the beginning of May. It purported to be a report of the cancelled Sydcon and was, apparently, a satire of Sydney fandom. Copies were sent overseas and Tucker, for one, took it at face value. Castellari may have been involved in this hoax because his letter in the September 1942 issue of *Startling Stories* referred to a convention held in Sydney which had been attended sixty-seven fans.

In August word spread that David Evans had committed suicide. On hearing this Veney decided to check and was greeted by Evans when he knocked on his door. Castellari and Levy admitted they had decided to play a practical joke on Molesworth by telling him of the suicide and blamed him for spreading the rumour to the rest of fandom. An unintended result of this hoax was to bring Evans back to the fringes of fandom though he took little further part in organised fandom and, in September, gave most of his fanzines to Stone and burnt the rest.

Also in August an unsigned note was sent to most Sydney fans announcing that the *Futurian Observer* was for sale. An issue of that fanzine was posted the same day and made no mention of the sale, apparently absolving the editors from perpetrating it.

To counter these hoaxes Molesworth proposed that the Society appoint an officer to witness and endorse statements and, at the end of August, they bought a rubber stamp bearing the words 'Witnessed and endorsed by the FSS'. Anyone who wanted to make a statement or issue a report was advised to send it first to the FSS to be stamped. This action might have had some

---

[17] Stone footnote in Molesworth, *A History of Australian science fiction Fandom*, Chapter 2.
[18] *Voice of the Imagi-Nation* 15.

effect because no more hoaxes worth mentioning occurred, or perhaps the hoaxer, or hoaxers, had simply lost interest in their pranks.

Molesworth appears to have lost interest in fandom around August when he sold and gave away most of his fanzines and some of his prozines, with most going to Stone. This could have been the result of his continuing health problems because he was back in hospital in early October 1941 and did not return to work until the end of November. During his stay most of the Sydney group visited him and gave him prozines and fanzines to read. He also spent time writing letters to friends overseas and working on his fiction.

When Molesworth had returned to take over the FSS earlier in the year he had also taken over the Futurian Federation of Australia and published two issues of the Association's fanzine, *Spaceward*. However, at the beginning of September, as he lost interest in the FSS, Molesworth also lost interest in the FFA and resigned as co-ordinator. Arthur Duncan, who had just joined the FSS, was convinced to become the FFA's coordinator and publish *Spaceward*. Stone decided to help Duncan by building a flatbed duplicator, but he had never seen one and didn't know how they worked with the result that the printing was so dreadful that Duncan was too embarrassed to distribute it.

Against this background of division, argument and bad feelings, in October members of the FSS began planning celebration of the Society's second birthday, to be held on 9 November. There would be very little business discussed but there would be quizzes, lectures, sf games and competitions. Publicity said it would be a big party rather than a meeting and it would be open to all.

Nine fans attended the party.[19] It began at two in the afternoon with a quiz which lasted about an hour, followed by a birthday cake and other delectables and then general discussion and activity. Molesworth auctioned off more of his fanzines and the remaining time was spent discussing things past and present, and the meeting ended at 6 pm.

At the meeting Molesworth caused a stir by reading a short speech calling for a 'Court of Inquiry' into aspects of the club's past because, he said, its records were in an 'unreliable condition'. He said nobody would be on trial, the only outcome would be a set of questions and answers which, when combined with the Society's existing records, would present an accurate record of its history. Everyone agreed, with the exception of the Russell brothers. It was the beginning of a period in which the FSS constitution and rules dominated its meetings and activities.

---

[19] They were; members Roden, Molesworth, Stone, Haddon and Eric Russell, and guests Evans, Veney, David Baodle and Ted Russell (who had resigned from the FSS to concentrate on his school work). The meeting received a telegram from Hockley in Melbourne.

Prior to the Court copies of Molesworth's speech were circulated and a list of about thirty questions were agreed to. Any fan could attend to ask questions or add to the statements already made and Molesworth was appointed Examiner because the court was his idea.

The Court of Inquiry was held at Stone's place on 28 December, starting at 8 pm. On the whole it was conducted in a friendly spirit of co-operation. Roden presided, Molesworth and Castellari took shorthand notes and there were another seven fans there.[20] The Inquiry looked into past events including the exclusion of Veney and his friend from a FSS meeting, membership of the FFA, unfulfilled Society plans and its actual membership following the 1940 collapse.

Within a month Molesworth had tabulated the evidence from the Court from the notes he and Castellari had taken and, at the FSS meeting at the beginning of February 1942, he presented the complete evidence of 21 pages which was read at the meeting and passed. He had yet to prepare an examiner's report but said there had been some perjury during the Inquiry that he would not discuss until his report was complete.

After the Court of Inquiry Veney and Levy were sent letters informing them that they had been banned for life from membership of the FSS, apparently because of alleged violations of the 'workable basis' agreement that had been made at the first Conference. This may have been done because Veney had already announced he wanted to convene a third Sydney Conference to discuss various subjects and find out if there were any matters on which all Sydney fans could agree.

That conference was held in the YMCA Building in Sydney, starting at 2 pm on 4 January 1942. Seven attended but Veney was absent because his mother was ill.[21] They began by discussing Australian representation at the coming American convention in Los Angeles, suggestions for science fiction social events such as visits to places of scientific interest and lecture and debates. When they came to the future of the FFA Duncan announced he would resign from it because he was unable to produce a duplicated copy of *Spaceward*. He was persuaded to stay on, probably because nobody else in the group wanted the job and the conference recommended that the FFA should remain a purely non-active organization. The rest of the afternoon was spent generally talking about science fiction. They tried to define fan, girls as fans, contact with fandom in America and agreed that there needed to be a better term than 'science fiction'. They then discussed the prozines

---

[20] The others there were Evans, Duncan, Levy, Eric and Ted Russell, Stone and Veney.

[21] The attendees were Veney, Castellari, Duncan, Jack Hannon, Eric and Ted Russell and Roden.

until the meeting ended at 4.30. Eric Russell said, 'This is the first time I've discussed science fiction in six months' and Graham Stone added 'Me too'.[22]

The Court of Inquiry and Third Conference had been held under the shadow of war. Australia had been at war before the first issue of *Ultra* had been published and the first FSS meeting held, but it was in far off Europe and North Africa and had little effect on the young Australian fans. However, when Japan invaded South East Asia and attacked the American Fleet in Pearl Harbour at the beginning of December 1941 the war in the Pacific threatened Australia directly. The nation went onto a total war footing and every resource was directed to only one purpose, holding back and defeating the Japanese threat. Now the rapid advance of Japanese forces into Asia and the Pacific made the invasion of Australia seem a real possibility and Australian fans were swept up in the national emergency.

All their future plans had to be abandoned. By 1942 many of them would have been old enough to have paying jobs so they could afford to travel a little. Bob Geppen in Hobart and Noel Dwyer in Sydney planned to visit Melbourne and Hockley, in Melbourne, looked forward to visiting fans in Sydney. They also hoped Sydney fans would be able to visit Melbourne in 1942 for a convention there. Now none of that would happen and every aspect of fandom in Australia was changed.

Almost immediately fandom in Hobart fell silent. Bob Geppen planned to publish a fourth issue of *Profan* but shortages of paper, his school commitments including the school cadet corps, and the lack of any science fiction to buy in Hobart all combined so that fourth issue was never published.

Tuck was on the verge of being called up for military service when he was offered an appointment in the munitions industry, but his new job was in Melbourne. He arrived there on 5 December and soon met Warwick Hockley. It was the first time fans from separate Australian cities had met and Hockley reported that they had a 'hellava party'. On the first evening Hockley took Tuck on the rounds of the second-hand shops where Tuck astonished him by spending £1 on magazines, and having twice that amount put aside for him. In following days they went to more shops, where Tuck bought more, and saw the sights of Melbourne. Hockley's only worry about meeting his new friend was that Tuck wouldn't leave anything in the shops for him to buy.

With both Hockley and Tuck in Melbourne there was potential for more fan activity, but they agreed to concentrate on collecting because they didn't have the time, energy or, to a certain extent, the inclination to do more. Tuck, Hockley and McLennan were all employed in protected services and, like almost everyone else engaged in essential war work, their jobs entailed abnormal working hours and often long periods away from home. On 30 December 1941 Hockley stencilled the ninth issue of *Melbourne Bulletin*, 'This

---

[22] *Science & Fantasy Fan Reporter* 22.

will be the last M-B for some time.' he concluded. 'Maybe I'll get another ish out some day, but it won't be soon'. It was Hockley's final fanzine and Melbourne fandom fell silent.[23]

The only fan group that remained active in Australia was in Sydney, and its population was much depleted. In preparation for his call-up Veney sold a lot of his collection and Stone bought much of it. By the end of January 1942 Veney and Castellari were both in camp, in a machine gun regiment, and within a few weeks Ralph Smith and Ken Jeffreys joined them in the Rutherford military camp. As others turned eighteen they were also called in for medical examinations and enlisted. In June 1942 David Evans wrote in *Voice of the Imagi-Nation* that most of Sydney's Futurians were by then in khaki. Exceptions were Evans, Eric Russell and Vol Molesworth who were ruled medically unfit for military service. Others, like Roden, Ted Russell, Stone and Duncan, were then still too young for military service but would take their turn later in the war. Others, like McLennan, Tuck and Hockley were exempt because they were employed in Australia's rapidly growing defense industries and were protected from being called up.

Those who were not enlisted into military service soon found the state of total war restricted their activities with jobs in protected industries that required many hours of additional work, volunteer work, civil travel restrictions, censorship, blackouts and rationing. Most of them understood that fan activity had to be reduced or put aside entirely until peace returned.

With their editors enlisted *Futurian Observer* and *Science & Fantasy Fan Reporter* ceased publication in the early months of 1942. The final issues of *Ultra* and *Zeus* saw the light of day, *Zeus* dated Spring 1942 and *Ultra* posted in September 1942, but both had been ready in December 1941. Molesworth and the FSS planned a new fanzine called *Futurian Digest* to keep fans in the services in touch, but only one issue was published, in February 1942. Between July and September Molesworth and Stone published nineteen issues of *Futurian Spotlight* and in September 1942 Roden published one issue of a *Bulletin* for the Futurian Federation of Australia. After that government regulations forbade any publication that did not have a licence, and none were granted for fanzines.

Fanzines had been the way in which Australian fans presented themselves to the rest of fandom, but that voice was now lost. Some Australian fans kept up correspondence with fans overseas so there were occasional hints of their presence. A letter or two from Alan Roberts were published in *Voice of the Imagi-Nation* and the June 1944 issue of *Futurian War Digest* mentioned that Bert Castellari was in New Guinea, Veney was operating a searchlight near Brisbane and Sawyer was somewhere in the Great Western Desert. It

---

[23] *Melbourne Bulletin* 9.

appeared that the only civilians still interested in science fiction were Eric Russell and Molesworth.

There was very little new science fiction to read in Australia, packets of prozines sent by American fans tailed off during 1941 and no fans had recently received parcels from overseas by the end of the year. British Reprint Edition prozines were slow to arrive, at least six months behind British publication.

Some hope for local science fiction publications came in January 1942 when Currawong published a sixpenny booklet, *The Living Dead* written by J W Hemming. It was about a mad scientist and crudely written with the science neglected towards the end but it was science fiction and raised hopes that more and better publications would follow. It sold out in Sydney in two weeks and *SFFR* encouraged fans to go to all the book sellers asking for it to encourage demand for more. Currawong published a second Hemming book *Subterranean City*, in February and, although the style was crude, *SFFR* reported that the ideas in it were good.

Spaceward Ho!, second of Vol Molesworth's Stratosphere Patrol Stories, Transport Publishing, 1943
(Merv Binns collection)

These two books encouraged Alan Connell and David Evans to submit stories to the Currawong. When Roden approached the publisher they said they wanted adventure stories with a scientific nucleus and Hemming had a third story, a time travel story, coming. They didn't want to put 'science fiction' on the cover because the new readers gained from the title would probably be less than the readers turned away by it. Currawong thought straight science fiction would fail but science-adventure might work. Sydney fans agreed that it was not very good science fiction but any type of science fiction was better than none. They hoped that a regular high quality science fiction magazine might appear in Australia but that would be impossible during the war.

Molesworth began selling novelettes to Currawong and the first appeared late in 1942, followed by others include a trilogy of 'Stratosphere Patrol' stories.

Molesworth also became the dominant figure in the FSS and his constitutional pedantry flourished. At a meeting in early in January 1942 he read the first chapter of a book he was working on called 'The Book of Futurian Law'. It was being organised and written to explain the various rules of the Society with the first chapter dedicated to 'Guests' with instructions explaining how the rules had been applied in the past and the rules that were then in force. The first chapter was read to and agreed by the meeting. Molesworth was working on a second chapter to be about 'Directors' and he planned the completed book would have many chapters, each one outlining and explaining a separate aspect of the FSS constitution.

Following the Court of Inquiry Molesworth revised the Society's minutes and prepared a condensed version which Ted Russell typed neatly and bound in light blue covers. They recorded all the club's important actions and were indexed for easy reference, with space left at the end for more notes if they became necessary. Ted Russell also began the work of retyping the complete minutes and records of the Society.

In February the group finalised plans to collect and send science fiction books and magazines to military hospitals for the wounded. They called it a Soldier's Relief Fund and Roden, who was in charge of it, called it 'Stf for the AIF'. The only person to object was Stone who thought that if members bought up books and magazines in secondhand shops for the fund they would not be available later for collectors. The group wrote to one of the Army base hospitals for permission to put their plan into action but before it was given the FSS's funds were seriously investigated by the police, who officially dismissed the group as 'Buck Rogers rat bags.'[24]

Attendance at Society meetings was small, five at a meeting at the end of March in 1942; the Russell brothers, Roden, Castellari and Molesworth. In July 1942 two fans from Brisbane, Bill White and Alan Roberts, arrived in Sydney and boosted numbers for a while. At a meeting in July Roden said the Society needed to build itself up by finding entirely new fans to join it. The meeting agreed and decided to seek new members through various bookshops and advertising in Currawong books. With nothing better to do, little new science fiction to read and discuss, the older and more mature members gone to the war, and encouraged by Molelsworth's legalistic tendencies, meetings degenerated into bickering and arguing over minor points of Futurian Law.

This achieved very little and the Society degenerated even further into meetings of endless petty disagreements and feuds. Moleworth, with some

---

[24] *Mumblings from Munchkinland* 13.

help from Duncan and Stone, engaged in endless argument over the Society's rules, electioneering and intrigue, leading to a split into factions called the 'new order' and the 'Neofan Party', which published the *Futurian Spotlight* devoted to criticism of Roden and Eric Russell.

Towards the end of September Roberts was elected Director and Duncan vice Director but Eric and Ted Russell resigned, objecting to Molesworth and Stone's 'party politics'. In an attempt to prevent the total collapse of the Society the lifetime expulsions of Levy and Veney were rescinded and they were invited to rejoin the club. The Society also decided to create goodwill by inviting all ex-members to the third birthday meeting in an endeavour to regain their support.

Disillusionment in the FSS was rife. Noel Dwyer declined the invitation to attend in a long letter explaining his belief that the FSS was a 'petty, paltry and deceptive thing' that was of no use at all. He wrote that the only use it had ever been was to give adolescents an interest, but that time was now over so the Society had outlived its purpose. He said the clubs should now direct its efforts towards the war and not science fiction. No member was doing anything at all to help the war effort and to carry on with meetings, discussions and putting out fanzines was 'disgusting'.[25]

The Futurian Federation of Australia was another source of problems and in March 1942 Duncan resigned from the FSS and the FFA, leaving it leaderless. It then fell to Roden to do something, but he made no attempt to revive it because he thought it could not be done until the war had ended. Others looked for a solution and at a meeting of Sydney members on 20 September they decided to resign en masse from the Association and set up a new, more effective, organization. Again, they sought to solve a problem they had created by abandoning one venture and starting out on another one, as they had done several times before. They then formed the Southern Cross Futurian Association with Roden as President and Molesworth as Secretary and the rest joined.

Creation of this new association created new possibilities. Eleven past and present Futurians were present at the third birthday celebration meeting of the FSS on 5 November 1942. Guest of Honour was the author J W Hemming. During the meeting they discussed, again, how to resuscitate the Society and get back all ex-members. At first they agreed to hold another conference to plan an entirely new club but Hemming offered another solution. He said the Society needed somebody older to direct their energies into the right channels or they would not succeed in promoting science fiction. Hemming was forty-two at the time and this seemed to offer the young group a way out of their problems.

At a Society meeting on 24 November Molesworth moved that the FSS

---

[25] *Science & Fantasy Fan Reporter* 26.

Fans in Australian Army Uniform, 1944. LtoR Bruce Sawyer, Bill Veney and Bert Castellari
(Chris Nelson, *Mumblings from Munchkinland* 14)

should be dissolved and it was passed, with the proviso that an emergency meeting could be called if it was considered necessary in the future. The Society was then dissolved and all the known Sydney fans, except Evans and Levy, joined the Southern Cross Futurian Association. Its policy and rules were then changed following Hemming's suggestion and he was elected as its President. He introduced several newcomers which brought the total membership to eighteen. The new club took over the Soldiers' Relief Fund but no other FSS responsibilities, so Molesworth resigned shortly afterwards.

Hemming said the Southern Cross Futurian Association would be more than just a science fiction club, 'It would be a Futurian club in the real sense of the word. It should be concerned not only with science-fictional subjects, but with anything that may help the future'. He argued that the reason for dissatisfaction with the old club had been that it provided no outlet and he introduced two new activities, debating and amateur theatricals. As a result meetings became more enjoyable but science fiction was pushed into the background. Hemming saw the Association as a social and political organisation and, as 1943 progressed, all pretense of concern with science fiction ceased and social matters were debated. The Association finally degenerated into a Sunday afternoon social group at Hemming's home devoted to amateur theatricals and informal talk.[26]

Soon after this change began Stone tried to organise a science fiction section of the Association but met with little success. Disillusioned by what was happening Molesworth and Duncan called a conference, on 9 May 1943, that was also attended by Eric Russell, Roden, Stone and new fan Stirling

---

[26] Molesworth, *A history of Australian science fiction fandom*, Chapter 2.

Macoby. They decided to reform the FSS and four meetings were held, attended severally by Molesworth, Stone, Roden, Duncan, Macoby and a new member, Victor Cowan. They disagreed over the club's name, outvoted Molesworth and Duncan and changed it to the Sydney Science Fantasy Society. At the fourth meeting Molesworth and Duncan pushed through a motion reverting to the original name and suspending activities until after the war.

Despite everything that had happened, during the war the common bond of science fiction and its fandom made friends out of fans who had earlier been enemies. The Russell home in Sydney was an open house and fans, in and out of uniform, arrived at all hours of the day and night. The first port of call for any interstate fan in Melbourne was to see 'Wog' and Pam Hockley and on one occasion a bunch of fans from Sydney made a rowdy entrance at Hockley's place, talked vociferously for an hour and then raced off to catch the train back to Sydney. If they met in the swamps of New Guinea or the inlands of Torres Straits they were instantly on the best of terms and on more than one occasion a bunch of ex-Futurians were seen rolling out of some Sydney pub calling on such deities as Smith and Campbell to damn their enemies.[27]

---

[27] *Ugh!*.

CHAPTER 4
1946-1952, Sydney

What remained of Australian fandom was spread out and disorganised when the war ended. Bert Castellari was in Borneo, Alan Robert was with the RAAF at Moroti and others were scattered wherever the war had tossed them. Later Castellari and Veney met in Japan where they were part of the British Commonwealth Occupation Force and some fans remained in military service for a few more years.

Fandom in Australia had been completely demolished, unlike fandoms in American and Britain, so it was not a matter of rebuilding what still existed but a matter of starting again. A few fans began writing to each other and meeting occasionally to talk about, among other things, what they should do next, but they held back, waiting to see what others would do to get the ball rolling. Maybe some were wary of committing themselves after their pre-war experiences, or perhaps they were busy finding their feet again in society after wartime.

Some time in early 1947 Bill Veney published a one-shot he called *Ugh* which included a letter Vol Molesworth had earlier sent to his 'old friendly enemy' Eric Russell, who had then passed it on to Veney. In it Molesworth wrote about the developments of the previous few years, the advances and inventions in science and technology which had been the dreams of science fiction fans but which the mundane world found amazing: atomic bombs, radar, jet engines, new drugs and much more. It would be a pity, Molesworth wrote, if science fiction fans could no longer share their interests as they had before the war. He went on to say that perhaps the war had done the Sydney Futurians a favour because they could now forget the personal conflicts of the past and attempt to rebuild, not a replica of the previous bickering fandom but a new organisation in which those interested in futuristic and fantastic literature could exchange ideas.

Warwick Hockley and Bill Veney in Melbourne, 1946

(Chris Nelson, *Mumblings from Munchkinland* 14)

Molesworth told Russell that he aimed, if possible, to reform the Futurian Society of Sydney on a more adult basis which would be independent from, but not necessarily oblivious to, the American prozines. He believed fans had now passed beyond the purely fan stage and reached a level where the club could be a meeting place for the discussion of futuristic and fantastic ideas in Australian publications, films and plays. He added that one or two better fanzines would provide a medium of communication with interstate fans and could be exchanged with fanzines being revived in America and England.

Only a few pre-war fans remained interested in an active involvement in fandom after 1945. When Castellari returned from the war he sold much of his collection and Graham Stone bought most of it. Alan Roberts had corresponded with *Voice of the Imagi-Nation* during the war but did not return to fandom after he was discharged. Others who had been prominent before the war but were absent from post-war activities included Levy, Smith, Dwyer, Evans, Sawyer, Roden and Ted Russell. Others including Hockley and Eric Russell remained in touch for a few years before also disappearing into the glades of gafia.

Science fiction was still ridiculed in the general community as 'Buck Rogers stuff' and demeaned as inferior escapist literature so science fiction readers rarely talked about it openly. However, science fiction's fans knew there was more to science fiction. Not only did they believe it valid literature, they thought reading it helped prepare them for the future. Castellari, for example, was in the Australian Army in Borneo in 1945 when he first heard about the atomic bombing on Hiroshima. He understood what it was and what it meant, and his first thought was that the future had arrived sooner than he'd expected. His army mates did not know or care about the future, to them it only meant the war would be over sooner. In 1952 Vol Molesworth told a meeting of the Book Collector's Society that science fiction had outlived its pulp origins and attained manhood, and that it embodied the spirit of the Atomic Age and looked towards the stars.[1] Graham Stone said that science fiction was not a means of escape but a means of catching a glimpse of the reality that everyday life obscured.[2]

The revival of Australian fandom was also hindered by the embargo on importing American publications that continued after the war because (the Australian government said) of the imbalance of trade between Australia and nations not in the British Commonwealth. This continued to starve Australian science fiction fans of what they considered to be the best science fiction.

---

[1] *Vertical Horizons* November 1952.

[2] *Sydney Futurian* 6.

The science fiction that was publicly available in Australia was mainly British books and reprint edition prozines which were reduced versions of the American originals. In the early 1950s British paperbacks (called 'pocketbooks') began appearing in bookshops, with some reprinted American science fiction among them, costing around 2/6 and 2/9 each. However hard-cover books, costing from around 10/6 to 16/-, remained prized by fans and collectors. The most common place to find them in Sydney at the beginning of the 1950s was McKays, a bookstall run by two brothers in the Royal Arcade between Pitt and George Streets. Some British reprint magazines were on display there and more interesting science fiction (and possibly pornography) might appear from below the counter if you asked.

Thrills Incorporated 1, 1950

Some science fiction was published locally, most notably *Thrills Incorporated* which ran for 23 issues from March 1950, the first twelve in pulp format and the rest in pocketbook size. Most of its stories were written by local hack writers who knew little about science fiction and eight stories were plagiarised by local authors from American stories. Descriptions of the magazine ranged from 'juvenile' and 'unpromising' to 'bloody awful'. Following the demise of *Thrills Incorporated* the Malian Press published American reprints and other short lived magazine titles included *Future* and *Science Fiction*. Newspapers and magazines occasionally published science fiction short stories, often reprints of American stories but also sometimes by Australian authors including Frank Bryning and Norma Hemming.

Molesworth and some of his friends attempted to launch a local science fiction press named 'Futurian Press' in 1948 but the deal to buy a printing press for it fell through. In 1950 Molesworth bought a small letterpress and, with the support of some friends, published a handful of booklets. The first was a *Checklist of Australian Fantasy* by Stan Lanarch that was launched at a cocktail party on 29 October 1950. Other titles included a volume of verse by Sydney fan Lex Banning (under the name John Hilbery), Molesworth's 'Blinded They Fly', 'Let There be Monsters', the first part of his *History of Australian Fandom*, and Graham Stone and Royce Williams 'Zero Equals

Nothing'. These were laborious to produce because each letter of the text had to be set by hand and it was printed one page at a time. The largest, 'Blinded They Fly' was 36 pages long with a print run of 200 copies, each numbered and autographed, at the cost of 6/-.

Overseas reviewers complained that Futurian Press publications were very expensive and there was little print on each page — which was due to the small size of the printing platen of the press. These booklets were not published for the general public but for collectors, not to make much money but to promote Australia to overseas fans and collectors and be a source of overseas money that could be used there to buy American books and magazines. The productions of the Futurian Press, the Malian Press, and even *Thrills Incorporated*, became collectors items that could be traded with collectors overseas for American publications and were a necessary part of any Australian science fiction collection.

Molesworth built up an impressive collection of rare and collectable books and magazines. Queensland collector Charles Mustkin had 500 science fiction magazines in 1948, including 50 post-embargo issues, and Stone had built up a collection of 117 books and 745 magazines, including almost complete runs of *Amazing* and *Astounding*. When established fans such as Eric Russell and Bert Castellari lost interest in science fiction they began selling their collections, often at auctions where the highest prices went for items that other fans needed to fill gaps in their collections.

Zero Equals Nothing title page, Futurian Press
(Doug Nicholson collection)

The paucity of science fiction in Australia forced fans to hunt for and hoard it, making collecting a major part of their fan activity. As their collections grew they began making lists of what they had and what they still needed, so collecting and bibliography became the central focus of many Australian fans' activities. Lanarch's bibliography of early Australian fantastic fiction was an early example and, in Tasmania, Don Tuck began listing his collection which became the basis of his later bibliographic work.

Collecting and the building large libraries also became one of the main reasons for the creation of science fiction clubs in Australia after the war because club libraries gave members access to more science fiction. One of the main objectives of the reformed Futurian Society of Sydney was to build up a club library from which members could borrow and which would become one of the club's main attractions for new members.

Vol and Laura Molesworth married in 1946 and hosted the first meeting of the revived Futurian Society of Sydney at their home in Kensington on 9 August 1947. Five people were present, Vol Molesworth, Laura Molesworth, Graham Stone, Eric Russell and Sterling Macoboy, who was an author, radio script writer and producer. They also had the support of letters from Bill Veney and Arthur Haddon (who were still away on military service), Ralph Smith and, from Tasmania, Bob Geppen and Don Tuck.

Molesworth's predilection for strong formal organisation was there from the start so the Society began much as it had previously ended. All five present were elected as members of the Society; Eric Russell was elected Director, Vol Molesworth Secretary and Treasurer and Laura Molesworth was appointed Librarian.

The next order of business was to ratify the Society's comprehensive new constitution which set out the details of how the club would operate. All prospective members had to submit applications and their membership be approved by the existing members. Under the constitution the Society was tightly regulated and everything was to be debated in parliamentary fashion. Subcommittees were often formed to examine proposals so, when the Society considered a proposal for Australian representation at an 'American' convention (now the 'World Science Fiction Convention'), a subcommittee of three was set up to recommend how that might be done.

Next the meeting resolved to set up a library comprising magazines that individual members did not wish to collect and any that were received in exchange for club publications. Full membership of the Society was one guinea and associate membership was half that, 10/6. Members and associates could borrow from the library at the rate of 3 pence per item per fortnight, plus postage. By the end of 1947 the library had 17 books, over 40 prozines and 200 issues of 47 different fan publications. The club had 17 members and eight associates, most of whom lived outside Sydney.[3]

The Society's constitution did not include the phrase 'science fiction'. Instead, it began: 'The Futurian Society of Sydney is an organisation of people interested in the discussion and promotion of science, weird and fantasy subjects'. This was in keeping with the Futurian philosophy of using a name that was more dignified than 'science fiction' and the claim that Futurians were not merely fans who read the genre, they were people who

---

[3] The membership of the Society in January 1948 were: full members Stirling Macoboy, Laura Molesworth, Eric Russell, Graham Stone, Vol Molesworth, Bill Veney, Stan Baillio, Stan Larnach and Jock McKenna. The Associate members were Warwick Hockley, Colin Roden, Ralph Smith, Arthur Haddon, Stephen Cooper, Don Tuck, Ken Slater and S Mustchin. *The Sydney Futurian* 5, January 1948.

had an interest in the changing world and looked forward to seeing something of their dreams for the future come true.

'Promotion' was the key word in their opening statement because the Society could not achieve its objectives if it did not first promote itself to gain more members. To do this the Society published a club fanzine to spread news of its activities. *The Sydney Futurian* was neatly and plainly duplicated on four, and later eight, pages in a folded-foolscap format which was chosen because, Macoboy suggested, copies could later be easily bound to preserve them. Its main content was reports on the progress of the Society, news of its activities, notices of the science fiction becoming available locally, and some interstate and international news. About 120 copies of most issues were printed and distributed as widely as possible in Australia and overseas to attract support from a wide fan base. It was free to members, cost 3 pence a copy to non-members and Americans could subscribe at the rate of one American prozine for six issues of *The Sydney Futurian*. (This subscription rate for non-Australian fans became a common asking price for Australian fan publications because it was one way Australian fans could get otherwise unaccessible American prozines and books.)

The Society believed it represented Australian fandom to the rest of the world and it comprised the majority of known Australian fans. An Australian Fan Directory published in Sydney in 1950 listed twenty-two names, all but five living in New South Wales.[4] As part of that representation to overseas fandom the Futurians organised contributions to be sent to overseas conventions including a sound recording of Sydney fans sent to the 1950 'American' convention and photographic displays to one or two later conventions.

Air transport had expanded and improved rapidly during the war, improving the speed of communication between fans in Australia and overseas. A permanent air mail service was opened between Australia and North America in mid-1947, initially every week-and-a-half, soon to weekly, and taking less than a week. As a result correspondence became more common and letters from Australians appeared occasionally in American fanzines and letters from fans in New Zealand, Britain and North America sometimes appearing in Sydney fanzines. This had the potential to integrate Australians more readily into American fandom and by 1952 nine Australian and New Zealand fans had joined the American National Fantasy Fan Federation.

Demonstrating their international interest, the largest issue of *The Sydney Futurian* was a special 'Torcon Issue' that the Society sent to the 'American'

---

[4] They were: David Cohen, P Glick, A W Haddon, D L Larnach, Harold Lennon, M MacGuinness, Jock McKenna, Stirling Macoboy, Vol Molesworth, Barry Reece, David Ritchie, Eric F Russell, Bruce M Sawyer, Nick Solntseff, Graham B Stone, Wm D Veney, Royce S Williams, Charles S Mustchin, Donald H Tuck, Roger N Dard, R H Harding and John C Park. *Woomera* 1, February 1951, pp.12-13.

THE SYDNEY FUTURIAN

No. 1. September, 1947. Price 3d.

FUTURIAN SOCIETY OF SYDNEY REFORMED

The seventy-eighth meeting of the Futurian Society of Sydney was held on Saturday, August 9, 1947, at 6 Balfour Road, Kensington. Present were Sterling Macoboy, Eric F. Russell, Graham Stone, Laura and Vol Molsworth.

The preceding constitution and rules were rescinded and the following constitution accepted in their place:

"The Futurian Society of Sydney is an organisation of persons interested in the discussion and promotion of science, weird and fantasy subjects. Persons living within 100 miles of Sydney are eligible for membership. Persons living elsewhere in the Southern Cross area may become associate members. Annual membership fee shall be one guinea, five shillings of which shall be payable on election. Associate members shall pay half a guinea per annum, of which half a crown shall be payable on election. Each member may invite one guest to any one meeting. Membership may be granted by a majority vote at any meeting. Membership automatically lapses after three months; non-payment of dues. Each member shall receive a copy of the constitution, and copies of any stationary, notices, publications, etc issued by the society. Meetings shall be held on the second Saturday night of each month, and shall be conducted according to the rules of debate. A quorum shall consist of two executives and two other members. Elections for the positions of Director and Secretary shall be held quarterly. This constitution can be amended by a two thirds majority vote at a meeting after all members have been notified by circular of the proposal to amend."

"The following persons then became members under the new constitution: (1) Sterling Macoboy; (2) Mrs. Laura Molesworth; (3) Eric F. Russell; (4) Graham B. Stone; and (5) Vol Molesworth.

Eric F. Russell was elected Director of the society and Vol Molesworth was elected Secretary. It was decided that the duties of Treasurer would be carried out by the Secretary until such
(contd. p.2)

The Sydney Futurian 1, September 1947
(Rare Books & Special Collections, Sydney University)

convention in Toronto in 1948. It featured a cover drawn onto stencil by Ralph Smith, a description of the Society and its activities, a list of the Society's by then 27 members, a description of the library, an article about Australian fantasy books and a letter column including letters from Canada and Japan. It highlighted the Futurians belief that fandom had to be organised to be successful and suggested that time was ripe in the post-war world to establish one global fan organisation to which national organisations and individuals could affiliate because, it said, 'there are many ways in which fans in different countries can assist one another in the collection and appreciation of stf, weird and fantasy fiction'.

The proposed constitution for a World Science Fiction League was drawn up in Canada and a Sydney Futurian select committee comprising Molesworth, Royce Williams and Eric Russell prepared a report about it for the November 1948 Society meeting. Despite the effort that went into this proposal, the Futurians had to tell fans overseas that they could not participate in an international fan organisation because Australian government regulations prevented them from sending money overseas to support it.

The Society received generous support from overseas fans in their quest for American science fiction. A letter from Molesworth published in the June 1948 issue of *Famous Fantastic Mysteries* about the need for magazines for the Society's library brought numerous letters from North America, so many that Molesworth could not answer them all and farmed them out to other Futurians to answer. Unsolicited parcels of magazines began arriving from the United States, Canada and Britain and donations from well known overseas fans including Ted Carnell and Ken Slater in Britain and Red Boggs in America. Australia's plight became so well known that the 1949 American convention in Cincinnati donated $100 to be spent on books and magazines for the Sydney Futurian's library.

A more promising and regular source of science fiction began with a letter from British fan Ken Slater that was published in *The Sydney Futurian* at the end of 1947. Writing as the trading section of the British Fantasy Library, Slater said he could send a large number of wartime American magazines. Slater's service became Operation Fantast and became a major supplier of science fiction to Australian fans. By the beginning of 1952 Australians also had access to other British book and magazine dealers including Milcross Book Service of Liverpool, Dell's of Bradford and, in London, the Fantasy Book Service, E J Carnell and G K Chapman. Most of the books and magazines they could provide were British but there were also some American publications so these services became very popular with the Australian fans who found out about them.

The Sydney Futurians held monthly meetings in members' homes. They were partly social but included an official business meeting that was kept as short as possible and at which 'no form of intense activity of a political or other nature would be encouraged'. To begin there was little disagreement because there was little to disagree about but Slater's letter and application to join the Society encouraged Futurians to expand their horizon and their view of the Society's place in the science fiction world. At the December 1947 meeting they decided to drop the word 'Sydney' from the Society's title to become simply the 'Futurian Society' with the objective of serving science fiction fandom globally by offering membership to anyone around the world. Those who could attend meetings paid a fee of one guinea a year, those who could not became associates at half that fee and Americans could pay their subscriptions in prozines or books. The use of the library, however, was limited to Australians.

By the end of 1948 the Society had 34 members including some North American associates and newcomers including Phinneas ("Bluey') Glick and Nick Solntseff whose family had recently migrated from Shanghai. The membership included a university lecturer, a writer, an editor, a pharmacist, an artist, a sailor, a store man, a musician, a tailor and a plumber. This growth was not a complete blessing because the larger membership brought a diversity of opinions which led to disagreements, and some members were quick to argue and did not like being challenged.

The first sign of friction came at the May 1948 meeting when some members wanted the Society to revert to its earlier name of the Futurian Society of Sydney and revert to being a purely local club. 'Animated discussion' occurred, no agreement could be reached at the meeting and the issue had to be decided by a plebiscite of all full members, resulting in the Society reverting to its original name. 'Animated discussion' had apparently become common at meetings and when Molesworth resigned as Director in March due to ill health Veney took his place and commented on earlier 'stormy periods'.

The Society met at first in members' homes but the growing membership led it to holding a meeting at the Quality Inn in King Street in April or May 1948.[5] Seven members and five invited guests attended, making it the best attended and liveliest Sydney Futurian meeting for a while. Encouraged by this success the Society decided to hold weekly meetings on Thursday night at the Quality Inn and 14 fans were present when the Thursday Night Group gatherings began on 10 June 1948. The Society's business was kept to a minimum and at the 98th meeting it lasted for two minutes, from six to eight minutes past 10 in the evening, during which the Director opened the meeting, the minutes of the previous meeting were read and, there being no further business, the meeting was closed. The rest of the evening was spent

---

[5] The Futurians recorded their meetings by number rather than by date so some dates are not usually mentioned so this date is an informed guess.

in talking, swapping and selling books and prozines and playing chess. The meetings were better attended than previous Society meetings and invariably very enjoyable.

Although its Thursday Night Group meetings were popular the Society began to struggle. When Molesworth had to withdraw from Society activities due to ill-health, Stone took over publication of *The Sydney Futurian* and wrote that the Society needed a couple of energetic and capable fans to maintain the club because the pace had proved too much for two secretaries so far — Molesworth and Eric Russell who said he couldn't keep up with it. A few Futurians began drifting away (including Laura Molesworth) and when Laura and Vol Molesworth hosted a party to celebrate the Society's ninth anniversary on Sunday 7 November, with a buffet provided by Laura, only eight members arrived. (The low attendance might have been affected by a strike in the coal fields which limited railway travel and also led to an 'occasionally tense' discussion of politics during the meeting.)

The Society's decline may have been partly because, by now, many of its most active members were beginning to move on with their lives with other interests and activities. This also led to frequent changes in Society leadership during 1948 as members found they had little time for club responsibilities. At one time or another Stone, Veney and Molesworth all held leading positions in the Society but had to withdraw due to other demands on their time. At elections in September 1948 Molesworth was elected both Director and Editor, Veney Secretary, Glick as Treasurer and 'Moby' Dick as Librarian. At the beginning of 1949 Molesworth announced he could not continue as Director due to pressure of work and study so relative newcomers were elected to the leadership: John Cooper as Director, Lennon as Treasurer and Williams as Secretary-Librarian.

Despite this decline and instability the Society was true to form and decided to embark on a new venture at the end of 1948. At Molesworth's suggestion *The Sydney Futurian* ceased publication and a new fanzine for local consumption was planned, along with a more ambitious but less regular 'high-grade' magazine for the Society's overseas members and for trade with overseas fan publications. An elected subcommittee comprising Cooper, Lennon, Macoboy and Russell was to edit the new magazine which they decided to call *Boomerang*. It would comprise about 40 pages and 'convey an idea of the nature of Australian fandom' but it never appeared and the new local fanzine, called *FSS News*, edited by Eric Russell, was only published three times during 1949.

By April 1949 nobody was interested in recording the minutes of Society meetings and it appears there were no meetings at all later in the year. In July Molesworth was again elected Director and said that unless something was done soon the Society would lose its members and the support of overseas fandom. By October little had happened and the Society's membership had declined to only seven full and 14 associate members.

Popularity of the Thursday Night Group was probably a significant cause of declining interest in the Society because it met the needs of most fans without any of the Society's formality. Friction developed between the Futurians and those who went on Thursday nights only to meet other science fiction fans and buy and sell prozines. Macoboy claimed that the Thursday Night Group meetings had become a 'magazine market' rather than a meeting where science fiction could be discussed, but he also acknowledged that the gatherings and magazines attracted more people than a Society meeting did. Meeting in a coffee lounge also made it difficult to hold formal Society meetings while people were eating and, when the Quality Inn closed in August 1949, the Thursday Night Group moved to another coffee inn, the Mariposa, where fans had to sit at various small tables rather than one big one, fragmenting the gathering.

The formality of Society meetings and informality of the Thursday night gatherings highlighted the difference between the two groups and raised the question of what the Society and fandom more generally exist to do. The Society existed, so its constitution said, for 'the discussion and promotion of science, weird and fantasy subjects' in the framework of a formally constituted and run organisation. On the other hand, the Thursday Night Group had no formal purpose except to create a place where science fiction could be found for the enjoyment and entertainment of those who attended. To set out the difference the Society's meeting in October 1949 formulated the statement that it was 'a group of active science fiction fans meeting to discuss and promote science fiction, to take part in international fan activities, and to publicsze FSS activities, and Australian fandom generally in other countries'. It emphasised the formality of its proceedings with the addition of: 'Meetings shall be conducted along Parliamentary principles'.[6]

Because of the difference between the two groups Molesworth suggested that the Society should withdraw from the Thursday night gatherings and hold separate meetings, while maintaining friendly relations with the Thursday Night Group. This decision made sense at the time but it left the Society without a purpose and a source of social energy so it continued to decline. At the end of 1949 Roger Dard, an associate Society member who lived in Perth, wrote to Operation Fantast that 'the Sydney Futurians seem to have become a thing of the past'.[7] He was almost right, but the Society didn't know how to die. When the Society met in May 1950 it was virtually defunct, half the executive had left Sydney, leaving Director Solntseff with most of the responsibilities. He was authorised to take over the treasury and library

---

[6] Molesworth, *A history of Australian science fiction Fandom*, Chapter 3.

[7] *Operation Fantast* 1/3.

funds for safe keeping and, when he retrieved the library he found it had dwindled from 36 books and 287 magazines to six books and 90 magazines.

At the beginning of June 1950 ten fans met to try finding a way forward, but instead of reaching agreement the meeting turned into a series of formal motions and counter proposals so that after two hours of 'bitter and acrimonious debate' nothing had been resolved. Eventually a motion that 'This meeting recommends to the FSS that it consider winding up its affairs' was moved, followed by another three-quarters of an hours of 'fierce and disorderly debate'.[8]

At a final meeting on 13 August Molesworth was again elected Director and Solntseff Secretary and Treasurer but membership had fallen to four full members and ten associates. All prospect of resuscitation seemed remote but the meeting decided to keep the club's machinery intact and carry on with a restricted program which might include meetings when possible and an irregular news sheet, but only one issue appeared. The Society's only visible achievement for 1950 was preparation of a double-sided 12 inch sound recording prepared by Sydney fans and sent to the American convention in Portland, Oregon, that year.

Molesworth blamed the Society's decline on outside factors including university studies, the ban on prozines and the lack of fan publications which would encourage new members. University studies were perhaps a major factor. During 1950 fourteen fans, including several Futurians, were students at the University of Sydney. An attempt was made to launch a Sydney University Futurian Society but it only met two or three times and was disbanded due to lack of support. At the end of 1950 Molesworth had topped his class in Philosophy, Solntseff had achieved a credit in Senior Physics and others including Stone and Michael MacGuinness had achieved good passes. Bluey Glick, who already had a Bachelor of Science degree, added to it a Bachelor of Engineering degree.

The Society's only real asset was its library which had been built up through donations, much of it from overseas fans and particularly the generous donation made by the 1949 American convention. To preserve it Solntseff recommended, at the Society meeting on 22 June, that the club should hand the library to a Trust to consist of seven trustees who would look after and administer it for the benefit of Australian fandom. A few days later the FSS Library Trust was established with seven members, three of them Futurians and three from the Thursday Night Group and about seventy books and 200 prozines were transferred to it.[9]

---

[8] Molesworth Chapter 3.

[9] The Trust's membership was Larnach, Macoboy, Molesworth, Russell, Solntseff, Stone and Veney.

The Thursday Night Group continued despite a change in venue to the Sun Si Gai Chinese restaurant, then to the Monterey Café in Castlereagh Street in the first half of 1950 and then to the Moccador some time later. Fans also begun gathering on Saturdays at the Molesworth's place at 160 Beach Street in Coogee to help with the Futurian Press. This developed into a social event where fans discussed sf generally, used the Library and shared tea en masse afterwards. When the Futurian Press's first book, Larnach's *Checklist of Australian Fantasy,* was launched at a cocktail party on 29 October, thirteen fans attended and Molesworth said that it showed Sydney fans could get on well together despite their differences.

Fanzines played only a small part in Sydney fandom after the war, in comparison to their central pre-war role — perhaps because of it. The first fanzine published in Sydney after the war was *The Sydney Futurian* which was a modest publication in comparison to the extravagance of many pre-war fanzines. Its purpose was limited to supporting and promoting the Futurian Society of Sydney. The first independently published fanzine was *Woomera,* the first issue published in August 1950 by Nick Solntseff and Mick McGuinnes. It was very neatly typed and duplicated comprising 12 pages in the folded foolscap format. Its intention was, its editors wrote, 'to foster the International flow of ideas on and of fandom'.[10] They said the decline in fanzine publishing in Australia was due to declining interest in science fiction which was a direct result of the paucity of magazines and books. *Woomera*'s content was serious and earnest with a short memoire by Eric Russell, a scientific article and some notes on current fan activities by Veney.

The second issue of *Woomera* appeared in February 1951. It was also called issue number one and was a fresh start, edited only by Solntseff and typeset in the style of the Futurian Press. It was a handsome publication of 24 pages with a red cover and serious content including part one of a serial by Molesworth (that was later reprinted by the Futurian Press), an article about the state of science fiction by Graham Stone, Roger Dard on British prozines and some news of Sydney fandom. Molesworth described it as by far the best fan publication in Australia with the printed format and neat layout that 'gave an appearance of permanence and dignity to the well-balanced contents'.[11]

Solntseff published another four issues of *Woomera,* each looking identical to the first with a mixture of sercon articles and some fiction. A second new fanzine was Stone's *Science Fiction Courier,* also typeset in the Futurian Press style, that saw three issues between March and August 1951. The third new fanzine was Arthur Haddon's *Telepath.* The first issue, published in December 1951, looked almost identical to the other products of the Futurian Press

---

[10] *Woomera* 1 August 1950.

[11] Molesworth, Chapter 3.

but was produced on a press Haddon had bought, similar to Molesworth's but with a cracked platen. The result was as handsome as *Woomera* with content just as sercon, but with a blue cover. The painstaking effort of setting type was too much for Haddon so when the second issue of *Telepath* appeared in October 1954 its interior pages were hectographed with the same printed blue covers, containing three sercon articles by Cockcroft, Tuck and Dard, and a note about the Thursday Night Group. All these fanzines reflected the Futurian attitude towards science fiction; serious, restrained and sober. A few years later Melbourne fan Lee Harding described them as being 'generally stuffy' with an 'unapproachable personality'.[12]

The failure of the Futurian Society led Stone to establish the Australian Science Fiction Society. He believed the Futurians had failed because they were unable to achieve anything co-operatively and suffered from lack of stable leadership, so he took it upon himself to launch and run the new organisation independently. It would be his organisation and he would keep control of it to prevent it from suffering the fate of all previous Australian fan clubs with similar plans. It had no rules, no elections, no constitution or planned activities beyond finding fans and introducing them to each other. It had one office bearer, a Secretary, and that was Stone. Having discussed the idea with some other fans Stone announced in February 1951 the formation of 'a national association to keep Auslans in contact'. He kept the new Society simple to reduce the effort it would require and its purpose was simple, to enrol as many science fiction readers as possible and give them an avenue through which they could make contact with each other. To achieve this goal Stone did what the early prozines had done, published the addresses of members so they could write to each other. This modest goal meant Stone would not over-extend himself in the way that the Futurian Society had in its attempts to create a national fan organisation.

Stone first published *Science Fiction Courier* for his new society. It was typeset in the Futurian style, but the work of typesetting each issue was too time consuming so, after issues published in March and April, the next one did not appear until August. After that Stone published *Stopgap*, a sheet or two of duplicated folded foolscap produced with no fuss or undue effort containing news and information that might be of interest to Society members. It was often quite chatty with news of fan doings in Sydney and, with increasing regularity, notes and reviews of books and magazines. With this simplified newsletter Stone kept up a good regular schedule and with each issued he also mailed out other flyers and fanzines that came to hand so *Stopgap* became the main avenue of communication for most fans in Australia. Initially the Society membership fee was 2/6, which Stone subsidised personally so the membership fee did not discourage prospective

---

[12] Lee Harding, 'I Remember AFPA', *Boys Own Fanzine* 3.

members. As a result membership grew rapidly from 10 in March to 55 by December 1951. The Society's membership had grown beyond Stone's expectations so the cost of postage had become too much for Stone's pocket and membership had to be increased to 5/- to cover costs.

The Thursday Night Group continued to meet regularly at the Moccadore, from about 8 pm. Attendance varied from six or eight to twenty and visitors to Sydney knew they would meet local fans there. Meetings were unstructured, people borrowed from the FSS Library Trust, prozines were bought and sold and discussion ranged wider than just science fiction.

Despite the success of the Thursday Night Group and Stone's ASFS, the uncontrollable Sydney urge to organise fandom reemerged. In the hope of creating a more formal fan organisation in Sydney Bill Veney called a conference, referred to as the Fourth Sydney Science Fiction Conference, in July 1951. It was attended by 17 fans and claimed to be the largest fan gathering held in Australia so far. Through periods of sometimes 'disorderly argument' the conference decided to organise a science fiction convention in Sydney and not to disrupt the Thursday Night Group. However the meeting also decided that Sydney needed a formal science fiction club and gave Veney and Haddon authority to decide what form it should take. They decided that it would be simpler to revive the Futurian Society of Sydney than set up a new club, even though that carried with it the danger of reviving old animosities and ever present problems of apathy and lack of support.

The first meeting of the re-revived Futurian Society of Sydney was held three weeks later and attended by eleven fans. Seven members were elected or reelected to the Society and its old guard of Molesworth, Veney, Haddon and Solntseff took charge. After going through a revised constitution point by point the meeting decided that the Society would be a purely local club while Stone's ASFS catered for fans outside Sydney. The Society's meetings were held on the fourth Monday night of each month in the Board Room of the GUOOF Building where the formal atmosphere provided a dignified change from previous meetings in lounge rooms and restaurants. To avoid confusion between the revived Society and the now separate FSS Library Trust, the Trust met a little later and renamed itself the Australian Fantasy Foundation.

The decision to organise a convention was made with little discussion despite other vigorous arguments at the meeting so Sydney's leading fans had probably already discussed the idea and agreed to it. It was a good decision because it energised the Society and gave it a common goal that helped create a spirit of co-operation and reduce conflict between the members. As a result a proposal to publish a new club fanzine, which previously could have caused much disagreement, was raised during the year but shelved and then dropped because Futurians were too busy organising their convention.

Organizing committee of Australia's First SF Convention. LtoR Graham Stone, Lex Banning, Bill Veney, Arthur Haddon, Nick Solnsteff and Vol Molesworth (who was not a committee member) (Chris Nelson collection)

To begin, a committee of four was formed separate from the Society to organise the convention but only Stone had put in much work for it by September 1951, so the Society had to take over responsibility for it or seeing it fail. Molesworth told Futurians it would mean a lot of work, that the Society's reputation in overseas fandom depended on the convention's success, and the meeting agreed unanimously to accept that responsibility. A committee, led by Veney and comprising virtually the entire Society membership, except Molesworth, was then appointed to organise the convention. The Futurians spent most of their meetings leading up to the planned convention date of 22 March 1952 in organising the details such as hiring a hall and film projector, catering, publicity and a convention dinner.

Haddon received permission from the publishers of the BRE *Astounding* to insert flyers into copies of the magazine distributed in Australia and they went out with the December 1951 issue. Haddon thought the Australian distributor was not very keen on the arrangement because they set him the impossible deadline of providing them with 1200 copies of the flyer by the beginning of business the following day. To meet their deadline Haddon went straight home to his printing press where he spent all night printing the flyers, before riding his bike into the city in the morning to meet the deadline. As a result the Society received about forty responses that brought into fandom new fans including Rosemary Simmons and Doug Nicholson, who found himself press-ganged into helping with the convention.

The increased interest and activity brought the Society's membership up to fifteen and there were 21 fans, including five women, at the Thursday Night Group gathering at the Moccadore Café in Market Street on 31 January 1952.[13] Gatherings of this size were too much for the Moccador and the

---

[13] They were: Lex Banning, Harry Brunen, George Dovaston, Sid Dunk, Bluey Glick, Elizabeth Gotch, Arthur Haddon, Keith Kennedy, Don Lawson, Michael McGuinness, Vol Molesworth, Madaline Moriarity, Les Raethel, Bill Russell, Rosemary Simmons, Nick Solntseff, Graham Stone, Ann Torrens, Bill Veney, Diana Wilkes and Alan Wilkes, *Stopgap* Jan 1952.

Thursday Night Group began meeting at the Katinka Library in Pitt Street on 6 March 1952.

By the beginning of 1952 most Sydney fans were well pleased with themselves and Veney wrote that a 'Pleasant aura of achievement' radiated from Sydney fandom and that plans made earlier in the year were, despite a few upsets, disappointments and disagreements, coming to fruition.[14] Molesworth said he was immensely pleased to observe the state of Australian fandom which, despite the ban on American science fiction, had seen the reestablishment of the FSS, the ASFS membership reach 70, the Australian Fantasy Foundation running like clockwork, a regular attendance of two dozen or more at the Thursday Night Group gatherings, three regular fanzines and the Futurian Press.[15]

Australia's first science fiction convention was held on 22 March 1952 in the meeting room on the 7th floor of the Grand United Building, 149 Castlereagh Street, Sydney. The organisers had hoped for a good showing but were amazed when 58 members joined. They had also hoped for some interstate members but the only one was Race Mathews who flew up from Melbourne. Roger Dard sent a telegram of congratulation from Perth, there was another from Tom Cockcroft in New Zealand and a radiogram came from the author A Bertram Chandler who was at sea (a ship's officer who visited fan groups around Australia on his travels).

The door of the convention was opened at 10 in the morning and within half an hour there were thirty fans inside mingling. Many may have known of each other before but few had met in person and it was the first time many had felt free to talk about science fiction openly and in public. The displays that had been prepared helped break the ice by giving members something to spark conversations. Stone had prepared a historical survey of science fiction that included professional and fan publications dating back to 1926 and he talked to newcomers about them. Vol and Laura Molesworth manned the Futurian Press stand and took orders. The next display was of about 150 items that were to be auctioned later in the day to raise funds for the convention and, finally, the Australian Fantasy Foundation had a stall where librarian Ian Driscoll displayed a selection of items from the library, and joined up 23 new members. Qantas contributed a display that included an aerial photograph of coastal New South Wales seen from the height of a trans-Pacific rocket and a Lunar landscape with rocket and space suited figures illuminated by ultra-violet light. As they arrived each member was given a 20 page souvenir program, a booklet prepared by Stone called 'What is Fandom' and a copy of *Stopgap*.

---

[14] *Woomera* 3.

[15] *Stopgap* February 1952.

Attendees at Australia's First SF Convention. Don Lawson first on left, Lex Banning third and Sid Dunk next
(Chris Nelson collection)

Attendees at Australia's First SF Convention
(Chris Nelson collection)

Veney, Chairman of the organising committee, opened the convention at 11.30 with a welcoming address, followed by Molesworth speaking on 'What is Science Fiction?' and Stone on 'What is Fandom?' The auction began at around midday and saw some keen bidding that raised £35 to help cover the costs of running the convention. In the afternoon Veney chaired a business session which received reports from various organisations and groups and then discussed several motions including one encouraging *Thrills Incorporated* to publish better stories and another welcoming the appearance of science fiction in general magazines that did not normally publish it. The meeting agreed unanimously that there should be another conference in Sydney later in the year and that another convention should be held in 1953.

There were problems with the Convention dinner but over forty fans attended at the Mayfair. The convention then resumed in the evening for films projected by Ian Driscoll and Lex Banning, even though the advertised films were not available and the projector broke down.

The program had been slight but the main purpose for the convention had been to create a space where science fiction fans could get together. That is what happened and the convention was a success. It broke up at about 11 in the evening but groups of fans kept talking until two or three in the morning. Nothing official had been organised for the following day, Sunday, but new friends congregated in several groups around Sydney to discuss science fiction and fandom. On Monday evening the Futurian Society held on open meeting which was attended by twenty-five and finally, on Thursday night about thirty fans gathered at the Katinka where prozines were auctioned and there was much happy conversation.

CHAPTER 5
1952-1953, Sydney

One new group was the North Shore Futurian Society which had no relationship with the existing Futurian Society of Sydney. It was launched on 1 April 1952 by Michael Bos and J C Crawford who had been inspired by the convention. It was created to serve fans along the North Shore Railway Line that ran over the Harbour Bridge into Sydney's northern suburbs. Its initial membership consisted of mainly younger fans who were at high school or college and its main purpose was to provide them with a library of science fiction books and magazines. Before long the group's membership was opened to anyone and one or two older Sydney fans joined Bos in running the club.

The new group's membership fluctuated with the school year and their ages varied from 11 to 50 though the majority were under 20. When the membership fell from 42 in October 1952 to 21 in April 1953 Bos explained it was due to exams at the end of the previous year before the club picked up again for the next school year. Membership fees varied from 1/- to 5/- (or a magazine for the library) and overseas fans could join for a book or three British or American prozines. Bos and some of the members began attending the Thursday Night Group meetings where their youthful enthusiasm might have reminded some of Sydney's now veteran fans what they had been like before the war.

Bos produced the *North Shore Futurian Society Notesheet*, which he later renamed *Sonic*. It contained news about the club, doings in Sydney and some snippets of science information. By March 1954 there had been eleven issues ranging in size from one to eight pages, none with any pretense of style or neat appearance. Not long before the next convention the club also published another fanzine, *Terrific*, with the help of other fans including Rosemary Simmons, Kevin Dillon and Graham Stone. At 32 pages it was one of largest and most adventurous fanzines published in Australia after the war with a three colour cover, fiction and science articles.

There were six women at the 1952 convention: Rosemary Simmons, Norma Williams and Norma Hemming (who had already had stories published in *Thrills Incorporated* and *New Worlds*) and the wives of existing fans, Diane Wilkes, Pauline Roth and Laura Molesworth. They decided to band together, calling themselves the Femme Fan Group, and to publish their own fanzine to give voice to local doings and overseas news. The first issue of *Vertical Horizons* appeared the month following the convention and contained an editorial by Laura Molesworth, a column of news and views by Rosemary Simmons and a story by Norma Hemming. Like most other Sydney fanzines of this time it was folded foolscap in format and neatly typed with no illustrations.

Post convention enthusiasm led to the publication of more fanzines. Veney, who had moved to Launceston in Tasmania at the end of July and then Brisbane by the end of 1952, published *Ugh*. No issue was longer than 10 pages, they were neatly presented without illustrations, were fannish in tone and generally encouraging of all aspects of Australian fandom with news of the development of fan groups in other states. In Sydney Molesworth and Ken Martin published three issues of *Notes and Comments* in the three months following the convention, and Molesworth published one issue of *Fantasy Impromptu*, another small folded foolscap fanzine of fan news.

More influential was Rex Meyer's *S-F Review* which aimed to give Australian fans a wide range of magazine and book reviews written by a few local fans. The first issue contained reviews of many current prozines by eight different reviewers, with reviews ranging from a few to 20 lines. Some reviews were very simple but others were analytic and literate to a standard not previously reached by fan writers and reviewers in Australia. Early issues were four or five pages long but by early 1953 they had grown to ten or more pages of considered and useful reviewing. It then began to shrink to about eight pages because Meyer was unable to keep up with the demands on his time of publishing it and eventually it was taken over by Stone and his ASFS. There was little pretense of attractiveness or style about *S-F Review*, its purpose was to inform its readers about what was available, not to look good.

The most ambitious publication of this period was Stone's *Science Fiction News* which first appeared in January 1953. It was intended to promote science fiction more widely than fandom with news and reviews of the field that would interest general readers. Stone's primary concern was that it had to look good to be accepted by the general public so he worked hard on its appearance and had it professionally printed so that good quality photos and book covers could be included. While *Science Fiction News* appeared more professional than any previous Australian fanzine, Stone did not call it a fanzine and it showed the direction he thought fandom should take with its unremitting proselytising seriousness. Others did not agree with Stone's approach and Veney said it was as though Stone had arrived at a picnic wearing a dinner suit. He said Stone had worked hard to make *Science Fiction News* as technically perfect as possible in the hope of getting a good response from people who didn't know about science fiction, 'But it has failed to

SCIENCE FICTION NEWS

No. 1   January, 1953

NICHOLSON MAKES GALAXY

Congratulations to R. Douglas Nicholson of Sydney on placing a novelette, "Far From the Warming Sun" with Galaxy S.F. — first Australian to appear in a S.F. magazine for eleven years.

New British Edition - GALAXY

(New York) Robert M. Guinn, publisher of Galaxy Science Fiction, has announced that two foreign editions of the magazine will be initiated soon: one in England and one in Italy. The British edition will be a complete and almost identical reprint of a single issue, and probably will commence from No. 1 of Galaxy (Oct. 1950) rather than a current issue. "The edition will be the same size, and have the same number of pages. They are also going to use a set of our plates for the covers...This magazine has been delayed but will definitely be out this year."

Galaxy was the first new science fiction magazine ever to offer a serious challenge to the long-standing leadership of Astounding Science Fiction, and has since remained dynamic and controversial, with a high standard of material and a strongly experimental outlook. The news of a British edition is thus most welcome. One was tentatively planned at an early stage, but shelved at the time.

The Italian language edition, retitled Urania, was scheduled for November 1952. No information is available as to its contents.

Artist Bergey Dies

(Doylestown, Pa., U.S.A.) Science fiction cover artist Earle K. Bergey, well known for his work on Startling Stories in particular, died of a heart attack on Sept. 29. He was in his late forties.

Mr. Bergey was one of the few artists to do considerable illustrating of magazine science fiction by cover paintings only. He did all covers for the thirteen issues published of Strange Stories, a Standard magazine issued in 1939-40, and thence began working for the associated Startling. From the July 1940 issue onward he painted numerous covers for the Standard group, Thrilling Wonder Stories, Captain Future, and the more recently launched Space Stories and Fantastic Story Magazine. He also worked for Ten Story Fantasy, Future, Out of This World Adventures and did covers for some pocket editions of books.

Although he continued a trend begun by his predecessor with Standard, H. W. Brown, Bergey more than any other artist has always been identified with the type of cover picture familiarly known as "Guy, Gal and Goon" or "BEM-Bum-Beauty".

Australian Reprint

(see p. 2)

capture the spirit of the times'.[1] Fun was not on Stone's agenda and there was no sense of it in *Science Fiction News*. Stone did not seem to appreciate others having fun either and his review of *Hyphen*, widely regarded as one of the best fanzines ever published, criticized it for having 'too much funny stuff' which was 'laid on more than a little too thickly'.[2]

Stone renamed his Australian Science Fiction Society the 'Australasian Science Fiction Society' to recognise its New Zealand members. His *Science Fiction News* replaced *Stopgap* as that society's publication so he made it available free in his regular mail outs to ASFS members that also included other material such as publishers pamphlets and fanzines including *Vertical Horizons* and *S-F Review*. By November 1952 the Society had 122 members, agents in Melbourne and Adelaide, and Lyell Crane became the Society General Secretary to help Stone cope with the heavy workload of running the growing Society.

The work of the ASFS, publication of other fanzines and enthusiasm following the convention stimulated the development of fan groups outside Sydney. A Molesworth letter published in *Famous Fantastic Mysteries* drew an astonished letter from Roger Dard in Perth who had long thought science fiction readers in Australia were too apathetic to form any kind of organisation. Dard became one of the most active fans in Australia with extensive correspondents in Australia and overseas. With other Perth fans and collectors, John Park and Ralph Harding, he formed the Perth SF Group which had little contact with the rest of fandom. They published one issue of the fanzine *Star Rover* in November 1950 in which a page of compact reviews of leading British, Irish and American fanzines demonstrated Dard's intimate knowledge of fan activities around the world. He became an Australian agent for the American National Fantasy Fan Federation and Britain's Operation Fantast but his increasingly bitter disputes with customs authorities in Perth over his attempts to import what they thought of as questionable literature soured his interest in science fiction and fantasy so he had handed his responsibilities for those organisations to fans in the eastern states by 1953.

Don Tuck had been an active fan in Hobart before the war and moved to Melbourne during it. He was still in Melbourne at the end of the war, then travelled back and forth between Melbourne and Hobart for some time before settling permanently back in Hobart by mid-1952. He knew of other science fiction readers in Tasmania including Bob Geppen and John Symmons but they were more interested as collectors and readers than in fandom and had little to do with the rest of Australian fandom. Tuck hosted fans if they visited Hobart and encouraged them with letters and articles for their fanzines. Encouraged by Roger Dard, Tuck began working on a compre-

---

[1] *Ugh* 2.
[2] *Science Fiction News* 5.

hensive bibliography, the *Handbook of Science Fiction and Fantasy*, that he self-published in 1954 to wide acclaim by fans around the world. Subsequently he devoted himself almost exclusively to his bibliographic activities.

LtoR, Don Tuck and Bill Veney in Hobart, 1952
(Chris Nelson, *Mumblings from Munchkinland* 14)

Fan groups formed in other Australian cities. There were periodic meetings at Ian Moye's home in Adelaide by early 1953 and he made his extensive library available to all Adelaide fans. A more substantial group formed in Brisbane when author Frank Bryning moved there and began contacting fans including Chas Mustchin and John Gregor, who were joined by Bill Veney when he moved to Brisbane. They held regular meetings every two or three weeks where they talked science fiction and exchanged prozines. After a meeting at Byrning's home in February 1953, attended by twelve fans, they decided to find a more suitable meeting place and were soon gathering at a coffee lounge in Queen Street on Thursday nights.

Veney met a fan group forming in Melbourne and reported to Sydney fans the progress being made there with meetings of about twenty led by Bob McCubbin and Race Mathews. Don Tuck, who visited them on occasions, reported that he was surprised by the enthusiasm of the group.

The emergence of new fan groups around Australia was encouraging but Sydney remained the centre of Australian fandom. Fans visited from interstate and overseas and attended Futurian meetings; Roger Dard from Perth, Don Tuck and Bob Geppen from Tasmania, Alan Roberts and Harry Roberts from Queensland, and Tom Cockcroft and Jack Murtagh from New Zealand. A regular visitor to most groups was the author A Bertram Chandler who was First Mate on a ship sailing the route from Britain to Australian ports on the south and east coasts.

As fandom blossomed Lyell Crane said they were living in stirring times. He worried, however, that fandom in Sydney had waned before and asked what could be done to keep the activity going while avoiding the dead ends that littered the history of fandom. Doug Nicholson and Kevin Dillon complained in *Stopgap* that Sydney fandom was essentially un-constructive because there was a preoccupation with the trivia of fandom rather than its purpose.

Some fans thought fandom had an important political or sociological role. In *Ugh* 3 Harry Brook wrote that science fiction illuminated the infinite possibilities of the future and that fandom was 'in the vanguard of the search after the ultimate truth with the goal which humanity cannot yet see clearly'[3]. Graham Stone wrote that fandom offered the complete freedom of perfectly voluntary association where fans could be themselves instead of harnessing their minds to a team and wrote 'There's nothing on Earth like it'.[4] A little later he had much less lofty ideals and wrote that 'Fandom is not an organisation or complex of organisations, but a state of mind which leads a great number of people to make themselves known to each other and to co-operate to serve their varied interests'.[5]

Fandom in Sydney became more lively and sociable after the convention but the growing fan population had to accommodate a wider range of opinions and a divergence grew between those who thought, as Stone did, that fandom's purpose was to promote science fiction, and those who felt the purpose of fandom was to enjoy science fiction in the community that gathered around it. In the post-convention glow these differences created few problems because the Futurians saw themselves as conducting the serious business of fandom and the Thursday Night Group were happy to let Futurians do what they liked while they enjoyed socialising with other fans.

Sydney fans have left us only hints of their active social lives that included parties, picnics, barbeques and a lot of drinking. Just before Christmas 1952 a small group including Norma Williams and Norma Hemming went to Manly Beach for the day and went paddling and looking at life in the rock pools. On another outing after Christmas two cars of fans went from Kings Cross to Garie Beach for a barbecue. Over the Easter weekend in 1953 a small group of fans traveled around the Bathurst region 'conducting scientific research into the alcoholic content of beer served in the district'.[6]

There was a lot of partying and drinking. Harry Brook spent three weeks leave from the Army in Sydney around the end of 1952 during which he attended a weekend gathering at Wentworth Falls, went to Thursday Night Group meetings, joined the Australian Fantasy Foundation and went drinking with fans on the weekends. Vol and Laura Molesworth hosted parties that were generally restricted to the Futurian Society crowd. On 4 May 1952 they hosted a cocktail party for the Futurians and the Femme Fan Group which was attended by thirteen. Twenty attended another party the Molesworths hosted at which 'an extraordinary time was had by all' and, on 5 September they hosted a party to raise funds for the coming convention that was attended by 47 fans. At it a serious-minded group gathered on the front verandah to discuss science fiction and other matters, some danced to the radiogram in the lounge and the rest adjourned to the back of the flat to

---

[3] *Ugh* 3.

[4] *The Sydney Futurian* 8.

[5] *Stopgap* December 1951.

[6] *Ugh* 3.

Fans at Wentworth Falls
(Doug Nicholson collection)

sing 'doubtful ditties'. Fans there had such a good time that one well known femme fan did not leave until 5 the following afternoon.[7]

During the second half of 1952 the Futurian Society organised three 'science fiction weekends' for all Sydney fans at the Grand View Hotel at Wentworth Falls in the Blue Mountains, though Rosemary Simmons wondered why they were called 'science fiction weekends' because that topic was rarely mentioned. There was no structure to the weekends but a lot of drinking as fans socialised and explored the countryside in the company of other fans. Activities included strolling down to the falls where fans could 'drink in the mountain and other things'. Seventeen fans went to the first weekend in May, twelve went to the second Wentworth Falls weekend around September 1952 and four more drove up from Sydney to join them on Sunday. Only eight attended another weekend towards the end of the year but by then university examinations were occupying many fans' minds.[8]

At the end of the 1952 university year Solntseff graduated from Sydney University with First Class honours in Science and the University Medal in Physics. Molesworth topped his year in Philosophy, for the third year in a row, and others including Rex Meyer, Arthur Haddon, Doug Nicholson and Judy McGuinnes all successfully passed another year of study.

The paucity of science fiction in Australia continued to limit public knowledge about and acceptance of science fiction. For a while towards the end of 1952 the government planned to lift the embargo on American magazines but a downturn in the sale of Australian wool overseas led to a decline in the

---

[7] *Vertical Horizons* May 1952 & October 1952, Notes and Comments 2 and interview with Doug Nicholson.

[8] Molesworth Chapter 4, *Vertical Horizons* May 1952, November 1952 & May 1953, *Stopgap* 10 and interview with Doug Nicholson.

Australian balance of trade so the government maintained its embargo, which lasted until the end of the 1950s.

The embargo did not prevent American books and magazines from entering Australia, it prevented Australians from spending their money in non-British Commonwealth countries to limit the flow of Australian money to America. Customs authorities were given the power to seize American publications they suspected had been paid for by Australians and customs regulations also allowed them to seize material that was banned on political, moral or other grounds. This left Australian fans in a constant state of apprehension about what might be let in or seized because officials in different States applied the rules differently, some officials were more lenient than others and there was no appeal against the decisions of individual officials. In Western Australia, for example, the post office had no objection to selling International Reply Coupons or Money Orders that could be sent overseas to pay for books and magazines but customs authorities were very enthusiastic about seizing anything they thought looked suspicious. In other States it was much more difficult, if not impossible, to send any money to America but customs authorities were often lax in their attitudes to material coming into the country. At one stage the customs authorities in Sydney placed a ban on almost everything coming into the country which was so severe that Sydney fans debated whether they should appeal to the Minister for Customs, but the seizures eased so they decided it was best not to make the matter official.

When Sydney fan Doug Nicholson had a story published in America in *Galaxy* he took part of his payment in the form of additional copies of that issue so he could give them to friends who could not buy them in Australia. When the parcel arrived in Australia it was stopped by the authorities so Nicholson had to explain why he wanted it before it was released to him.

Nicholson attempted to encourage writing and publishing science fiction in Australia with *Forerunner* which he intended to pave the way for a professional, adult, Australian science fiction magazine that would grow out of

Forerunner 1
(Merv Binns collection)

Australian fandom and have the interests of fandom at heart. He saw that many fans in Sydney wanted to write science fiction but had nowhere to publish it except in fanzines, so he wanted to create a magazine that was between a fanzine and a prozine to encourage Australian writers by giving them a place where they could be published to gain experience and learn the art of writing. At eighty pages the first issue of *Forerunner* was more ambitious than anything published in Australian fandom after the war but inexperience marred it so it was a jumble of styles. Some pages were run off from stencils that Nicholson typed himself, several with interior illustrations hand-drawn onto stencil, and some pages were photo-litho printed in a very small font. There was a two-tone printed cover of Nicholson's design and everything was held together by a big metal clip. The result looked far from professional but it was a promising start with the first episode of a serial by Vol Molesworth, fiction by Norma Hemming, C Gilbert, Royce Williams and Norma Williams, verse by Lex Banning, and an article by Nicholson.

The second issue of *Forerunner* was dated Autumn 1953. Nicholson had learned a great deal about production from the first issue so the second one was a much slicker 46 pages with a neat wrap around cover. All the pages were printed from stencils with right hand justification and some electrostencilled headings to enhance the tidy appearance. It contained stories by Frank Bryning, Royce Williams, Vol Molesworth and Dough Nicholson, and an article by Norma Williams.

However, *Forerunner* was doomed to failure almost before it began. The standard of the fiction and the production values were adequate but Nicholson's big hurdle was distribution. There was no commercial interest in science fiction in Australia, the only avenue of distribution he had was through fandom so he promoted the magazine as much as he could, took copies to club meetings and conventions and sent many copies overseas in trade for overseas fanzines. The contents of the third issue were ready when Nicholson took a job in Ballarat, Victoria, and handed it over to Kevin Dillon to publish, which never happened.

For a short period in 1953 Kevin Dillon published a weekly sheet listing the science fiction on sale at the various shops in Sydney, usually no more than a page listing the titles, shops in which they were available, and their price. The largest range could be found at Angus & Robertson which had, in March 1953, eleven science fiction and fantasy titles of which only one novel was by an American author. This scarcity of science fiction gave strength to the FSS and its associated library and the Thursday Night Group because they were the best sources of science fiction in Sydney.

Sydney fandom, which had been a small group leading up to the 1952 convention, became a much larger swirling pool of personalities united by almost only one thing, their enthusiasm for science fiction in a period when it was frowned upon by the general public. Not long after the convention Stone conducted a survey of Sydney fans and received 35 responses including five from women. A tabulation of the results showed that the average Sydney fan was male, 26 years old, 5' 9" tall, weighed 10 st 6 lb and had brown hair and blue eyes. They smoked, drank, were unmarried and had no religion. Their ages ranged from 17 to 48 and only two were under 20. They had been reading sf for fifteen years, liked *Galaxy* best and their favourite author was A E van Vogt. Most were white collar workers and had, on average, reached at least Matriculation, and nine had university degrees or equivalent. Some looked like mad scientists or anarchists, some looked a little weird and some would not have looked out of place at business meetings. Almost without exception they wore collars, ties and jackets for anything but the most informal occasions.

Partying Sydney Futurians. LtoR Brian Finch, Norma Hemming, Dave Cohen, Graham Stone and Don Lawson
(Chris Nelson, *Mumblings from Munchkinland* 34)

Some fans stood out. Bill Veney was genial and friendly and liked the social side of fandom. He was eloquent, a talented but insecure salesman who left Sydney for Launceston and then moved to Brisbane in November 1952. Lyell Crane, the one fan in Australia who had been overseas and attended conventions in North America and Britain, was an Australian by birth who had gone to Canada after the war. He returned to Sydney in May 1952 and played an active role in fannish organisations and tried to keep the peace between warring factions. Harry Brunen was a short-sighted tailor with a little shop near Royal Arcade who hated anything that brought science fiction into disrepute. He had a close to eidetic memory and entered a big quiz show with the topic of the works of E E Smith and walked away with a very big prize. Lex Banning was brilliant but was severely disabled and could move about only with difficulty. His poetry was admired by many but he could barely write or type so Rosemary Simmons helped him in many ways including doing the typing that helped him gain his Masters degree. Norma Hemming and Norma Williams (known as Mark I and Mark II), made an impression on Sydney fandom's social life. Williams, who was ten or fifteen years older than the other women, often strode around in jodhpurs and riding boots and turned up with her own bottles in hand when she heard there was some serious drinking going on.

As the number of women in fandom grew relationships, engagements and marriages followed: Lorelie Giles and Phinneas Glick, Valerie Pauline and Doug Nicholson, Betty Such and Bruce Purdy; and babies too, a daughter to Len and Pauline Roth. There were also unrequited longings and secret, often fleeting, relationships, or rumours of them. It was whispered that Rosemary Simmons was Vol Molesworth's mistress and the relationship between Laura and Vol Molesworth was volatile because she learned to have a sharp tongue to survive his attempts to undermine her. There were also fallings-out over relationships and Nick Solntseff and Doug Nicholson fell out over a girlfriend. Most notorious was a liaison between Diana Wilkes and Arthur Haddon which led to a fight between Haddon and her husband, Alan, which started in the Lincoln Inn (another fannish meeting place) and continued outside. Through their association with Sydney University a few fans drifted into the circle of Professor Anderson's free thinkers and bohemians who became known as the Sydney Push that also met at various places around Sydney including the Lincoln Inn.

Friendships and alliances were like the tides, ebbing and flowing due to the volatile natures of some Sydney fans who drew others into their disputes. In some disputes friends were allies and other fans might not be friends but they became allies. A few, like Lyell Crane, tried to keep the peace and gained little thanks from their attempts. Two of the most disruptive fans were Graham Stone and Vol Molesworth who were usually allies but not really friends.

Graham Stone cut a debonaire figure who could party with the best of them when the mood took him, which may have hidden a reserved and insecure nature behind the bravado. He was the most active fan in promoting science fiction in Australia, serving in almost every official capacity in the Futurian Society, editing its publications and setting up and running the ASFS. He was also opinionated and often intolerant of others who did not agree with him. Molesworth called him a 'stormy petrel', a person who delights in conflict and attracts controversy, and he did not go out of his way to avoid it.[9]

Vol Molesworth was a veteran of pre-war Sydney fandom and one of the original Sydney Futurians. Being a diabetic he was often in poor health and unable to enlist in the Army during the war so he spent the time working as a journalist and writing a series of widely circulated juvenile novels. When the opportunity arose after the war he set out to study literature at Sydney University but discovered instead his forte in philosophy, which he then went on to study, teach and write. His father had been a conservative politi-

---

[9] *Stopgap* February 1952.

cian and he shared the inclination towards parliamentary forms of organisation and debate which shaped the Futurian Society into an organisation driven by its constitution and formal debate. He was among the brightest Sydney fans and was probably the Secret Master of Sydney fandom in the early 1950s, sometimes acting through the agency of Graham Stone. Like some other Sydney fans he had a prickly ego and his intelligent personality included a cruel streak which he could use to manipulate and upset other fans if he so chose. He was eloquent, in a scholarly fashion, and his fondness for arguing fine constitutional points made many of his friends (and enemies) think he had missed his calling as a constitutional lawyer.

Major alliances formed around the FSS and the Thursday Night Group because of their differing attitudes towards science fiction. The weekly focus of fan activity in Sydney was the Thursday Night gatherings which was sponsored by the FSS but had an almost separate existence. When the weekly meetings became too big to continue at the Katinka Library, Rosemary Simmons suggested the Sydney Bridge Club located on the third floor — to the left of the lifts — of 160 George Street, about 100 yards from Wynyard Station. Thirty one fans attended the first gathering there on 5 June 1952.

The room with its bare wooden floor and pressed metal ceiling was large enough for fans to move around the tables freely to look at books and prozines and socialise in what Stone called an 'unorganised social affair with no purpose beside providing a handy meeting place for anyone interested in sf'.[10] Usually there was no formal program but on some occasions there were talks and on others Don Lawson set up his film projector and showed movies of interest to fans. The weekly meetings started at about 7.30 and ran to about 11.30. By the end of 1952 about thirty people were attending the meetings. There were disagreements and fights, sometimes people flounced out in anger, but generally they calmed down and returned. Les Raethel managed the venue for the Futurian Society and collected small fees to pay for the room hire and supper. Gradually he built up a small reserve to be put back into improving meeting conditions.

The FSS was more argumentative because its participants took seriously their objective of promoting science fiction in Sydney and because the club had a thorough constitution and a tradition that encouraged debate and argument. Unlike the Thursday Night Group, membership of the FSS was limited to those who were considered suitable and had been elected by existing members so those with different ideas or attitudes were not welcomed and, from the outside at least, it looked like a secret society. The Society took itself seriously and encouraged that view by the way it presented itself publicly with a booklet of the Society's constitution and rules beautifully

[10] *Stopgap* 10.

printed on Arthur Haddon's letter press and a bound book of FSS minutes, carefully typed and preserved. Argument was never far from the surface and attempts to organise the rest of Sydney fandom later in 1952 came to nothing, partly because outsiders were not interested but mainly because Society members could not agree on what they should do to achieve that goal.

This serious attitude may have been the result of a conservatism rooted in the desire to make science fiction presentable and acceptable to a conservative general public. This echoing of traditional conservative values emerged at the open Society meeting immediately after the convention with a proposal to create a Women's Auxiliary for the Society, which was a common practice at a time when women were excluded from many organisations. Rosemary Simmons then asked whether women could join the Society and Molesworth said that the admission of women had caused problems in the pre-war Futurian Society and a heated debate followed. The motion to admit Simmons was defeated by six votes to three but, unsatisfied with this result two members, Banning and Stone, demanded a special meeting at which three men were elected to membership without debate but Simmons application was again rejected, on Molesworth's casting vote. A series of quasi-parliamentary maneuvers followed during which the Society passed a motion that it did not discriminate 'on the grounds of race, creed, party or sex', Molesworth was then forced to withdraw his casting vote and Simmons was finally elected to membership by six votes to four. Norma Hemming was then unanimously elected to membership at the following meeting.

Another dispute arose a couple of months later over how fandom in Sydney should be organised, ranging from establishing a council of the various Sydney fan groups to an internal reorganisation of the Society, which appears to have been snuffed out by 8 votes to 3. These small numbers demonstrate how much effort and emotional energy so few fans put into trying to create formal structures and activities for fandom in Sydney. While this was going on three times that number regularly turned up at the Sydney Bridge Club on Thursday night to borrow from the Foundation library, look at and buy the science fiction that might be available and enjoy themselves in each other's company.

A much more bitter dispute within the Society, which occupied the second half of 1952 and spilled into 1953, was the standing and future of the Australian Fantasy Foundation and its library. The problem might have been solved easily but for the form in which Futurian debates were conducted, the seriousness with which Futurians took themselves, and their argumentative natures that drew out the whole process.

The problem arose because of the seven Trustees who had been appointed when the Foundation was set up, two had left Sydney (Macoboy and Veney) and three more had lost interest (Larnach, Russell and Solntseff). The library itself had been housed by the Molesworths and they asked for it to be moved elsewhere. Two fans, Stone and Haddon, offered to take it and when it was given to Haddon, Stone resigned and claimed that the library should have gone back to the Society, which probably meant him. At the next Society meeting in August 1952 Haddon claimed that Stone did not give him all the Foundation's money and records but Stone replied, making much of little in typical Futurian style of arguing over formalities, that since the Foundation no longer existed there was nobody he could give them to.

The argument could have been easily resolved but instead the Society worked its way laboriously and painfully to the question of whether or not the Foundation had been properly established to begin with. To resolve the issue the Society decided to conduct a 'Futurian Court of Enquiry' at which the legality of the situation would be examined. The Society debated the problem for two following meetings and the Court of Inquiry was conducted on 17 December with a lawyer present as a 'Judge-advocate' and Molesworth as 'Examiner'. Evidence was taken from seven people and a transcript of the proceeding running to 23 closely typed foolscap pages was entered into the Society's records. While all this was going on the library itself was closed and missing from the Thursday Night Group meetings, which did not impress the wider Sydney fan community and did not enhance the Society's reputation. The lawyer who has been appointed for the Court reported that it appeared the Trust had not been legally constituted in the first place but, he said, the problem was really a practical rather than a legal one and depended on what the original donors to the library had intended.

The library was returned to the care of the Society in early 1953 — what else could have been done with it? It was again open for borrowing by the general fan community but the Society, and Stone and Molesworth in particular, were criticised for the way in which they had dealt with the problem and the general feeling that the Court had been a farce that was held to put certain fans on trial.

A little more animosity entered Sydney fandom in February 1953 when the Futurian Press published Vol Molesworth's *Outline History of Australian Fandom, Part 1, 1935-1940*. Reviews in *S-F Review*, *Woomera* and *Vertical Horizons* were supportive or positive but fans who had lived through the period, such as Veney, did not think it was entirely accurate and that it gave too much emphasis to a Futurian perspective. Consequently a number of fans who had offered to help with the publication withdrew their support before it was published, creating more bad feeling in the group.

Against this background of growing discord Sydney's fans began organising Australia's second science fiction convention. Planning for the convention began at the Fifth Sydney Conference held on Saturday 19 June 1952 that was attended by 19 fans. The conference began with reports of various fan activities and then discussed the coming convention which, they decided, would be spread over three days. A tentative list of committee members was drawn up and referred to the Society for approval. At the following Scoeity meeting Haddon, Martin, Molesworth and Nicholson were nominated and additional members were appointed to take care of various responsibilities.

The proposed program, which had been drawn up by Molesworth and Stone, was adopted. The convention would begin with a cocktail party on Friday night, exhibits on display on Saturday morning, a general 'Exposition of Science Fiction' in the afternoon and films on Saturday night. There would be an auction on Sunday morning and a formal business session on Sunday afternoon. This program was relatively informal and designed for relatively new fans, offering plenty of opportunity for mingling and meeting other fans. It appears that Arthur Haddon ended up with most of the responsibility for running the convention, he again arranged for publicity pamphlets for the convention to be circulated in an issue of BRE *Astounding* and placed advertisements in several overseas magazines to attract the interest of overseas fans.

The Second Australian Science Fiction Convention was held in Sydney from 1-3 May 1953. Before the event Nicholson wrote that, despite differences in Sydney fandom, the convention committee had minimised that intrusion into the convention which showed that fans of violently differing views could co-operate on something like a convention.[11] However, the management of the convention showed otherwise and Melbourne fan Ian Crozier wrote that it reeked of 'bad organisation'.[12] Later examination of the things that went wrong found that the main problem had been lack of communication between members of the organising committee, many of whom were highly antagonistic towards each other.

Eighty-four people attended the convention, the vast majority from Sydney. Joyce Joyce and Ian Moyes came from Adelaide, Harry Brook and Bill Veney from Brisbane, Ian Crozier from Melbourne and two

Second Australian SF Convention. LtoR Judy McGuinness, Joyce Joyce and Bill Hubble
(*Australian Women's Weekly*, 13 May 1953, p.31)

---

[11] *Ugh* 3.
[12] *Etherline* 5.

national service trainees stationed in Sydney, one from Western Australia and the other from Tasmania, were also there. On the Wednesday evening before the convention the 'King's Cross Ludo, Science Fiction and Glee Club' staged a cocktail party for the benefit of interstate visitors and the following evening the Thursday Night Group welcomed visitors at their weekly gathering. The following evening things started to go off the rails.

Second Australian SF Convention interstate delegates. LtoR Ian Crozier, Joyce Joyce, Bill Veney, Harry Brook and Ian Moyes
(*Science Fiction News* 5)

The Society had organised an elaborate cocktail party at the Woolhara Golf Club to begin the convention but Haddon failed to confirm the booking so the event had to be moved somewhere else at the last moment. As a result several interstate visitors were stranded in pouring rain, wondering what was going on while alternative arrangements were made. Nicholson found an alternative venue at the last minute but, while an enjoyable party for thirty-eight finally got going, the venue was more expensive and put the convention into the red almost before it had started.

The convention itself also began badly the next day. The plan was that fans would congregate at the Bridge Club on Saturday morning and then go to the GUOOF hall for the afternoon sessions. Nobody turned up in the morning to start proceedings so fans were left to mill about until about 11.30 when Vol Molesworth learned there were problems and, with the help of Lyell Crane, saved what he could of the situation and then led the group to the afternoon's venue.

The session began with a souvenir program and fanzines being handed to members and Stone and Nicholson giving informal talks explaining various exhibits arranged around the hall. Molesworth opened the formal program with a welcome and then a lecture on 'Science Fiction and the Development of Modern Literature'. Next Nicholson talked on 'Science Fiction as a Specialist Literature' which traced the development of the field, illustrated by images from prozines (that was marred by problems with the slide projector). Glick followed with a talk on 'Science Fiction and Science' and then Rex Meyer on 'Biology in Science Fiction'. Stone then talked about fandom and fan publishing and Dave Cohen spoke about Operation Fantast. The work that had gone into preparing these talks helped smooth over the convention's earlier problems and created plenty of topics for fans to discuss later.

During the dinner break Crane held an informal meeting with several local and interstate fans including Ian Moyes from Adelaide, Ian Crozier from Melbourne, Harry Brooke and Bill Veney from Brisbane, Ted Butt from Newcastle and Dave Cohen. Crane was apparently trying to create a network of Australian fans to circumvent the divisions in Sydney that affected the rest of Australian fandom. However, divisions in Sydney fandom were becoming so deep that there was nothing the rest of Australian fandom could do about it.

In the evening Don Lawson showed some short films of interest to fans and then the Czech fantasy of Karel Capek's '*Krakatit — An Atomic Fantasy*'. After the film show fans broke into little groups and headed off for various coffee shops, sly grog joints and the hotels where interstate fans were staying.

Sunday was supposed to begin with the auction but the auctioneer and material failed to make an appearance. Eventually Jack Legget found the auction material and Bluey Glick started the auction. There were 200 items, a lot of them of little interest, but American prozines fetched fabulous prices, as was expected.

A formal business session occupied the afternoon, chaired by Molesworth. It began with a series of reports from various fan groups: the FSS, NSFS, Melbourne, Brisbane and Adelaide groups, Operation Fantast, the FSS Library, Forerunner, the Femme Fan group and the Thursday Night Group. Then things became lively when Molesworth opened the meeting to motions from the floor.

A motion that Australian fandom should show its appreciation of US fandom's help by sending a parcel of Australian science fiction to the coming American convention in Philadelphia was passed without argument. Next Veney moved that Stone be forced to include interstate fans more in the workings of the ASFS. This came about because Veney had failed to get any satisfaction from Stone by letter and so brought it up in public. He wanted from Stone a clear picture of what the ASFS's policy and position was and interstate fans agreed that they did not feel included in the Society's business. The thin veneer of civility in Sydney fandom was quickly ripped off and their ability to disagree violently emerged between those who supported Veney and those who supported Stone. Stone refused to take part in the argument except to say 'No comment', and eventually when he was asked to explain where the authority of the Society lay he replied 'I am a law unto myself'. Veney, seeing that nothing could be achieved, withdrew his motion and the meeting calmed down.

The final item of business was the next convention. Wally Judd, a relative newcomer to fandom, said he had observed the errors in the current convention and thought he could correct them. He asked that the Society be given another opportunity to stage the convention so Australian fandom could see what it could really do, and the meeting resolved that the FSS should run the

Group photo taken towards the end of the business session of the Second Australian SF Convention
(Doug Nicholson collection)

1. Phil Royce; 2. Ian Moyes (Adelaide); 3. Walter Judd; 4. Terry King; 5. Fred Fredrickson;
6. Rosemary Simmons; 7. Alan South; 8. Des Conley; 9. Vol Molesworth; 10. Padraic McGuinness;
11. Christine Davison; 12. Harold Nicholson; 13. Dave Cohen; 14. William Veney; 15. Don Lawson;
16. Lloyd Fisher; 17. William Hubble; 18. Rex Meyer; 19. Graham Stone; 20. John Earls;
21. Royce Williams; 22. Kevin Smith; 23. Laura Molesworth; 24. Phineas Glick;
25. Ian Crozier (Melbourne); 26. Patrick Burke; 27. Lyell Crane; 28. Joyce Joyce (Adelaide);
29. Brian Finch; 30. Ted Butt; 31. Sidney Dunk; 32. Nicholas Solntseff; 33. Michael McGuinness;
34. Charles LaCoste.
Photo: probably Jack Leggett

next convention. To overcome the communication problems that had marred the current convention the FSS would appoint one person to take responsibility for the next convention and he would pick a committee of his choice and report progress regularly to the FSS. (At the next FSS meeting Judd was appointed to organise the 1954 convention.)

At the conclusion of the 1953 convention Molesworth talked about the splendid work Haddon had done in the early days of preparing the convention and took on himself the blame for the problems that had so marred the convention. In concluding he stressed that the fundamental aims of the convention had been to bring Australian fans together and that, in doing so, the convention had been an 'unqualified success and promised well for the successful meeting in 1954'.[13]

---

[13] Reports of the convention which differ in some details but agree on most points appear in *Mumblings from Munchkinland* 22 (reprinted from *Fantasy Times* 179), *Etherline* 5, *Wastebasket* 1, Molesworth, Chapter 5.

CHAPTER 6
1950-1953, Melbourne

Melbourne was a drab and dour city at the beginning of the 1950s. Its 1.3 million inhabitants had experienced two decades of depression, war, rationing and regulation and all that most people seemed to want was a nice suburban block of land where they could build a home and raise a family. It was the dream of suburban prosperity that their politicians had promised them. The habits of frugality learned through the depression and obedience learned during the war lingered and gave most people comfort and a sense of security. They had become used to a world of grey conformity where fitting in was what counted.

Australia was a provincial backwater of British and American culture. Like the food they ate and the clothes they wore, everything was uninspiringly British and cultural life was sober and conformist. Shops closed after noon on Saturday and the city's streets were empty of life so most people entertained themselves with sport, almost exclusively football, cricket and the horses. At night they flocked to the city's picture theatres, many located close to suburban railway stations because cars were still uncommon. Week after week families sat in the same seats to watch whatever was being shown, usually a British B-grade movie before interval and something American after.

Melbourne was a highly conservative city imbued in traditional Christian values. The bars shut at six in the evening and the only form of public entertainment on Sunday was the churches that were packed. There was little else for the populace to do. Life was dominated by a kind of puritanism that demanded and enforced high standards of morality, in public at least. Public drunkenness, lewd behaviour and possessing immoral reading material were all punishable offences and censors protected the public gaze from anything that might offend. They banned many publications, some music and films for moral or political reasons, and it was common for them to remove questionable scenes from films so that they did not offend or arouse public passions. The paperback anthology that included John W Campbell's novelette 'Who Goes There' was banned in Australia and, in Perth, Roger Dard and the Customs department were in a state of perpetual war over his attempts to import such questionable material as *Weird Tales*.

Australian politics were also conservative and repressive. After almost a decade of national ALP government, and a rapid succession of radical social changes, a conservative government was returned to power that appealed to conservative middle-class values. Victorians experienced the solid, patriarchical and restrictive Bolte government — with the exception of a mere two and a half years in the early 1950s — which made Melbourne the most staid and tedious of Australia's state capitals.

Melbourne was a more relaxed, slow placed and welcoming city than Sydney. In its own way Melbourne accepted, for example, gays and managed them. Sydney's narrow gloomy streets gave it a closed-in feeling unlike the wide and open main streets of Melbourne. Sydney was about money and, while money counted in Melbourne, so did other things. There was a string of live theatres, most of it amateur, and J C Williamson dominated with American musicals at the Her Majesty's and Comedy theatres in Exhibition Street. There was some night life for the sophisticated and monied class such as The Chevron in St Kilda Road. For that class overseas trends were followed seriously and women wore the current year's fashions

There were pockets of less restrained culture, some of it provocative, such as Frank Thring and his group that titillated Melbourne tastes. Jazz and folk music clubs, sub-cultures and pockets of deviance dwelt in the city's back streets. A seedy night life could be found at the Spring Street end of Bourke Street and parts of Little Lonsdale Street with offerings such as prostitution, sly grog joints and, if you knew where to look, gay enclaves. A bohemian demi-monde sustained itself in cafes and coffee shops, but nothing as brazen as the Sydney Push because, after all, this was Melbourne. Political deviance also flourished in political movements including various factions of the Communist Party but everything was managed by the state to keep it out of public view. There was the Special Branch and the Vice Squad to keep deviance under control so it did not sully the calm and conservative waters of Melbourne life.

Melbournians could glimpse the rest of the world, tantalisingly out of reach, through the windows of cinema. Even with heavy handed censorship it showed worlds of experience and excitement that Melbournians who wanted more could only imagine. The immense wave of migration that would transform Australian life was only beginning and television and 'rock and roll' were still six years in the future.

Science fiction had almost no place in this conservative and constraining world and its relative scarcity and pulp origins made it socially unacceptable. The science fiction that most Australians saw was comic strips in newspapers and carttoons and movie serials made for Saturday matinees, so it was inevitably described as 'that Buck Rogers stuff'. People who insisted on reading it in public did well to hide their books and magazines inside something more respectable like *The Sporting Globe* or *Man Magazine* to avoid public stares and ridicule. Fans of the genre did not discuss science fiction in company and any friends who learned that they did politely did not raise the topic or mention it to others. At school boys who read it were ridiculed as 'a dill, a drongo or a wet weed'.[1] This attitude made the people who read science fiction feel outsiders in Australian society, but they also believed that what they read was important because it pointed the way to the future and offered insights into life that others ignored.

As it was in Sydney, science fiction was hard to find in Melbourne. There were comic strips such as Speed Gordon, Brick Bradford and Mandrake the Magician in the newspapers and magazines and the fantastic elements in the boys' papers, but the pulp magazines that were freely available in the drug stores of America were rare in Australia. Some was brought in by individual science fiction readers through the postal system but it might be seized by the Australian Customs on suspicion that it had been paid for with Australian money or because it fell foul of the censors who were particularly sensitive to anything that was tinged with licentiousness or horror, so almost every issue of *Weird Tales* was routinely banned in Australia.

The few science fiction fans in Melbourne before the war had ceased to be active. Some kept in touch with each other as friends and collectors but did not continue their pre-war activity. Thus it fell to a new generation of science fiction readers to recreate fandom in Melbourne and four of them were the teenagers Race Mathews, Dick Jenssen, Lee Harding and Mervyn Binns. They were all children of the Great Depression who grew up during World War II, so they suffered all the privations of that period, shortages, regulation, rationing and housing shortages. What they had in common was their love of the printed word in general and science fiction in particular. They came from different backgrounds and economic

Early Melbourne fans. LtoR Merv Binns and Dick Jenssen. Front row LtoR Bob McCubbin, Bert Chandler (visiting author) and Race Mathews. (The photo was most likely taken by Lee Harding)
(Merv Binns collection)

---

[1] Interview with Dick Jenssen.

and educational circumstances but their love of science fiction and the need to share that enthusiasm with others brought them together.

Race Mathews' parents read to him while he was still a babe in arms. He was a sickly child and insisted that his parents read to him constantly and, after he learned to read at a very early age, he learned how to use libraries and select his own books. He also developed a love for the British boys' magazines of the time; and discovered his grandparents cache of similar magazines from the previous generation and read them avidly. There were many fantasy elements in this reading; lost worlds, strange powers, time travel and other flights of fancy so he was no stranger to science fiction when he finally discovered it.[2]

When he was nine, in 1944, Mathews started at Melbourne Grammar School's preparatory school in East St Kilda and got there from Brighton by tram, with a change at the junction of High Street and Balaclava Road in St Kilda. Before long he discovered a nearby second-hand shop which had comics in the window and he regularly went to look at them. One day the comics had been shuffled aside to make room for something he had never seen before, an issue of *Thrilling Wonder Stories* (the Tenth Anniversary issue published in 1939). It was love at first sight. The price was 2/6, a week's pocket money which was not due until the following Saturday so he feared that somebody else would buy it before he could. But it was still there when he arrived on Saturday, he bought it and started reading on his way home.

Dick Jenssen (properly 'Ditmar' but always called 'Dick') was born in Shanghai in 1935. His father worked for the Shell Oil Company which moved him to Sydney in 1941. When Jenssen arrived in Australia he was exposed to the same kinds of fantastical literature as Mathews, comic strips such as Buck Rogers and the same British boys' papers. However, his sense of wonder was fired at school, first when he saw a book of (possibly) Chesley Bonestell astronomic art in breathtaking colour, the beauty of which made him gasp and opened up for him a new world of imagination. The other was a story read to him by a teacher about travelling back to the time of the dinosaurs that stimulated his imagination and helped him to see this new world and its inhabitants. He was also a student at Melbourne Grammar where he met Race who introduced him to the term 'science fiction' and directed him to the couple of science fiction anthologies in the school library.

Lee Harding (known as 'Leo' during this period) had a less settled childhood after his mother left his violent father and they spent the war years struggling to find a permanent place to live because a single woman with a child was not acceptable to most landlords. Consequently he had an education at several schools but, after the war, they found a spacious place in

---

[2] For more information on these fascinating magazines Dick suggests looking at E R Turner, *Boys Will Be Boys*, Faber & Faber, 2012.

Gertrude Street in Fitzroy where life became more settled. In 1949 his mother remarried and the family moved to a semi-detached house at 510 Drummond Street in Carlton. It was a solitary childhood and he was an empathetic, shy boy who felt himself an outsider to the world he found around him.

Harding's mother read to him when he was a child. She read him poetry and fiction and taught him to read and write and do 'sums' before he began primary school. He loved to read, had an enquiring mind, was interested in science, particularly astronomy, was curious and imaginative and could dream up his own stories that he started scribbling in books in primary school. He too found the science fiction comic strips including 'Silver Starr' that was drawn in Sydney by Stan Pitt. Like Dick he suffered the ridicule of those who found out that he read science fiction, sneering at him, 'There goes Harding, he thinks people are going to fly to the Moon'[3]. When he was twelve he discovered the Franklins Lending Library in the Eastern Market (later the site of the Southern Cross Hotel) from which he borrowed old prozines and read them avidly. At technical school he discovered photography and started working in a photographic studio around the end of 1951.

Mervyn Binns grew up in a family that also encouraged reading and an interest in science. He was a happy but friendless boy at school because he didn't know anyone who shared his interests. He found the Buck Rogers comic strips in his mother's copies of *New Idea* and then the strips that the others had also found. He was an avid reader and discovered the same boys' comics and magazines as the others. His revelation came one day when his parents bought him a copy of Vol Molesworth's *Spaceward Ho!* so after that he went to the Preston Library and asked for more books like it. The library didn't know what science fiction was so they gave him books about science instead which he found interesting and enjoyed reading. In 1951 his interest in science led him to begin a career as an electrical apprentice but he didn't like that so he sought another job. Since he was interested in reading and books, he was sent to work at McGills Newsagents and Book Seller in Elizabeth Street where he found out about science fiction.

These boys were dreamers. They thought about more than the simple world around them that seemed to be enough for most people. They thought about the universe and what was possible in it. Science fiction fired their imaginations about the world and stimulated them to think more broadly, combined with adventure yarns that fired their sense of wonder. It gave them new ways of looking at human problems. Science fiction exposed them to the wonder of the universe and the intellect, promoted and fed their imaginations and gave them something against which to measure their everyday world. It cultivated and fed their inquiring minds and often made

---

[3] Interview with Lee Harding.

them feel like outsiders in the mundane world. Those who made fun of them called their literature 'escapist', but to them it was liberating.[4]

Being a fan of science fiction in Melbourne at the beginning of the 1950s was a solitary occupation because they had no one to share their enthusiasm with and the literature they wanted to read was hard to find, which led them to build up collections which became prized possessions. Binns, for example, built up a collection of books, magazines and comics that he kept in a large box in the family's garage, which was stolen and then sold by the thief to a nearby second-hand shop.

To build up their collections fans found second-hand bookshops where they could occasionally find a book, prozine or American comic, apparently sold by people who were selling their collections or had friends in America who sent them those things. Mathews and Harding had regular routes of second-hand shops near tram lines they visited regularly, trawling to find anything that looked remotely strange and fantastic. For Mathews the shops included Birds, Hanley's, Quaine's in Commercial Road, Halls in Chapel Street and Franklin's and Hall's in the city.

Franklin's had a lending library behind its second-hand shop which contained a rare treasure trove. It had acquired hundreds of American prozines including *Astounding*, *Amazing*, *Thrilling Wonder Stories* and *Startling Stories* and had them hard bound with the covers cut off and glued to the front. For a hefty joining fee of £2/10/- and a lending fee of 6 d each they could be borrowed, and Harding struggled home on the tram with five or six to devour on weekends. He favoured *Thrilling Wonder Stories*, *Planet Stories* and *Startling Stories* because, in addition to the fiction, they also had letter columns and fan sections which other magazines, and the BREs, did not have. Through them he began to learn about fandom.

Harding wondered how Franklin's got so many American prozines, despite the restrictions, but he soon discovered there were ways to do it. Through advertisements in magazines he discovered the book sellers Ken Chapman and Ted Carnell in Britain who could supply the latest books and, through a mention in the fan column in *Startling Stories*, he found out about Operation Fantast, a mail order business run by Ken Slater, a British soldier based in Germany with the British Army of the Rhine that was part of the Allied occupation of Germany after the war. Slater could obtain copies of American books and prozines which he then sold to fans around the British Commonwealth. He published catalogues of his offerings and his customers sent in their orders, paid for with International Money Orders, and waited expectantly. Many years later Harding could still recall the delight and wonder when he opened his first package from Operation Fantast that

---

[4] Readers will recall, of course, that J R R Tolkien pointed out that the people most afraid of escape are the jailors of the world.

included an issue of *Thrilling Wonder*, issues of the new British magazines *New Worlds* and *Science Fantasy*, the first *Wonder Story Annual* and a couple of paperbacks. Many other Australians also discovered Operation Fantast and it also became the way in which some fans first made contact with each other.

Roger Dard saw Molesworth's address in an issue of *Famous Fantastic Mysteries* in 1948, wrote to him and soon found himself invited to join the Sydney Futurians. He was soon probably Australia's best-known fan overseas through his correspondence and a regular column in a prominent American fanzine so Ken Slater asked him to become the Australian agent for Operation Fantast. Dard put Mathews in touch with Don Tuck, who was still living in Melbourne after the war, who introduced him to another Melbourne collector, Gordon McDonald. Through Tuck Mathews also came to know of Melbourne's pre-war fans, Hockley and McLennan.

Mathews and Jenssen first met in Grimwade House, Melbourne Grammar's preparatory school, and Mathews introduced Jenssen to the second-hand shop in St Kilda and its treasures. Mathews introduced Jenssen to other science fiction and fantasy, including more sources of science fiction in second-hand bookshops and the Franklin's lending library where Jenssen borrowed the same hardbound American prozines that Harding was also reading.

Mathews also learned about fandom in Sydney and Graham Stone appointed him the Melbourne agent for the ASFS — an agency which did not last long when, due to his studies and other interests, Mathews failed to live up to Stone's high administrative expectations. Harding also joined the ASFS and began receiving regular packets from Stone which included the latest Sydney fanzines including *Stopgap*, *Vertical Horizons* and *S-F Review* which impressed him with its literate reviews of recent prozines and hardcover books.

Dard put Mathews and Harding in touch with each other. They corresponded for a while and then Mathews invited Harding to visit him in his parent's home in Barnett Street, Hampton, a Melbourne bayside suburb. When Harding arrived on a lovely Sunday afternoon he found Mathews sitting on the front lawn reading *Wonder Stories Annual*. They talked about science fiction for a few hours and Harding left after giving a vague promise that he would return a few weeks later to attend a meeting Mathews was arranging with some other science fiction fans.

Bob McCubbin was a middle-aged teacher who had served as an education officer with the Australian Army in the occupation of Japan after the war and worked as a teacher when he returned to Australia. He was a compulsive collector and when he returned to Melbourne he began trying to collect as much science fiction as he could and, like others, had a circuit of shops that he visited regularly. One day he fell into conversation with Mathews as they were standing next to each other fossicking in McGills and McCubbin noticed that Mathews looking at a copy of *Amazing* he had already read. He commented on it, they exchanged names and then went together to another shop, Hanley's, where Mathews had heard there was a sale of second-hand magazines.[5]

Slowly a few fans began to establish a loose network and some occasionally visited each other's homes and loaned each other books and prozines. McCubbin's network grew to include Harding, Jenssen, Mathews, Marshall McLennan and Gordon Kirby, but these fans did not necessarily know each other. Mathews was the one who brought these individuals together. He was only 16 and baby faced, but he seemed to have a wisdom beyond his years, a strong and mature personality and unlimited energy.

Everyone who bought science fiction at McGills knew Binns, the jolly seventeen-year-old shop assistant who built up a small section of science fiction in the shop. One day McCubbin asked him if he would like to attend a meeting at Mathews' place in Hampton where they would talk about forming a science fiction club in Melbourne and he agreed.

The meeting took place on 9 May 1952. There were about ten people there including Mathews, Jenssen, Harding, Binns, McCubbin, Jack Keating and two pre-war fans, Hockley and McLellan. It was the first time any of them had been at such a large gathering of science fiction fans.

By coincidence Harding and Jenssen met on the bus travelling up South Road from the railway station to Mathews's place in Barnett Street. They became instant friends and spent the bus trip in animated conversation about what they had read and what they liked. They were an odd couple, Jensenn a well-off Melbourne Grammar boy and Harding from working class Fitzroy, but they shared the same enthusiasms and vision so where they came from counted for little and they became lifelong friends.

At the meeting Jenssen and Harding were initially shy but felt accepted in this group among people who were happy to talk about science fiction, understood what they were talking about and what they saw in it. Harding, who was 15 at the time, found his first friends in this group, particularly Jenssen who was, like him, younger than the others. He found that fans weren't concerned about a person's religion, whether they were straight or gay and if they had physical handicaps, what mattered was that they read and liked science fiction and wanted to talk about it. He found it very liberating to be part of the group. Jensen found that the group, by their acceptance of him, was enormously effective in helping him to build up his confidence.

---

[5] Most accounts of first encounters with other fans vary in slight details but I have tried to use the version that is most likely to be the correct one or, if that is not possible, the more entertaining one. If you want to be pedantic you can look up the stories for yourself using the sources listed at the end of this history.

Following that initial meeting the group met about monthly in the homes of some of its members, usually at Mathews', McCubbin's or Kirby's places. Meetings revolved around talk, letters, barter and chess. New members were recruited by Binns who promoted the group at McGills so numbers gradually swelled to about a dozen.

During these meetings the idea emerged of creating a broader organisation so there would be even more people to talk to. The decision to establish a formal group was made at a meeting at Mathews' place which the Sydney fan Bill Veney attended while moving from Tasmania to Brisbane. He argued strongly for a highly structured organisation similar to the Futurian Society of Sydney but Melbourne fans resisted and instead decided on a much less formal organisation with no formal office holders, formal meetings, subscriptions, minutes or any of the other trappings of the Sydney Futurians. It had five conveners: McCubbin, Mathews, Jenssen, McLennan and Kirby, with McCubbin the prime mover who also published a newsletter for the group. They called themselves a 'group' because they felt they would be getting closer to a Sydney style arrangement if they called themselves a 'club'. So the Melbourne group remained a bunch of people who got together regularly to swap yarns and trade a few prozines in the hope of avoiding many of the problems that occurred in Sydney and, while there were occasional disagreements, there was little that disrupted the general harmony of the group.

The group grew and after a meeting at which nineteen people packed into McCubbin's modest living room in his home in suburban Auburn they decided to find a meeting place that didn't also involve spouses having to clean up after them. Somebody suggested Val's Coffee Lounge at the top of a flight of stairs leading from a doorway in Swanston Street opposite the Town Hall. It was an ideal venue in some ways, a convivial spot in the heart of Melbourne that served coffee and snacks and where people could sit for ages talking to friends. It was also a place where Melbourne's newly emerging lesbian and gay community met, apparently known to many people but not to others because such things were not common knowledge in the repressive climate of early 1950s Melbourne. The science fiction group began holding fortnightly meetings there on 14 August 1952 with five around one table and, by November, the meetings had grown so large that there were twenty-nine people who occupied the whole of the west end of the Lounge.

Some found the atmosphere of Val's disagreeable though others might have found it convenient and more than once a member of the science fiction group disappeared for a time into the company of the others there. The Melbourne SF Group did not meet at Val's for very long but their time there became vivid in the memory of the group. McCubbin wrote that 'the odd characters frequenting Val's soon made it imperative that we move to a more healthy position'.[6] Apart from Val's sexual overtones, and the sometimes questionable quality of the food it served, the Group was beginning to build up a collection, a library of books and prozines that were initially kept in a large box that McCubbin had brought back from Japan. As it grew the Group needed somewhere more permanent to meet where it could also keep a permanent library. Keith McClelland found a basement room in the Oddfellows Hall at 30 Latrobe Street that cost 12/6 for each meeting, and the Group began meeting there on 14 November 1952.[7] It was much more austere than Val's and fans felt a little out of place there, but it gave the Group space to itself where it could lay out books and prozines for sale or swap and build up a library that was kept in a cupboard in the hall outside their room.

In February 1953 the Group decided to meet weekly on Thursday evenings. Despite the suggestions of some, including Mathews and Harding, that the Group become more organised, it continued on with no formal organisation and McCubbin as its informal leader, collecting cash to pay the rent and holding brief informal sessions where he delivered news of general interest, introduced new members and kept attendance records. By September 1953 the Group had a roll of 58 names but the usual attendance at meetings was about fifteen, roughly ten of them regulars. Bert Chandler visited when he was in port and other fans including Don Tuck, Doug Nicholson, Mick McGuinnes, Bill Veney and Rex Mayer visited when they were in Melbourne. The evenings were spent in informal discussions, swapping books and prozines (sometimes for cash) and playing chess. After the meetings members adjourned to Mirka's, another convivial central Melbourne meeting place that was more acceptable than Val's.

Also in their Oddfellows Hall basement room the Group watched movies after Dan Bicknell brought a movie projector and occasionally brought it in to entertain the Group with trade and educational films that were of interest to the members. Almost all Group members were film fans and Group members went together at times to see science fiction films that were screened commercially. They went to a preview screening of *The 5000 Fingers of Dr T* at the Windsor Theatre in Chapel Street and when *Fantasia* was re-released the group went to see it. Individually and together. Mathews, Jenssen, Harding and Binns went to see any movies that displayed reality from slightly different perspectives including some early French and Russian films. However Australia's harsh censorship rules meant that many movies never made it onto Australian screens or, if they did, scenes that were

---

[6] *Etherline* 12.

[7] Bob McCubbin suggested that the move was made in November 1952 and Bill Veney gives, in *Ugh*, the precise date of 14 November. On the other hand Race Mathews writes that the agreement with the Oddfellows was signed on 17 December 1952. Who is right and does the precise date matter?

offensive to the censors were cut out, no matter what they did to the rest of the film.

Most Group members knew little about the state of fandom in Sydney. As far as they understood the situation the fans there were nasty and back-stabbing with combative personalities so they could always find something to argue about. A few Melbourne fans had more direct contact with Sydney. Mathews attended the first Sydney convention where he felt immediately at home with the other attendees in discussing science fiction unguardedly. He met most Sydney well-known fans including Molesworth, Castellari, Stone and Dillon. Veney met him at the airport, took him to his accommodation, to the convention and to a famous Kings Cross night club one evening. Mathews' attendance at the second convention was very short. After he left his wallet in a taxi he had only enough spare change to get back to the airport and home again.

Harding's enthusiastic correspondence with Roger Dard introduced him to the schism in Sydney fandom. He formed a rapport with Veney when he visited Melbourne and was included in a group letter circulating between Dard in Perth, Veney (by then in Brisbane) and Lyell Crane in Sydney. When the group letter arrived he was surprised to find page after page of typing, none of it about science fiction but instead about fan politics and the general world situation. He loved it. After the initial shock he looked forward to each new instalment, but it petered out after about nine months, probably after Crane tried to play peacemaker with the Stone and Molesworth group, but Dard would have nothing of it.

Harding's irrepressible energy and enthusiasm had helped support the formation of the Group and kept it going. Next he turned his enthusiasm to building relationships with overseas fans. Shortly after he joined Operation Fantast he began writing to fans and fanzine editors overseas and established a few contacts there, one of the first was Bob Silverberg who was then publishing the fanzine *Spaceship*. Fanzines began to arrive such as *Slant*, *Hyphen*, *Spaceship*, *Peon*, and others. He was flabbergasted and inspired. He didn't think about anything except the fanzine he wanted to publish but, always at the back of his mind, was a professional aspiration because he thought it would be a way of getting into professional publishing and learning how to deal with contributors and things like that. He had bought a typewriter with the intention of trying his luck with the prozines but, having met with poor response to his first story, he decided to turn to fanzine publishing.

Around the time the Group began meeting at Val's Harding said to Jenssen, 'We must put out a fanzine.'[8] Jenssen agreed, he was happily drawn into Harding's project and, as the two youngest members of the Group, it

---

[8] *Boys Own Fanzine* 3.

was natural that they should plan this venture together. Jenssen was also looking for an outlet for his creative energy and, while he tried his hand at writing, his greater interest and skill lay in drawing and illustrating and that became his responsibility in the fanzine they began planning.

Harding and Jenssen thought big. Their fanzine was to be called, *Perhaps: The International Magazine of Fantasy and Science Fiction*. They had seen Doug Nicholson's *Forerunner* that came out in September 1952 and planned something similar but not quite so elaborate. Harding wrote to his contacts, overseas and in Australia, asking for contributions and gradually their fanzine began to take shape. Jenssen prepared a scraper-board cover, Roger Dard and Ken Slater provided autobiographical contributions, Veney contributed an article on Australian SF writers, Bob Silverberg in New York provided news about fandom in America and Bert Campbell, editor of *Authentic* in Britain, also provided a contribution. Jenssen also wrote a short story and provided fillos.

The content for the first issue was far more adventurous and wide-ranging than any Australian fanzine for years, but planning was the easy part. Apart from McCubbin's news sheets for the Group nobody in Melbourne had published a fanzine since 1941 so Harding and Jenssen had nobody to teach them how to do it and they learned the hard way, through experience. At first they planned to produce their fanzine in the traditional folded-foolscap format but then discovered that Harding's new portable typewriter would not take stencils sideways. Instead they had to redesign their fanzine in a quarto format and found that it had the advantage of allowing more space for art and headings. Harding also had no experience with cutting stencils and had not heard of corflu, so when he made a typo he either struck it out or planned to cross it out later on the printed pages.

More challenges followed. Planning was more or less completed by mid-November 1952 so they decided to spread the news of their forthcoming opus by publishing a two page Preview. Binns suggested that they could use the McGills Rex-Rotary duplicator to print it so, eager and excited, the three went to McGills after work one evening to print it with the two stencils Harding had typed, complete with typos and strikeovers. An evening of frustration and disillusionment followed when the pages from the duplicator came out with a two-inch-wide stripe on black ink on the reverse side. Binns tried to fix the problem by cleaning the rollers but the black stripe reappeared no matter what he tried. Eventually they gave up, printed the second stencil on a second sheet of paper which Harding then stapled together and sent out to roughly a hundred fans listed in the ASFS directory and a separate bundle mailed to Dave Cohen in Sydney to distribute to the Thursday Night Group. Later they found out that the problem had been caused because the stencils had been two inches too short for the duplicator.

The response to their effort was a stony silence but they continued with preparing their first issue. Harding had almost completed stencilling the issue when he heard that Mathews was planning to publish his own fanzine, initially to be called *Xanadu* but later *Bacchanalia*. Graham Stone had loaned Mathews copies of two outstanding American fanzines, *Nekromantikon* and *Fanscient* and Mathews hoped to produce an antipodean counterpart. Harding was alarmed that a second fanzine from Melbourne would be competition for *Perhaps* so he and Jenssen visited Mathews and suggested that they combine their resources rather than compete. Mathews agreed that they would pool their cash and the material for *Perhaps* and *Bacchanalia* in an alliance they called the Amateur Fantasy Publications of Australia (AFPA). They would concentrate on publishing the first issue of *Perhaps* and then the first issue of *Bacchanalia*. Both would be in the same format but *Perhaps* would be mainly about science fiction and *Bacchanalia* devoted mainly to fantasy. When Harding wrote to Dard about their arrangement he replied with a cheque for £10 and became a silent and unacknowledged partner in AFPA.

The wrap-around cover for *Perhaps* was at the printer when they again approached the McGills duplicator, more prepared than last time. But their problems were far from over. Harding had recently received a copy of Silverberg's *Spaceship* duplicated on shiny, semi-slick paper in contrast to the customary American twilltone paper. He was so impressed with it that he scouted around Melbourne's paper houses until he found something similar. It cost twice as much as the regular duplicating paper and he bought four reams of it. They found it was a quarter of an inch larger than their usual paper and soon also discovered that their duplicator ink was incompatible with their new paper and refused to dry on it.

With only a few pages of duplicating to go the Rex-Rotary stopped working and they left it for McGills to repair. They knew that McCubbin had an old-fashioned flatbed duplicator that he used to run off the occasional Group newsletter and asked him to help complete printing the issue. He did what he could but they soon discovered that the flatbed delivered only about fifty to sixty copies before the stencils started to crease and fall to pieces while they had hoped to print an optimistic hundred and twenty copies. A few weeks later the Rex-Rotary was repaired. Harding had retyped the butchered stencils and they ran off the remainder of the first issue.

When the covers arrived from the printer they were finally able to publish the first issue of their fanzine in February 1953. Harding and Jenssen had laboured hard to produce a superior fanzine but what they ended up with was a great disappointment. At every stage of production the fanzine of their imaginings had crumbled into dispiriting reality. Harding was dismally disappointed because nothing had turned out the way he had hoped due to his youthful lack of experience. He hand trimmed the pages into a semblance of unity and mailed out copies with a heavy heart. He sent a few dozen copies to Cohen in Sydney for distribution, the nominal cost was one shilling a copy but he told Cohen there was no charge if the buyer felt it was unwarranted, and most did not pay.

On top of a muted response Graham Stone's review in *Science Fiction News* was short and condescending. 'A fine effort marred by childish drawings and bad typing and duplicating' he wrote. 'A lot of hard work goes into a fanmag. Without care, common sense and taste it is work wasted. We expect better next time.'[9] Others were more encouraging. Dard was conciliatory and Tuck was enthusiastic. In *S-F Review* Nicholson wrote that *Perhaps* was 'characterised by energy, enthusiasm, inexperience and general untidiness', which was a very good summary.[10] The letters of comment that came in were mostly generous and supportive and Harding and Jenssen were thankful that a few people had thought the effort had been worthwhile. It was enough to encourage them to do better with the next issue of *Perhaps*.

Perhaps 1
(Merv Binns collection)

Veney wrote that *Perhaps* was 'like a breath of fresh air in a musty room'. It was, he admitted, full of every error imaginable but also that; 'The happy renegades, who hold the theory that the spirit is more important than the form, will find more enthusiasm and vitality than in any other Australian fanzine since FUTURIAN OBSERVER'.[11] He was right. *Perhaps* looked sad, due to Harding and Jenssen's inexperience, but its content was a vivid departure from everything that had previously been published in Australia. It was lively, energetic and enthusiastic and bubbled over with new ideas and content. Previous Sydney post-war fanzines had spent more effort on looking neat and tidy but their content had been staid, provincial and conservative. Harding had been inspired by the best of American fanzines of the period and tried to do what he had seen in them. He had sought and

---

[9] *Science Fiction News* 2, February 1953.
[10] *S-F Review* 6, March 1953.
[11] *Ugh!* 2, February 1953.

received support from overseas fans so *Perhaps* was international rather than parochial. The issue of Stone's *Science Fiction News* in which the *Perhaps* review had been published was carefully laid out and expertly printed but its tone was unexciting and uncreative in comparison. *Perhaps* might have seemed like a poor effort to Stone, but it showed what fanzines published in Australia could become.

Chastened, Harding and Jenssen began planning the second issue of *Perhaps* which would have none of the faults of the first issue. The big hurdle to their plan was money. Many of the problems of the first issue could be overcome by publishing the second in photolith, but a thirty-page issue would cost in the vicinity of $120-160. Where could AFPA find that kind of money?

A partial solution came in the shape of Ian Crozier who found out about and joined the Melbourne Group through Dard and Operation Fantast. He was more than five years older than Jenssen and Mathews and seven years older than Harding, was employed as a Customs Agent and experienced in business. He was smooth, affable and extraordinarily hospitable, and the Group was awed by his talent for organisation. The Group was lethargic with little or no inclination to become organised, nor had much of an idea about how to do it, so his influence on the club was felt from the start.

Crozier did the lettering for the cover of *Perhaps* but his influence on AFPA came from his experience and knowledge about business and office equipment, and his ideas about what fans should do. The group wanted to produce expensive photolithoed fanzines because it was the only method they knew that would reproduce artwork well. Crozier told them about an alternative method of electrostencils that could reproduce half-tones and photographs on a duplicator. He brought samples of what the method could do to a Group meeting and they were quickly convinced. The catch was that old duplicators like the McGills one could not use electrostencils so they would need to buy a new one. The cost was an astounding $300 but one photolithoed issue of *Perhaps* would cost almost half that, and with the grand plans the group had, it made economic sense to buy the duplicator. The purchase also came with two drums of different colour that would give them a great deal of flexibility with future publications.

The original idea had been for each AFPA member to contribute $20 each towards the cost of photolithing *Perhaps 2* but this was rearranged so that the money went towards the purchase of a Roneo 500 which was to be paid off over three years from what they expected would be the profits from their publishing ventures. Crozier became a member of AFPA and not long after another Group member, Kevin Whelahan, also joined.

Buying their own duplicator freed the group to think more imaginatively about what they wanted to do. Crozier was not very keen on most fanzines and saw AFPA as a vehicle for publishing semi-professional magazines to be marketed through various fan outlets across Australia and by direct retail sales. Harding's imagination was much broader and less business like. In addition to the next and improved issue of *Perhaps*, he began thinking about and gathering material for a smaller and frequent news fanzine for Australia. He had devoted some space in *Perhaps* to news from overseas under the heading 'Etherline' and decided to use that title for his new project. He talked to Binns and Jenssen about the idea and they decided to go ahead with a sort of Victorian newsletter on a fortnightly schedule to compete with the Sydney fanzines. He dummied up the first issue but was not keen on cutting the stencils sideways on his typewriter so, when Crozier offered to do the typing for him, he agreed. McCubbin was happy because *Etherline* meant he didn't have to continue publishing a newsletter for the Melbourne Group.

Binns ran off the first issue of *Etherline*, dated 1 March 1953, on the McGills Rex-Rotary but when Harding saw it he was upset. Apart from his initials at the end of the editorial on the front page and a couple of interior contributions, there was no mention of him or his role in the fanzine. Harding felt slighted because, after all, *Etherline* had been his idea, but they talked the matter over at length with Crozier and finally came to an agreement that Crozier would take over *Etherline* and Harding would concentrate on *Perhaps*. There was, Harding said, no point in being greedy, Crozier was enthusiastic and eager to get started and Harding doubted his ability to stick to a fortnightly schedule. The second issue of *Etherline* acknowledged Harding as publisher but after that *Etherline* continued on with only Crozier as editor and Binns as publisher, under the AFPA banner.

Mathews' *Bacchanalia* appeared in April 1953, looking quite like *Perhaps* with a printed wrap around cover and duplicated interior pages. There were many less mistakes and the content was mainly fiction of a fantasy flavour including an article about H P Lovecraft. A month later, in May, the second issue of *Perhaps* was published and it was a marked improvement over the first issue. It made full use of corflu, electrostencils for most of the artwork and a red duplicator drum to add colour to the issue. Dard had told Harding how to create an even right-hand margin — a laborious process of typing everything twice — so this issue looked much tidier. It featured a long article by the American fan Hal Shapiro, that came to Harding through Dard, about witnessing an atomic bomb test and a few other well written and generally lively pieces, including a letter column. Among its features was three pages of thoughtful book reviews in the style of Rex Meyer's *S-F Review*. It was in many ways a good Australian version of an American fanzine of the times and quite a contrast to the earnest Sydney fanzines. When Stone reviewed this issue in *Science Fiction News* he commented favourably on the Hal Sapiro piece but, as for the rest, he wrote, 'Some of the rest of this issue is good

FLASH!!!!! SEE PAGE 5

ETHERLINE

THE SCIENCE FICTION NEWSLINE

No. 1 — March 1st 1953

Published fortnightly by the Amateur Fantasy Publications of Australia

---

Arranged and edited by
Ian J. Crozier.
on behalf of A.F.P.A.

Production:
Mervyn Binns.

Correspondents:
Capt. Ken Slater
Roger Dard
Charles Anderson
Bob Silverberg
H.J. Campbell
and
A.F.P.A. Members

Classified Ads. Rate
2d. per word or
Full Page   15/-
Half Page   7/6
Q'tr Page   3/9

6d. per issue

This Issue Gratis.

TALKING POINT

The idea of a regular Australian newsletter has been knocking around in our collective editorial minds for some time now. It began with "PERHAPS", was pushed on a bit more when it became established, and now becomes a reality. Our aim is to pump the news out as fast as it comes in, and fear the not that you will have to put up with an editorial every issue -- that's for "PERHAPS" and "BACCANALIA", our companion magazines, as if you had'nt heard. Our duty is to supply NEWS, and that is what we will feature, not long solemn heddy-torials.
With the co-operation of a bunch of British and U.S. fans and professionals, as well as an odd - very odd- Aussie or two to dish out the news from this side of the globe.
Before I leave you, in this, my first and last editorial, I will put in a plea for "PERHAPS". We want artwork and articles by our own Australian fans. The U.S. and British fans are only too willing so what about it, Aussies.   LJH

Etherline 1
(Merv Binns collection)

enough to sort out from the rubbish' but 'The standard of grammar, spelling and typing is low, and rather spoils the issue'.[12]

By this time Harding had little regard for Stone and his opinions, and his fevered fannish brain was hatching another project. Publishing an issue of *Perhaps* took a great deal of effort and organisation but what he needed was an outlet for his fannish energies and enthusiasms, something more immediate, fannish in the American style and less sercon than *Perhaps*. The result was *Wastebasket* which he put together quickly using a few items lifted from American fanzines to fill out the issue. His intention was to make *Wastebasket* a fanzine of fannish fun not seen in the Australian fan scene, modelled on American fanzines and poking some fun at Sydney fanzines and what *Etherline* had become under Crozier's editorship. *Wastebasket* bore the sub-title 'What the Good Editors Reject — We Print!' but the content was good so this was more a statement of self-denigration than a statement of fact. The production was even more assured than *Perhaps 2* but there was no attempt to include electrostenciling, rather the interior art, of which there was a lot, was all drawn onto stencil, and there was no attempt at right-hand justification which showed the production was more spontaneous. In contrast to *Perhaps*, *Wastebasket* bulged with energy and enthusiasm at the cost of intent and appearance.

Response to *Wastebasket* seems to have been stunned silence. Harding later recalled that Doug Nicholson told him; 'This sort of thing just wasn't proper for Australian fans' and that, chastened, he wrote to Cohen asking him to destroy the copies that he had sent him to distribute in Sydney. What probably happened was that Australian fans did not realise the enormity of Harding's transgression until a second issue of *Wastebasket* appeared a few weeks later. There are two versions of *Wastebasket 2*, a lively 16 page issue dated July 1953 that appeared to be thrown together enthusiastically, containing generally well written and lively material, illos drawn direct onto stencil and a few scurrilous comments thrown in for good measure. There is also a second 12 page version dated 30 July bearing the sub-title 'News, Views and the Lighter Side' but containing much more sercon material, no illustrations and all but the final couple of pages right margin justified. It could not have looked more like a Sydney produced fanzine or *Etherline* if it had tried. Perhaps Harding had been chastened by response to the first version, recanted his evil ways and shown that he could conform to the expectations of others. Or perhaps there is a touch of parody about the second version. It looked more worthy but, of the two versions of *Wastebasket 2*, the first is much more interesting and entertaining.

Wastebasket demonstrated the divide between the fannish and sercon values in Australian fandom with only Harding visibly deviating from tradi-

---

[12] *Science Fiction News* 6, June 1953.

tional Australian sercon values to the fannish side. Fandom should be for fun, he declared, but others did not agree and Harding began to feel that he was on the outer. There was nothing of the cultural cringe about *Wastebasket* as there was in most Australian fanzines of the time. Rather than the tidy, self-effacing and anemic nature of those, Harding took the energy of American fannish fandom and tried to give it an Australia, or more precisely a Melbourne, voice. Like many other Australians at that time who were trying to find an Australian voice in the arts and Australian culture more generally, he and his work was not understood or appreciated.

Harding also began to feel that he was being pushed to the outer in AFPA where Crozier and *Etherline* had become the main publishing activities. Harding and Crozier had quite different personalities, Harding was young, enthusiastic and keen to engage with difference and change while his enthusiasm bubbled over into publishing fun fanzines. Crozier, on the other hand, was a conservative businessman who expected general orthodoxy of behaviour in the fan group that should do things in what he considered to be the right way. He took his science fiction seriously and thought that AFPA should publish material that contributed to the betterment of the genre, not for fun. Harding began to feel that Crozier was edging him out by not talking to him and deliberately avoiding him. What, Harding wondered, had he had done that was wrong, what was Crozier planning, and did he want Harding out of AFPA so he could take over control? He began to notice that Crozier and Kevin Wheelahan were often seen in earnest conversation about something, but he was not included in their plans. He began to see Crozier as underhanded and a sinister person who manipulated people, so he withdrew his support for *Etherline* and concentrated on his own fanzines.

The third issue of *Wastebasket*, dated August 1953, probably bought to a head the issues bubbling below the surface. It was published in the same folded foolscap format as *Etherline*, bore the sub-title 'The Science Fiction and Fantasy Review' and had 24 pages of generally excellent content of which a highlight was seven pages of good, literate book reviews. In comparison, the tenth issue of *Etherline*, which was published at the end of July, contained 12 pages of news from Australia and overseas, book lists and news about forthcoming books and magazines, a page of Melbourne Group news, film news and reviews and ads for Operation Fantast and McGills in a style that had no hint of levity.

Talk openly began about reorganising AFPA along lines preferred by Crozier during August 1953. He announced in *Etherline*, on 20th August, that, in future, the book and magazine reviews which normally appeared in *Perhaps* would be included in *Etherline* and the fiction and other material would appear in AFPA's new fanzine, *Question Mark*, while *Bacchanalia* would continue to feature fantasy and allied subjects. A much more intense discussion, which Harding recalled as a 'Court of Enquiry' in the Sydney style, was convened by Crozier the following week. Harding was accused of publishing 'a magazine in direct competition with an AFPA publication' and copies of worthy *Etherline* and unworthy *Wastebasket* were produced in evidence. Harding was then expelled from AFPA, but after the experience of the previous few months he was glad to go. The expulsion was cordial enough — Melbourne fans wanted to avoid the acrimony they saw in Sydney — and Harding was allowed to recoup his investment in AFPA by running off fanzines on their duplicator.[13]

The next issue of *Etherline* announced that AFPA had been reorganised with three full members: Mervyn Binns, Kevin Weelahan and Ian Crozier, and associate members Keith McLelland and Bruce Heron. Its publications would be *Etherline* and *Question Mark* and all other publications previously under the control of AFPA would revert to the care of their editors, though AFPA would print any fanzine or other material at a low charge.

By the time that Harding was expelled from AFPA Mathews and Jenssen had already ceased to be active in it. Mathews had continued to talk about a second issue of *Bacchanalia* and planned a fanzine of fantastic verse but his interests had begun to shift elsewhere and his attendance at Group meetings became less regular as he drifted into the glades of gafia. After high school he enrolled at the Toorak Teacher's College which offered many new distractions so he developed new interests and his reading widened beyond science fiction. There he met Geraldine McKeown, who attended Group meetings on occasions. He began courting her and started selling parts of his science fiction collection in the process, part at Group meetings and a large part to an academic in Sydney. In July 1954 he sold *Bacchanalia* to AFPA and at the end of the year he and McKeown were posted to begin their teaching careers, he to a single teacher school of 21 students at Yinnar South in East Gippsland and McKeown to a similar school about 20 miles away. They married in 1955 and when they returned to Melbourne in 1958 for him to teach at Blackburn South, his family, and the home he was building in Croydon allowed no time for fanac.

Jenssen was also finding his way into other endeavours. Science fiction had revealed to him the beauty and adventure of science and that was the direction he took. His father never refused to buy him a book of any sort when he asked but he also discouraged him as a 'dreamer'. In the Melbourne Group he had found friends who shared his passions, saw him as an intelligent person and encouraged him. The Group gave him the confidence to believe in himself and to follow his interest into a career in science. Serious study kept him away from the Group but resulted in him completing Matriculation with honours and enrolling in a Bachelor of Science course at

---

[13] *Boys Own Fanzine* 3.

Melbourne University in 1954. At university he also discovered another group of people he could relate to, where intelligence counted and where some people read science fiction but had other things to talk about. His increasing interest in science also affected his tastes in science fiction and he sold his complete run of *Galaxy* to help build up his run of *Astounding*.

Dick Jenssen at the control of CSIRAC
(Dick Jenssen collection)

After he completed his Science Degree in 1956 Jenssen was invited to study for a Masters, working on Australia's first digital computer, CSIRAC, which had been relocated to Melbourne University that year. He thought it was like living science fiction in real life. On this computer he did the first weather modeling in the southern hemisphere and also some of the first computer graphics when he produced weather maps on the computer's printer.

Harding produced one more issue of *Perhaps* after he was expelled from AFPA. It showed how much he had learned so quickly about writing, editing and production. Dated January 1954 it impressed with an elegant Jenssen scraperboard cover and a full range of contents from well-known and respected Australian and overseas writers. It was the equal of all but the very best American fanzines but the response was minimal, in contrast to the mail he had received on *Wastebasket*, and he was ready to move on to something new.

Harding aspired to become an author so that is where he turned his energy next with a project to publish a semi-professional magazine in Australia to be called *Tomorrow*. Despite his energy, efforts and the letters he wrote to authors soliciting advice and submissions, the project was not viable and ended before a word had been published.

Like Mathews and Jenssen, Harding had to become serious about his future so he dedicated himself more fully to photography and, feeling unwelcome in the Melbourne Group, was rarely seen there. His creative fannish spirit could not be subdued completely and in 1956 he produced two more fanzines on the AFPA Roneo at the cost of 30 shillings a ream. *Antipodes* was subtitled 'The Friendly Fanzine from Down Under' and was entirely fannish, inspired by American fanzines of the time. The second issue featured a long amusing story about AFPA's first encounter with the McGills

Rotary Rex, a couple of pages of extensive fanzine reviews, notes on Wellington (New Zealand) fandom, a contribution from Don Tuck and a long rambling fannish editorial. There was no artifice of right justified margins and all the illos were drawn direct onto stencil and looked to be an expression of unrestrained fannish enthusiasm.

Antipodes was not published for Australian fans, it was published for fans overseas. Nevertheless the animosity between Harding and Crozier emerged in some of Harding's comments about *Etherline* that stirred Crozier into response by questioning Harding's comments and reminding his readers that *Etherline* was a registered name and infringement left one open to be sued. His comments about *Antipodes* were dismissive, he wrote that despite its mild attack of typos, *Antipodes* was well produced and readable. Bob McCubbin summarised his review by writing that Harding had learned moderation since *Perhaps* and *Wastebasket* and if he continued to improve he might 'yet carve a niche in the fannish Hall of Fame'.[14]

Of the four original AFPA members Binns remained closest to it. He remained active in the Melbourne Group and published *Etherline* for Crozier. He continued to work at McGills, building up their science fiction offerings, building up the Melbourne Group and its library and building up his own clientele of customers for overseas science fiction.

It was through Binns that AFPA's influence on Australian science fiction fandom extended many years beyond its short life. Although AFPA had ceased to exist in all but name by 1954 its heritage continued through its Roneo 500 duplicator that stayed in the Group where Binns continued to use it and where he later taught a new generation of fans to use it, launching several fan publishing careers. More than a decade later it was still in use so when Harding, who had been lured back into fandom in the early 1960s, helped produce the first issue of *Australian SF Review* in 1966 and, when the first issue of *SF Commentary* was published in 1969, it was on the old AFPA Roneo 500.

---

[14] *Etherline* 76 (undated).

CHAPTER 7
1953-1954, Sydney

Sydney's science fiction fans had tried to suppress their differences for their second convention but they were not successful and the result had only made the situation worse. Perhaps it was inevitable, or perhaps they were swept up in the spirit of the times.

The post-war world had brought new technologies to Australia that would have seemed the dreams of science fiction only a decade earlier. The Woomera rocket range was established in Central Australia in the late 1940s to test British long-range rockets. Atomic energy and weapons came to the country with the government's decision to develop Australian uranium deposits in January 1953, establishment of the Australian Atomic Energy Commission and approval given for British atomic bombs to be tested in Australia, commencing in October 1953.

Equally fantastic developments included the CSIRO's construction of Australia's first computer, involvement in the development of radio telescopes and the establishment of a permanent Australian base in Antarctica in early 1954. In March 1953 the Commonwealth Parliament passed the Television Act which would lead to the first television broadcasts in Australia in 1956. (Before then Sydney fan Stirling Macoboy sailed for New York to learn about this new form of entertainment so he could be in at its beginning in Australia when he returned.) Reel-to-reel tape recorders became available in the early 1950s and science fiction fans were very early users. In November 1953 Sydney Futurians Crane, Molesworth and Stone, and a visitor Geoff Bennet, recorded a tape to be sent to a fan in Canada. When Robert Heinlein visited Sydney on a round-the-world cruise in February 1954 he recorded a message to be played at a convention later that year and the whole of that convention was recorded on tape.

These exciting innovations were overshadowed by the fear and paranoia that infected Australia in the early 1950s. The Iron Curtain had come down across Europe, the Russians had atomic bombs, the French were losing to Communists in Vietnam, the Communists had taken power in China and another world war, that would surely end civilization, seemed inevitable. When war broke out in Korea in June 1950 the Australian government quickly committed troops to it and one to go was the fan Harry Brook. When he was at the front in mid-1953 he met other science fictions readers and wrote home asking for Australian fans to send him prozines that he could read and share with his mates.

Science fiction was hard to find in Australia due to the government's embargo on importing American books and magazines. There were a few attempts to publish science fiction locally. Malian Press printed slim volumes containing some American stories and a handful of Australian magazines contained mainly reprints of American stories with the rare story by local authors including Frank Bryning and Norma Hemming. Two Australian magazines, *Popular Science Fiction* and *Future Science Fiction* were launched in mid-1953 but folded a year later because the publisher felt they were not a paying proposition and not worth the effort. Another new magazine, *Science Fiction Monthly*, that also published American reprints, was launched in September 1955 but soon also failed. While science fiction books and prozines were becoming available in major cities, readers in regional and rural areas had to rely on news of what was available from sources such as *Science Fiction News, Etherline* and the mail order services of a few capital city book shops.

Science fiction had gained a small but unsavory reputation in the general public and most people knew about it. Newspapers occasionally published a science fiction short story, usually reprinted from overseas, and radio stations sometimes broadcast science fiction and fantasy stories. High budget science fiction movies such as *War of the Worlds* were well promoted and when *Forbidden Planet* was screened in Sydney 'Robbie the Robot' made appearances in the city streets. In 1953 and 1954 two Sydney bookshops dedicated full-window displays to science fiction and the Winter 1954 issue of *Meanjin* featured articles by Frank Bryning and Bob Brissenden about science fiction.

The Sydney press had published short but reasonably accurate reports of the two conventions so far held in Sydney so fans like Graham Stone began to hope that they were making progress in their crusade to make science fiction popular and respectable. But public attitudes became muddled by the new developments of Dianetics and the Unidentified Flying Object craze which detracted from science fiction's credibility and contributed to the unsettled spirit of the times.

Overwhelming these developments in an unsettled world were the threats of war with Russia and of communism that would, it was said, destroy western society. In response to them the Australian government introduced the National Service Act in March 1951 which forced all 18 year old Australian males to register for 178 days of national service, and most Australian fans of this period did their term in Australia's armed forces. In September 1951 Australia formed a mutual self-defense pact with New Zealand and the

United States (ANZUS) and in September 1952 a similar treaty with several South-east Asian countries (SEATO).

In the United States the rabidly anti-communist McCarthyist movement hung over the lives of Americans and in Australia the conservative government brought in the Communist Party Dissolution Act that may have done the same thing, but it was ruled unconstitutional by the High Court and narrowly defeated at a nationally decisive referendum in September 1951. Even so, the fear of communists and their fellow travellers possessed the minds of governments and infected Australian life. The Australian Security Intelligence Organisation, which had been established in 1949 to detect and defeat Soviet spy rings in Australia, carried out widespread secret investigations which could include anyone who was suspected of left wing tendencies. State governments also conducted secret investigations into unusual and deviant behavior. The fear and hate of communism also destroyed Australia's most important political party, the Australian Labor Party, in a bitter struggle between its anti-communist and left-wing members. It ripped the Party into two bitterly opposed political parties in the middle of the decade and gave Australia almost exclusively conservatives governments for the coming decade and a half.

Enmity, fear and loathing split friendships and alliances so those who had once been good friends would have nothing to do with each other. Rumours and innuendo spread and fueled disagreements and hatreds. This cancer infected many corners of Australian life and gave approval to those kinds of attitudes and actions in daily life. The Futurian Society of Sydney, which had been no stranger to enmities in the past and had personalities who seemed to prefer conflict to co-operation, could not help but take the same path in its own small way.

The Society considered itself the organisational force behind Sydney fandom and said that what it did was for the benefit of all fandom. For most of this period its membership hovered around the high twenties, a handful of them women and about half of them newer members brought into fandom by the conventions the Society had run in 1951 and 1952. It operated under a strict constitution which, by December 1953, ran to eight pages, not including the standing orders, rules of debate, index and cross referencing. Non-members were usually allowed to attend FSS meetings but only financial members were entitled to vote. There was little serious disagreement in the group after the success of their second convention and the only serious disagreement, at first, was over whether or not the Society should buy a typewriter for use by members. The disagreement became deadlocked and had to be resolved by a plebiscite of the entire membership, which failed.

The Society's most important asset and attraction was its library which grew rapidly from 56 borrowers in May 1953 to 86 by the end of the year. It offered 784 items including hardcovers, paperbacks and prozines. The membership fee was increased from 5/- to 7/- in August to enable improvements and additions to the library and Stone prepared a catalogue for borrowers because not all the library was readily available to members and only a selection of around 200 items could be carted to Society meetings in suitcases.

The Society's major project during 1953 was organising the 1954 convention. Wally Judd, a peaceable, calm and reasonable fan who got on with most fans in Sydney, was appointed its organiser. He said that all fandom would benefit from the convention and asked everyone to set aside their past differences and work together to put on the best Australian convention yet. He was given authority to pick his organising team which included Rex Mayer, Jack Leggett, Graham Stone, Lyell Crane, Rosemary Simmons and Vol and Laura Molesworth. Later Bruce Purdy was appointed to handle the auction and Don Lawson to organise the films.

Laura Molesworth took charge of the fund raising for the convention with guessing competitions and raffles that had raised £11/11/- by September 1953. On 5 September she and Vol hosted a fund raiser at their home which contributed another £13 and attracted 47 fans who had 'a whale of a time'. More funds came from a barbeque and from a chess tournament organised by Don Lawson on Thursday nights.

The Society's most popular activity was the Thursday Night gathering at the Sydney Bridge Club room. It was large, square and big enough for people to circulate around the tables and chairs where they could also sit and talk. An average of 29 fans met there with over forty on occasions. Les Raethel managed the evenings unobtrusively and collected the weekly charge of 3/- and, by September 1953, he had collected a surplus of more than £60 which was being saved to buy furniture for an official clubroom in the future. The weekly fee included supper which was initially served somewhat chaotically and later by the Ladies Committee with everyone seated to be served. Sometimes there was organised entertainment such as a Yugoslav fantasy film shown by Don Lawson and watched by 46 in May 1953.

Science fiction was the major attraction on Thursday nights with the FSS Library open for borrowers. The North Shore Futurian Society also began setting up a table so its members could borrow from their library. The North Shore Futurians were generally younger than the rest and their youthful enthusiasm entertained some but annoyed others. Dave Cohen, who had taken over the Operation Fantast agency in Australia and operated it as Blue Centaur Books, also set up a table where he bought and sold books and prozines and arranged subscriptions for people.

Some Futurians regarded the Thursday Night Group as a necessary evil because it brought new people into the group and kept them interested and entertained. However some, most actively Graham Stone, deplored the rowdy behaviour of some who came to the Bridge Club later in the evening after drinking sessions at a nearby pub. He wanted science fiction to be respectable so it did not shock or outrage ordinary people as it had previously done with its outlandish ideas, badly written stories, lurid magazine covers and juvenile fan behaviour.

Sydney fans about 1953. LtoR Vol Molesworth, Graham Stone, Doug Nicholson and Nick Solensteff

Molesworth wanted more for science fiction than mere respectability. Reviving the old ideal of Futurians as people who thought about the future and wanted science fiction to help shape it, he saw a grander future for science fiction and the Futurian movement. He was elected again to the position of Director of the Society at its Annual General Meeting on 27 July 1953 with a vigorous plan for the Society's future which would make it what he called 'a fighting force for fandom'.[1] In October he said he hoped to see Futurian Societies established in 'every city, town and hamlet in Australia' and that the FSS would give fan groups that wished to set up a 'properly constituted organisation' all possible assistance, including copies of the Society's Constitution — which had been drawn up to cover all possible fan activities and had been 'thoroughly tested in law'. The Society could also give advice on holding meetings, setting up a library, organising social activities, publishing fanzines, holding film screenings and organising conventions. He said that the concrete results the Sydney Futurians had accomplished could only be achieved by a well-organised body of fans, properly constituted and working towards common goals. Inspired by this the editor of *Futurian Society News*, Brian Finch, added that the privilege offered to members of the Society could be summed up in one phrase, 'the opportunity to work for fandom'.[2]

Molesworth's dream of a spreading the Futurian spirit was starting to show success. A small group in Canberra, encouraged by Molesworth and Stone, adopted the Sydney Futurian's constitution with some amendments

---

[1] At that meeting were Director Ken Martin, Vice-Director Graham Stone, Treasurer Arthur Haddon, Secretary Rosemary Simmons and members Laura Molesworth, Vol Molesworth, Lyell Crane, Rex Meyer, Kevin Dillion, Wally Judd, 'Bluey' Glick, Les Raethel, Don Lawson, Clive Mellor, Bruce Purdey, Jack Leggett, Pat Burke, Mike McGuiness and Brian Finch. *Etherline* 13, 17 September 1953. *Futurian Society News* 2 & 4.

[2] *Futurian Society News* 6,

to create the Futurian Society of Canberra which held its first meeting in November 1953. A science fiction group that formed in Adelaide adopted the Futurian Society of Canberra constitution. Another small group that formed in the region centred on Newcastle north of Sydney called itself the Hunter River Futurian Society. The North Shore Futurian Society had 63 members and 550 items in its library by August 1953 and held regular meetings, film nights and published a regular news sheet. Most of its members were under 20 and Michael Bos, its President, said it was a club for younger and enthusiastic fans who were part of the 'ever growing ranks of fandom'.[3] The science fiction groups in Brisbane and Melbourne remained, however, stubbornly unorganised.

Graham Stone's Australian Science Fiction Society had 172 members by the end of 1953. Most lived in Sydney but there were also members in every state and territory except the Northern Territory. They supported Stone's aims and when he appealed for funds to buy a Remington typewriter for £29 the money was quickly donated. For some time Stone supported the expense of running the Society from his own pocket with its biggest single expense being publication of *SF News*. An increase in the membership fee to 10/- helped balance the budget. By the beginning of 1954 the ASFS had agents in Adelaide (Joyce), Melbourne (Crozier) and Canberra (Bennett).[4]

Sydney fandom was very social with the regular Thursday night meetings and drinking sessions in nearby pubs. Other social events included a barbeque organised at Fullers Bridge near Chatswood in July 1953 which was catered for by Clive Mellor, with ample supplies of beer provided by Loralie Giles and entertainment by George Dovaston on the squeezebox. There was a lot of singing and noise, which attracted a visit by the police, and the event was a raging success judged by the state of disrepair everyone was in at the end of the night.[5] In August Norma Hemming hosted a science fiction fancy dress ball with attendees including Jack Leggett sporting an awesome raygun and a group of Grey Lensmen. It was an elaborate event where a luminescent sign advised 'Time Travellers' to check their 'Entropy' before entering and the entertainments included reports of flying saucers landing in Hyde Park in Sydney and Lords in London during a cricket broadcast which included a BBC interview of a Martian. 'Dancing was had and all enjoyed themselves immensely'.[6] In November a group of seventeen fans

---

[3] *NSFS Notesheet (Sonic)* 7, *Etherline* 20.

[4] The membership breakup of the Australian SF Society in January 1954 was: Sydney 79, rural New South Wales 12, South Australia 22, Victoria 19, Queensland 11, Western Australia 7, Australian Capital Territory 4, Tasmania 2, New Zealand 9 and Overseas 6 (including four expatriates, Boyd Raeburn and Bert Chandler), ASFS Membership List, January 1954, ASFA circular to members undated, 19/6/53 & *Futurian Society News* 8.

[5] *Futurian Society News* 4 and *NSFS Notesheet* 6.

[6] *NSFS Notesheet (Sonic)* 7.

joined nearly 200 revelers at the Trocadero in fancy dress for the Artists Ball where they had another great time and planned to go again next year.

Another social event was a conference in Albury, on the border between New South Wales and Victoria, over the weekend of 8-9 August 1953 that was hosted by local fan John O'Shaugnessy. Five fans from Melbourne and six from Sydney attended — there should have been seven but Don Lawson expected to board the Albury express when it stopped at Strathfield Station, but it didn't stop and he was left standing on the platform.[7] There was a formal business session on the Saturday at O'Shaugnessy's home where reports were heard about fan activities and plans made for the future, but most of the time was spent in social activities including seeing the sights around Albury. On Saturday evening some fans went the movies (to see *Frankenstein meets the Wolf Man* and *The Cat Creeps*) while the rest stayed in the hotel lounge drinking and chatting until there was no liquor after midnight. The event was considered a great success and plans were made for other border conferences including one at Mildura so that Adelaide fans could join and a conference at Coolangatta on the New South Wales and Queensland border, but neither of these eventuated.

Sydney fandom's active social life did not encourage fanzine production. The fifth and final issue of *Vertical Horizons* was published by Rosemary Simmons in October 1953. Three issues of *Trial & Error*, published by Doug Stanborough, an ex-Japanese POW, contained mostly fiction and multi-coloured, hastily drawn full page illos, but demonstrated almost no relationship with mainstream Sydney fandom. Rex Meyer's *S-F Review* faltered and, after issues in May and June 1953, the next issue was dated July 1953 but not circulated until February 1954. In it Graham Stone and Lyell Crane announced that the Australian SF Society had taken over publication, and the first issue of the second series was published in August 1954.

Other Sydney fanzines were published by clubs. Brian Finch and later Bob Thurston (and possibly Graham Stone from December 1954) published *Futurian Society News* for the Society, a regular and informative newsletter for Society members. It was in the traditional folded foolscap format, about eight pages long and contained news of the Society's activities. Michael Bos, sometimes with the assistance of Bill Hubble, published the *North Shore Futurian Society Notesheet*, usually a one or two page sheet of news for that Society's members that grew to become the larger *Sonic* with its seventh and final issue in August 1953. Graham Stone published an irregular *Australian SF Society Circular to Members*, another short newsletter, and *Science Fiction News*

---

[7] The Sydney fans attending were Lyell Crane, Nick Solensteff, Loralie Giles, Brian Finch, Graham Stone and Michael McGuinness. The five Melbourne fans were Geraldine McKeown, Race Mathews, Merv Binns, Bob McCubbin and Ian Crozier. *NSFS Notesheet* (*Sonic*) 7 August 1953.

which was sent free to members of the ASFS. Early issues made some mention of fan activities in Australia but, as time went by and Stone's attitude to fandom changed, there was almost no news of Australian fan activities because he wanted to attract a wider readership outside fandom. He said he printed 1000 copies and distributed most of them, though paid subscriptions were, as he wrote, 'in the minority'.[8]

Movies were always popular with fans although there were few decent science fiction and fantasy movies available in the early 1950s. There were the occasional film showings at Thursday night gatherings, groups went to see *War of the Worlds* and the North Shore Futurians also organised a group to see *Bud Abbott and Lou Costello go to Mars* on a Saturday night in August 1953. To help meet fans' insatiable desire to see science fiction and fantasy movies Don Lawson launched the Sydney Imaginative Film Society in July 1953 which promised to show a minimum of three movies, with the first to be the classic *Metropolis*. Screenings were to be held in the Public Library Lecture Theatre using a projector that the group would install there, but it seems this plan did not reach fruition. Another group that began at this time was the Science Fiction Drama Club, later called The Arcturian Players. It was formed in October 1953 by a group including the author Norma Hemming and immediately began planning and rehearsing with the objective of staging a production at the 1954 convention.[9]

The Sydney Futurians planned that one day their club would be large and prosperous enough to have its own clubroom where its library could be permanently housed. It would be a base from which Futurians could work for the future of science fiction and fandom and it would give them an image of permanence and respectability in the wider community. That time came, perhaps earlier than expected, in late 1953 when attendance at the Thursday Night meetings had become too large for the Bridge Club room and the Society was notified that it could no longer rent the GUOFF Board Room for its formal meetings. This forced the Society to begin looking for new premises for both meetings.

Suitable space for a clubroom was found on the third floor of the McIlraith's Chambers at 126 Oxford Street in Darlinghurst, up Oxford Street from the city and next to Taylors Square. There were some conditions attached to using the space and the rent was six guineas a week, but that was within the Society's budget. A large group of fans went to inspect the

---

[8] *Mumblings from Munchkinland* 12, *Science Fiction News* 1, 2, 3, 5 & 10.

[9] The initial members of the Group were Christine Davison, Norma Hemming, Loralie Giles, Joan Russell, Bruce Purdy, Clive Mellor, Doug Nicholson and Jack Leggett. Lyell Crane and Lex Banning were also enlisted to help. *Vertical Horizons* 5, October 1953, I 15, and *Futurian News* 6.

space and a Society meeting of 18 members held on 19 October 1953 agreed unanimously to take up residence there.

The owner allowed the Society to make the improvements it needed and redecorate the space, and the work began almost immediately. A number of fans installed florescent lights, resurfaced and painted the walls, constructed wall seats, made a kitchenette from which supper could be served and also a lock-up section for the library with shelves and a cupboard. Loralie Giles, Judith McGuinness, Betty Such and Laura Molesworth provided afternoon teas for the men who did the work. The decor was restrained and respectable, the colour scheme consisted of pinks and maroons: the walls were a delicate pastel shade of shell pink and the wooden fittings were in orchid. There was seating around the walls with steel tubular chairs that were mahogany upholstered, plenty of colourful card tables and notice boards on the walls. Molesworth described the environment as gaily painted and modernly furnished.

The new Futurian Society of Sydney clubroom at Taylor Square was officially opened on Thursday 3 December 1953 with 43 people present. It would be open for fans to use the library and socialise from 7.30 on Monday and Thursday evenings and on Saturdays from 10 am to 5 pm.[10]

After a pause for the Christmas and New Year the Society began a program of activities which included a lecture on space flight given by Dr John Blatt from the University of Sydney and a light hearted Parliamentary style debate on the question 'should extra-terrestrials by subject to the Compulsory Unionism Bill' (which was a hot political topic in New South Wales at the time). The highlight of the year was on 25 February 1954 when 48 people crowded into the clubroom to meet Robert Heinlein who was in Sydney with his wife on a round-the-world cruise.

Despite this promising start things began to go wrong almost from the beginning. There were two main reasons. One was that the Taylor Square clubroom was not located in central Sydney, as the Bridge Club had been, so fans had to travel into the city and then make their way up Oxford Street to get there and that discouraged some from attending.

The second reason was more complex. It began at a Society meeting on 23 December 1953 when Les Raethel resigned as Librarian and Clubroom Manager and Laura Molesworth was elected Librarian and Graham Stone as Clubroom Executive. This may have been the single biggest mistake the Society made. Stone was a dedicated and hard working Futurian who had

---

[10] The FSS had 24 members at this time. They were: Harry Brunen, Pat Burke, Kevin Dillon, John Earls, Brian Finch, Loralie Giles, 'Bluey' Glick, Wally Judd, Don Lawson, Jack Leggett, Lyell Crane, Ken Martin, Rex Meyer, Vol & Laura Molesworth, Clive Mellor, Jock McKenna, Doug Nicholson, Bruce Purdy, Les Raethel, Len Roth, Rosemary Simmons and Graham Stone. Michael McGuinness and Stirling Macoboy were overseas but still counted as members. *Futurian Society News* 8.

only the best of intentions for the Society and science fiction, but his strengths were not in his people skills and he could be single-minded, aggressive and blunt to the point of rudeness, particularly in handling people he didn't like and didn't agree with. He did not like or agree with some members of the Thursday Night Group and the North Shore Futurian Society. For their part, most members of the Thursday Night Group did not think very highly of Stone who, Veney described later in 1954, as Molesworth's 'little idiot mate'.[11] This set the scene for trouble.

Friction between Stone and his opponents reignited old grievances and personal animosities. Most sincerely wished the best for science fiction and fandom in Sydney but they could not agree on what that was or put their differences aside for the common good. When the Society had reformed in 1947 it had been with the hope that the rivalries and animosities that had tainted pre-war Sydney fandom could be put behind them, but that had not happened. To make matters worse, by the beginning of 1954 most of the protagonists knew each other very well and knew how to wound and upset their opponents, which made the atmosphere in Sydney fandom even more poisonous.

Organisation for the 1954 convention also created friction. It emerged that there had been a lack of communication between Wally Judd, the convention organiser, and the Society, which led some to question how the Society was being run. At the meeting on 8 February 1954 Doug Nicholson (seconded by Kevin Dillon) moved a censure motion that questioned the abilities of the Society's executive. It moved that the entire executive be asked to tender their resignations because they had 'interfered with, attempted to dominate, control, and bleed funds [from] every activity related to science fiction which Sydney had seen', because the Society's veteran members had 'systematically maneuvered inexperienced individuals into key positions, then as often as not caused them humiliation by direct and indirect attacks on their conduct, and also on their character' and because the executive had laid out 'what is for this Society an enormous sum of money on a pathetic little room'.[12] Whatever the validity of these allegations the feelings they unleashed led to a heated debate that lasted for an hour and ten minutes. When Nicholson's motion was finally put to the vote it was passed by ten votes to five but, although some changes resulted, Molesworth was again elected Director.

The main source of friction came from the use of and conduct in the new clubroom. The agreement between the clubroom's owner and the Society had two major conditions; that there would be no alcohol allowed and that the meetings would not infringe upon other occupants in the building —

---

[11] *Scansion* 22, 30 December 1954.

[12] Molesworth, *A History of Australian science fiction Fandom*, Chapter 5.

meaning that they would be quiet and orderly. Stone agreed with these conditions because he wanted to attract respectable middle-class people to the club and science fiction, so he hoped these rules would restrain the rowdy behavior of some members. However he had great difficulty in controlling them and some seemed to have enjoyed baiting him, which created more tension in the club. One method Stone hoped would bring civility to the room was a swear box, six pence for every strong word uttered. This had some effect and Ian Driscoll, an impoverished student at the time, could not afford to visit the club because of how much it would cost him. However, one evening he arrived at the club with a fist full of sixpence coins, marched up to the swear box, bellowed 'cunt!' and dropped in a sixpence. He then proceeded to spend the rest of his money on more swearwords than most people knew.[13]

Other irritants to Stone's management of the clubroom were the North Shore Futurian Society and Dave Cohen's Blue Centaur Books. When the Society moved to its new clubroom from the Sydney Bridge Club, Cohen and the North Shore Futurians and their library moved in as well. Stone found the North Shore Futurians particularly annoying because they set up their library table in the middle of the clubroom and touted for business, to the expense of the Society's Library which was located discretely in one corner. At first he endured this intrusion but, by March, he had had enough, asked the North Shore Futurians to move their table to somewhere more discrete and talked with Molesworth about throwing them out of the clubroom entirely. When less drastic methods failed Stone's ultimate sanction to protect the Society and its membership from the unruly element was to ban them from the club.

The situation had reached breaking point by late March and Cohen resolved it on 1 April 1954 when Blue Centaur Books opened for business back in the Sydney Bridge Club on Thursday nights. With him went the North Shore Futurians and six Sydney Futurians. There are several accounts of how this happened but the most likely is that Cohen, dissatisfied with conditions in the Taylors Square clubroom, talked the matter over with some of his friends and decided that they would be better off back at the central city location they knew and away from Stone's harassment. Doug Nicholson probably played a key role in this because of his feelings about the Society's management and his prominent part was shown when the breakaway group was sometimes called 'The Forerunner People'.

The ramifications of this breakaway were not immediately evident and, at the next Society meeting, a motion that the organisers of the walkout be banned from the Taylors Square clubroom was soundly defeated. Perhaps the meeting felt the split could be healed later and the Society had other

---

[13] *Mumblings from Munchkinland* 34.

priorities in the first week of April 1954 because the convention it was to host was only a fortnight away.

CHAPTER 8
1954-1960, Sydney

The third Australian Science Fiction Convention was held in Federation Hall, Phillip Street, Sydney over the weekend of 17 and 18 April 1954. The registration fee was 10/-. It was the Easter weekend and Good Friday was set aside for fans to travel to Sydney and congregate at the homes of local fans where, doubtless, recent events in Sydney were discussed from several conflicting perspectives. Most interstate fans met at Lyell Crane's place where 'liberal doses of refreshments were imbibed'.[1]

On Saturday morning displays of early science fiction magazines and fanzines were set up, a selection of covers from books in the Society Library and a display of recent AFPA publications. Fans milled around looking at them, meeting each other and looking at the souvenir convention program book and a special 48 page Convention issue of *Etherline* members were given. Two floors below and separate from the convention, Cohen's Blue Centaur Books and the North Shore Futurians also set up for business.

The afternoon's program began at about 2.15 with an informal welcome followed by a brief history of science fiction and science fiction film. The set piece for the afternoon was a symposium entitled 'The World of Tomorrow' to discuss the ideas underlying science fiction. It comprised talks about 'The Future of the Machine', 'The Future of Man' and 'The History of Culture' followed by a discussion of the topics raised and then questions from the floor. The symposium demonstrated the founding Futurians' belief that they should be interested in more than science fiction and in understanding and helping to shape the future. Ian Crozier described the talks as 'ponderous and boring' and wondered why science fiction fans did not talk about science fiction.

The film showing in the evening was well received with a number of interesting movies including *The Beginning of the End* about a nuclear war in the near future. The start was delayed because the screen had been accidentally locked in the Society's clubroom and could only be liberated with a hacksaw. Disorganisation continued the following morning when the auction could also only be opened with a hacksaw. The attendance was poor and prices for most items was not high, except for the American books and magazines. The

---
[1] *Etherline* 28.

Attendees at the Third Australian SF Convention
(Doug Nicholson collection)

1: Arthur Haddon; 2: John Earls; 3: Bob McCubbin; 4: Doug Nicholson; 5: Mervyn Binns;
6: Michael Duggan; 7: Michael Bos; 8: Bill Hubble; 9: Terry Clarke; 10: Rosemary Simmons

usual Business Session occupied the afternoon and the evening's entertainment was a highlight. There were a couple of short taped dramas, a short film and the Arcturian Players performed Norma Hemmings play 'That's the Way it Goes'.

The total convention membership was over 135, the most attended sessions were 61 on Saturday and only 40 attended the Sunday night performance. It was regarded as being a well-run convention, for the most part, but the Business Session overshadowed the convention and set the scene for what would follow.[2]

As usual the meeting opened with reports presented by Australia's various fan groups which all reported growth.[3] When debate from the floor opened Lyell Crane said he and Stone wished the convention to recommend a future direction for the Australian SF Society. With fan groups being established and growing in other cities the purpose for which the Society had been created, registering science fiction fans in Australia and New Zealand, had been achieved to a considerable extent so it was not clear what should be its future. Several members made suggestions leading to a 'heated discussion' which ended when the Chair closed that debate, saying that sufficient suggestions had been made for the Society to decide its own future.[4]

The meeting became more heated when Arthur Haddon moved that the 1955 convention be hosted by the North Shore Futurian Society. This shocked many Sydney fans because Melbourne fans had previously hinted that they might like to run the 1955 convention and, after the crisis in Sydney fandom, most fans probably felt it might be a good idea to put the convention in the hands of Melbourne fans. However, fans in Melbourne had decided they wanted to hold a convention in 1956, the year of the Olympic Games in Melbourne. Hubble and his supporters argued that the younger fans of the NSFS should be given the opportunity to show what they could do and that the FSS deserved a break after having run three conventions for three consecutive years. Fans in the Society's circle, including Stone, were outraged because the North Shore Futurians were part of the breakaway group that had gone back to the Bridge Club, so giving them the next convention was like handing it over to their enemy. Bitter debate followed but eventually the North Shore Futurians were given the 1955 convention by a vote of 22 for and 14 against.

[2] Five convention reports give different accounts of the performances on Sunday evening so this is not certain. *Operation Fantast* 16, *Etherline* 28, *Mumblings from Munchkinland* 23, *SF News* 9 and Molesworth, Chapter 5.

[3] The reports included the Futurian Society of Sydney, the Futurian Society of Canberra, the Melbourne Science Fiction Group, the Australasian Science Fiction Society, the Adelaide Science Fiction Group, the Newcastle and Hunter Valley Science Fiction Society and the North Shore Futurian Society. Ian Crozier, *Operation Fantast* (New Series) 16.

[4] *Operation Fantast* 16 and Molesworth, Chapter 5.

Things turned even nastier when Doug Nicholson moved that the breach in Sydney fandom should be healed. Melbourne fans, having just seen the hostility of some Sydney fans, knowing what was likely to happen next and not wishing to be drawn into the Sydney feud or be asked to comment or criticise, wanted nothing to do with the debate. So Bob McCubbin led other Melbourne fans out of the meeting. After that Sydney fans got seriously stuck into each other as old hostilities and hatreds were unleashed. Things were said that could not be unsaid and emotions unleashed that would only make the divide between Sydney's fan groups worse so that a healing became all but impossible. When the meeting was adjourned at 5.15 nothing had been resolved but much had been done to wreck what had been built in Sydney fandom in the previous two or three years.[5]

At the following Society meeting Wally Judd reported that the convention had achieved a greater attendance, greater profits and less friction than the two previous conventions. Molesworth had edited the tape recordings of the convention down to a 50 minute documentary tape which the Society endorsed as a precis of the convention. But Sydney fandom was changed and for some it was the end of their involvement. An 'open house' had been planned for the Monday following the convention at the Society's Clubroom but there is no record of it having taken place.

Upset and disgusted by what had happened some fans gafiated quickly and others drifted away more slowly. The effort of organising the convention killed Wally Judd's interest in fandom and he disappeared. Another stalwart, John Earls, joined others drifting out of fandom. In May Bluey Glick and Loralie Giles escaped to Melbourne to get away from it all. Les Raethel, who had been one of the hardest working and most reliable fans in Sydney, moved to Ballina later in the year. Lyell Crane and Nick Solnsteff, two of Sydney's most prominent fans, became so disgusted with fandom and fans that they refused to have anything to do with them and, even though they lived only two or three hundred yards apart, consciously avoided each other. When Macaboy returned to Sydney from New York in September 1954 he said he was too busy to become involved with fandom again and when Bill Veney returned to Sydney from Brisbane the following month he excused himself from fannish activity because, he said, he was travelling outside Sydney during the week.

Graham Stone made matters worse when he published his response to the North Shore Futurians being given the 1955 convention in a pamphlet titled 'The Stone Report: No Sydney Convention in 1955'. It implicated Melbourne fans in a conspiracy to hand the 1955 convention to the North Shore Futurians and denied the convention's validity. It also demonstrated Stone's ability

---

[5] The full transcript of this business session can be found in *Mumblings from Munchkinland* 35.

to alienate people. The Thursday Night Group regarded it as sabotage by creating bad publicity for the coming convention. It confounded Melbourne fans who had been at the business meeting and knew the meeting has resolved that the North Shore Futurians were to organise the 1955 convention. In the next issue of *Etherline* Ian Crozier tried to make light of Stone's pamphlet by expressing surprise at his announcement. Crozier wrote that the pamphlet was a poorly done attempt to widen the ridiculous rift between the factions in Sydney and told Stone not to involve Melbourne fans in Sydney's disputes, concluding 'GROW UP, SYDNEY!!!!'.[6]

This exchange widened the rift between the Sydney Futurians and fans in Melbourne. The Society took Crozier's comments as an 'unprovoked and unjust attack' that showed 'unfair prejudice' which was also demonstrated, it claimed, because *Etherline* did not publish any Society news but did published reports from the Thursday Night Group. Crozier responded that an iron curtain seemed to have come down around the Society when it came to news.[7] This lack of news about the Society may have been the result of Stone's common response to people he didn't approve of, refusal to have anything to do with them including sending them news or copies of fanzines.

At the FSS Annual General Meeting on 5 July 1954 the retiring Director, Molesworth, summarised the Society's achievements of the past year including holding Australia's most successful convention, the growth of science fiction fandom in Sydney and the rest of Australia, the expansion of the Society's library and its new clubroom. Only obliquely did he mention the breakaway group when he mentioned that the Society had gained twelve new members and lost six. He did not stand for reelection and Graham Stone was elected as the Society's new Director with a Council of five to support him.[8]

Under Stone's leadership the Society sought new ways to keep the interest of members, attract new members and increase the club's revenue. It introduced a Quarterly Associate Member's ticket for £2 which gave readers access to the clubroom and library and was a saving for those who attended regularly. It began selling the current BRE prozines through an arrangement with the distributor which, the club said, would save members the trouble of going around Sydney trying to find them among the floods of western and detective magazines.[9] Regular auction and film nights were also introduced,

---

[6] *Etherline* 33.

[7] *Etherline* 34.

[8] The Council comprised: Bruce Purdy (Vice-Director and Club Room Manager). Leslie Raethel (Treasurer), Alan Smith (Librarian), Jock McKenna (Assistant Librarian), Robert C Thurston (Public Relations Officer) and William W Turnbull (Entertainments Organiser). Harry Brunen was appointed Secretary.

[9] *Futurian Society News* 17.

although sometimes the movies were only borderline science fiction or fantasy because there were very few good science fiction or fantasy movies in 1954.

By July 1954 the Society's library had 91 borrowers, membership was separated from Society membership and cost 5/- a year plus a small charge for each book borrowed. A major library attraction was its collection of American prozines, some dating to back before 1930 including a donation of magazines sent by Heinlein. The Society began a chess championship in September and Stone gave an illustrated talk on early science fiction at the clubroom in October. At the end of December the visiting British author Arthur C Clarke gave a talk which included coloured slides and a short colour film taken in Florida waters because he had come to Australia to film scuba diving on the Great Barrier Reef. The Society celebrated its fifteenth anniversary on 4 November 1954 with a showing of a good quality privately owned print of *Metropolis*.

When Molesworth announced his retirement as Society Director he said it was because he and Laura had done all they could for the Society and felt it had reached the stage where it 'will run more or less of its own accord'.[10] However, he must have known that he was handing Stone a potential disaster because the Society's future was far from bright. The Society's clubroom had been rented at the cost of six guineas a week and in expectation of having at least sixty visitors a week paying 2/- each with the break-even point of 61 visitors. Visitor numbers had not reached that level from the beginning with the highest attendance being when Heinlein visited. After the breakaway group had returned to the Bridge Club the average weekly attendance was 45 which meant the Society was losing an average of 32/- each week. Attendance at the clubrooms appears to have been low in the second half of 1954 and only nine members attended a meeting on 2 November. Because of declining income the premises owner agreed to a rent reduction to £4 a week from July 1954 and Saturday openings were abandoned. The club now needed only 40 visitors a week at 2/- each to break-even but the average attendance for the second half of 1954 was 23 a week, leading to a weekly deficit of 38/-, which cost the club a total loss over the six months of £47/10/-.[11]

In an attempt to attract new members and overcome the disability of the clubroom's location in Oxford Street, the Society planned to launch a branch in the western suburbs of Sydney, probably at Strathfield. It held an initial meeting in the Melody Hall at Burswood on 3 December 1954 which included short films, Stone's illustrated talk on early science fiction, playing taped excerpts of the most recent convention and brief speeches by

---

[10] *Futurian Society News* 15.

[11] Molesworth, Chapter 5.

Molesworth and a local fan, James Murphy. However, nothing seems to have followed from this meeting, perhaps because of the Society's other problems.

The Thursday Night Group (also known sometimes as the Sydney Science Fiction Group) faced few of the Society's problems because it existed as nothing more than a place where people who shared an interest in science fiction could go weekly to find it and socialise with others who shared the same interest. They could borrow books and magazines from the North Shore Futurian Society library run by Bill Hubble or buy them from Dave Cohen's Blue Centaur books. Rules were kept to a minimum, sufficient only so people did not cause offense to others. Apart from a supper of rich cream cakes and tea provided by the ladies of the Bridge Club, no regular activities were planned. A few chess games might be played in one corner, a discussion group might form and others might simply talk or read as the mood took them.

No real records were kept but weekly attendance began with about a dozen and grew to a regular attendance of twenty or thirty, with occasionally more than fifty.[12] Some regulars turned up every week and a larger number floated in occasionally to borrow or buy science fiction and keep in touch with their friends. As an evening progressed numbers gradually built up from a quiet beginning to reach a crescendo with the arrival of the 'Scansion drunks' from a nearby pub.

To bring some continuity to the Thursday Night Group Doug Nicholson and Pat Burke launched the fanzine, *Scansion*, a weekly page or two published in turn by several members of the group which contained news of the group or whatever took the fancy of the editor that week.[13] One recurring topic was the Sydney Futurians. The Thursday Night Group did not take the Futurians very seriously, perhaps because the Futurians took themselves more than seriously enough, so their criticisms of the Society often took the form of condescending ridicule.

The financial arrangements of the Thursday Night group were much less taxing than the those of the Sydney Futurians. There was an attendance fee of 2/6 that included supper and Cohen made up the difference between what was collected and the Bridge Club rent. By around September 1954, when finances became tight because attendance number were sometimes low, the

---

[12] The roll for Thursday 9 September 1954 was: Arthur Haddon, Merv Bone, Michael Duggan, Lloyd Fisher, Kevin Pickling, Kevin Dillon, Bruce Ikin, Bill Hubble, Mick Bell, Doug Nicholson, Fred Fredrickson, Norma Williams, Sherrington Maclean Cohmann, Padraic McGuinnes, Laurie Bannatyne, Tom Hubble, Michael Baldwin, Dave Cohen, Pat Burke, A P Jaundrell, Bill Veney, Henry Tucke, Terry King, Nick Solnsteff, Tex Clarke and Len Goldobro. *Etherline* 36, 23 September 1954.

[13] They were Mike Baldwin, Pat Burke, John Earls, Fisher, Glick, Haddon, Hubble, Nicholson, R Seber and Norma Williams. Molesworth, Chapter 6.

fee was increased to 3/6 a night, and the North Shore Futurians also made a contribution for a while. Eventually Cohen decided to take full responsibility for the gathering's financial obligations because that gave him the autonomy to act as he pleased, including expelling anybody he didn't like. Members of the group did not always agree with or like some of Cohen's actions but they coexisted happily to present a regular friendly environment for Sydney's science fiction readers and fans.

Although the schism in Sydney fandom was fueled by individual personalities it was fundamentally a difference in philosophy between those who believed fandom had to be organised to effectively promote science fiction and those who didn't. Molesworth, Stone and their allies believed that the interests of science fiction in Australia could only be advanced through formal organisation and pointed to the Society's achievements to prove their point. On the other side, Doug Nicholson disagreed in an issue of *Scansion* when he wrote that most of the things achieved in fandom had been done by individuals acting individually. Minimal organisation was the most efficient form of organisation in fandom because it required less time and money than creating and maintaining an organisation to do the organising. In this he said the Society's lack of achievement and its problems were also an excellent example.[14]

Despite their differences science fiction fandom in Sydney could only survive if the two groups mended their differences and co-operated because neither was strong enough to prosper in competition with the other. Personalities, long held grudges and the circumstances of the times made this impossible. The Thursday Night Group had no formal leadership but Cohen was probably closest to being the group's leader. He had nothing to gain from returning to the Taylor Square clubroom and was said to have 'an intense personal dislike of Molesworth'.[15] Doug Nicholson wrote to *Etherline* that there were only two people in Sydney responsible for Sydney's reputation for brawling and there had never been a feud in Sydney without one or both of them playing a leading role. (He did not name them but they were clearly Molesworth and Stone.) He suggested that without them there was a reasonable chance that the rest of Sydney fandom could get together and share their science fiction in the same companionable atmosphere apparently enjoyed in Melbourne.[16]

The Thursday Night Group's main targets of criticism were Molesworth and Stone and some members found pleasure in baiting Stone and the Society, often in issues of *Scansion*, in the same way small boys enjoy stirring up ant nests to see the activity that follows. For example, a comment about

---

[14] *Scansion* 25.
[15] Molesworth Chapters 6.
[16] *Etherline* 34.

'the seemingly feeble-minded and spineless rank and file' that allowed Stone to dominate them, and Pat Burke's reference to Stone as the 'ignorant, ill-mannered psychopath'.[17]

The Thursday Night Group passed around rumours about Stone and the Society. One was that Stone had warned a well-known fan that she would be expelled from the Society if she did not stop helping with organisation of the coming convention, so she resigned from the Society instead. They heard that when a science fiction reader in Brisbane had written to Stone asking if there was a club in Brisbane he replied that there was no fan club in Brisbane because there were no known fans there. They also thought that he cut his opponents off the Australian SF Society mailing list.

Stone said that the Futurians were the intellectuals of Sydney fandom and the Thursday Night group the 'bobby soxers'.[18] Under Stone's Directorship the Society responded to the Thursday Night Group's taunts, officially and in print at least, with stony silence as though the Group did not exist. At one time the Society considered launching a vigorous publicity campaign to offset 'the constant streams of abuse against the Society, most of it inaccurate' but nothing came of the suggestion.[19]

Apart from being topics of conversation the two Sydney groups had little to do with each other and went in separate groups to see *War of the Worlds* in July 1954. The factions met occasionally but not always happily. Barbs published in *Scansion* by Pat Burke brought Society stalwart Bruce Purdy to a Thursday Night Group gathering demanding to know where Burke was, saying, 'I'm going to flatten him'.[20] Other occasions were more friendly. A few Futurians went to Thursday Night Group gatherings, but not as Futurians, and when Harry Brunen went to a gathering to find out how arrangements were going for the next convention he was received warmly and spent the night chatting with the fans there. On 11 December 1954 the Arcturian Players hosted a party at the Bondi School of Arts that included a short comic sketch written by Norma Hemming. Members of Sydney's two factions, and a few people who had dropped out in disgust, attended and mingled. Bill Hubble, organiser of the coming convention for the North Shore Futurians, Harry Brunen, secretary of the Society, and long-time fan Clive Mellor, were seen talking happily together for once.

Possibly preoccupied with their feud Sydney fans published few fanzines during this period. The Thursday Night Group published around 41 issues of *Scansion* between July 1954 and December 1955 in its typically anarchic

---

[17] *Scansion* 18 & 26.

[18] A derisory term referring to the wildly enthusiastic teenage female fans of 1940s popular music, in particular Frank Sinatra. *Scansion* 6, 18.

[19] *Scansion* 4, Molesworth, Chapter 5.

[20] *Scansion* 18 & 22.

fashion with the quality and content, sometimes frivolous, entertaining, thought provoking or angry, depending on the editor. The Society published the *Futurian Society News*, a newsy little fanzine directed almost exclusively at members which ran for nineteen issues between May 1953 and January 1955, by which time it had become infrequent. Although Stone took over Rex Meyer's *S-F Review* with the intention of publishing it for the Australian SF Society, only one issue appeared in August 1954. Stone's publishing energy went into *SF News*, which was distributed to fandom through the ASFS, but only seven issues were published between the beginning of 1954 and the end of 1955.

The only traditional fanzine to be published in Sydney was the second issue of Arthur Haddon's *Telepath*. A modest 16 pages published in October 1954, it contained articles on science fiction and fantasy by Tom Cockcroft, Roger Dard and Don Tuck, short contributions about fandom in Brisbane and the Thursday Night Group and a short parody of a Futurian Society meeting. Unlike the first issue which had been laboriously typeset and published in 1951, the second was produced on a hectograph because, Haddon said, typesetting was okay for 500 copies but not 130. Haddon wrote that he planned to publish *Telepath* monthly to create a forum for contentious viewpoints for all concerned but the environment was not welcoming and there was no third issue.[21] Thursday Night Group members Kevin Dillon and Michael Duggan also planned to produce fanzines but nothing came of them.

Both Sydney groups led active social lives. The Society clubroom was open twice a week and some Futurians probably met for dinner before going to meetings (but there is no mention of this in the *Futurian Society News*). *Scansion*, on the other hand, records a very busy Thursday Night Group social life including gathering for a meal before going to the Bridge Club on Thursday nights and Saturday lunches from about 1.30 at the Sun Si Gai in Castlereigh Street (later the Tai Ping Café in Hay Street after the Sun Si Gai closed). This lunch group called itself the 'Hay Street Irregulars' and had a private room there where everyone was welcome. Drinking was a popular Thursday Night Group activity and the Tai Ping Café being next door to the Burlington Hotel was probably part of the restaurant's attraction.

To raise funds for the 1955 convention Arthur Haddon hosted a Sunday evening party at his home from the end of September 1954 where eight fans indulged in talking, 'some slight drinking' and had a good time. There was a small charge for supper with half the amount going towards the coming convention. These parties became a regular event and convention fund raiser. Other money was raised for the convention from the Thursday Night

---

[21] *Telepath* 2.

Group parties which went to see *War of the Worlds* and *Creature from the Black Lagoon*.

The North Shore Futurian Society had almost lost its geographic association with the north shore and was part of the Thursday Night Group by the time of the 1955 convention. Bill Hubble was the Organiser, Arthur Haddon the Secretary, Pat Burke the Chairman, Michael Bos the Local Publicist and Dave Cohen the Treasurer.[22] They were angry with the FSS because Stone's 'No convention in 1955' pamphlet had put them on the back foot with their publicity. They believed the Society had sabotaged their convention because they received no support from Futurians who were the more affluent Sydney fans, so they had to plan on a more modest scale than might otherwise have been possible.

Bluey Glick unwittingly fanned the flames of discord when he returned to Sydney at the beginning of 1955. He had friends in both groups and hoped to bring them together again, but in doing so he only intensified the feud. At a Society meeting on 6 February 1955 he said that Melbourne fans deplored the situation in Sydney, urged the Society to support the coming convention and seek a reconciliation with the breakaway group because the Society was in a poor financial situation. In response Molesworth told Glick that he was out of touch with current events and the breakaway group was at fault because it had rented the Society's earlier meeting place, unlawfully used the word 'Futurian' and vilified the Society in its publications. He denied there was a feud and claimed the whole affair was due to the animosity of the people at the Bridge Club.[23]

The next Society meeting was called to discuss the Society's financial problems. Glick tied its financial problems to the feud between the two groups and said he believed the Society was responsible for the split in Sydney fandom and was partly responsible for keeping it going. He believed that if the Society took the first step the split could be ended, which would incidentally also solve the Society's financial problems. He said that many old Society members had ceased to support it because of the feud, that many had allied themselves with the Thursday Night Group under the impression that it had taken little action against the Society, and that a banned list and threats of banning had insulted many of the neutral members' friends. In reply he was told that the Society did not have such a list, although some people claimed they had seen one.[24]

Lists of fans banned from each other's rooms became another cause of discord. Cohen may not have had a written list but he probably had in mind

---

[22] *Etherline* 31.

[23] Molesworth, Chapter 6. This account reads as though it was lifted directly from FSS meeting minutes, which I have not seen.

[24] Molesworth, Chapter 6,

the names of several Futurians he would not allow into the Bridge Club room on a Thursday night, with Molesworth and Stone high on the list. There was a list of fans banned from the Taylor Street clubroom, apparently not a Society list but Stone's personal list which included Burke, Haddon, Veney, Nicholson, Bos, Hubble and three others.[25]

On the steps of Dunbar House at the Fourth Australian SF Convention.
LtoR Ian Crozier, Bill Veney, Bluey Glick and Doug Nicholson
(Doug Nicholson collection)

To keep the lines of communication open the Society moved a motion that it did not oppose the coming convention, issued a pamphlet denying that it had a banned list and resolved to send five delegates to the coming convention; Glick, Martin, Mason-Cox, Molesworth and Traeger.[26]

The fourth Australian science fiction convention was held over the weekend 19-20 March 1955 at Dubar House, a heritage building on the waterfront in Watson's Bay not far from the South Head of Sydney Harbour. It was a picturesque spot with a clear view down the harbour to the Harbour Bridge. On the whole it was a great success and probably the best organised convention so far held in Sydney. The warm weather made the venue more attractive but perhaps the location also limited the attendance which was lower than the most previous conventions. The low attendance was also due to the lack of Futurian support.

Forty fans attended the fancy dress ball on Friday evening. Bill Veney and partner were dressed at 'Salome and the Wandering Jew', Bill Hubble as a Sprague de Camp character and Doug Nicholson as a ghoul. Norma Hemming went as the Venusian Swamp Girl from the cover of a recent issue of a BRE *Dynamic* and Arthur Haddon as a green Martian Grub. (Hemming's skin colour washed off easily but Haddon's didn't and he was still tinged green by the end of the convention.) The ball went off with a bang and set the tone for the rest of the convention.

---

[25] Molesworth, Chapter 6.

[26] Molesworth, Chapter 6.

Sharing a meal at the Fourth Australian SF Convention
(Doug Nicholson collection)

On Saturday morning about 30 fans mingled informally and admired the artwork donated by *New Worlds* and *Nebula* which was auctioned on Sunday evening to support of the convention. Fifty-one people were present when the formal program began at about 2.30 with a speech by Dr Blatt of Sydney University on the 'Science in Science Fiction' and then a less interesting talk on 'Transportation in the Future'. Next the convention's Guest of Honour, Arthur C Clarke, joined Blatt for an extensive question and answer session which included news of American plans for an earth orbiting satellite within ten years. After tea two movies, *The Day the Earth Stood Still* and *Metropolis* were shown.

Only about twenty fans attended the convention auction on Sunday morning, resulting in low prices. The afternoon was occupied by the Business Session and in the evening 45 people attended when the *New Worlds* and *Nebula* art works were sold at high prices and the Arcturian Players performed Norma Hemming's clever play 'Miss Denton's Dilemma' with gods, goddesses, and nymphs 'wandering around in gay abandon, and very little else.'[27]

Despite the success of the rest of the convention the Business Session was its dominating moment. It began traditionally with reports from various fan groups and then congratulated Don Tuck on the publication of his *Handbook of Science Fiction and Fantasy* and unanimously moved a motion condemning literary censorship in Australia.

---

[27] *Etherline* 47.

The meeting turned nasty on the topic of trying to find a way to heal the rift in Sydney fandom. Ian Crozier, a neutral Melbourne fan, was talked into chairing the debate but he was unable to restrain the animosity and heated emotions that erupted. Nicholson and his allies suggested that the major participants on both sides should withdraw from activity for a set term so the two groups could reunite and Molesworth suggested that Stone should be expelled from the Futurian Society so that everyone else could rejoin it. Neither proposal was acceptable and the debate degenerated into what Crozier said was little more than a clash of personalities and childish wrangling. 'This type of thing', he wrote, 'was alright when they were immature schoolchildren, but one expects something a bit better from them now.'[28]

The only tangible outcome from the debate was a resolution that the two groups would meet on Monday 4 April at the Society's clubroom to try to resolve their differences. Eighteen people attended the meeting which was a 'dismal failure', marred by all the usual intolerance and personality clashes that had become typical of Sydney fandom.[29] In the following issue of *Etherline* Crozier published a drawing of a tombstone bearing the inscription; 'Sacred to the memory of ORGANISED SYDNEY FANDOM which passes away after a lingering attack of SCHIZOPHRENIA April 1st, 1955, Resting in the hope of a GLORIOUS RESURRECTION'.[30]

Some leading Sydney fans had already decided that the existing conditions made the situation impossible and they would start again. The following Sunday they launched the Albion Futurian Society (Albion being an early name for the Sydney district). It was a closed group with members only admitted on election by the existing membership, probably to keep out the undesirable element. Although it followed the Futurian model some old wounds were forgiven and Arthur Haddon was elected Director and Vol Molesworth Secretary at the first meeting.[31] The group started with five members and held meetings on the second Sunday of the month in members' homes. They were apparently charming social events but the

---

[28] *Etherline* 47. Crozier added in exclamation, 'My God, the Labor Party hasn't got anything on Sydney fandom!' but one would have to know something of Australian political history to see how prophetic this statement was. Fandom in Sydney would not recover from this turbulent period around the same time that the Australian Labor Party regained some of its strength at the end of the 1960s.

[29] The attendees were: Baldwin, Butt, Brunen, Gore, Haddon, Hemming, Hubble, Leggett, Mason-Cox and wife, Molesworth and wife, Nicholson, South, Thurston, Turnull, Veney and Williams. Molsesworth, Chapter 6.

[30] *Etherline* 48

[31] Arthur Haddon later had no memory of the group and suggested it might have been a hoax because the mere idea of he and Molesworth working together was laughable. *Mumblings from Munchkin Land* 31.

group had given up any pretense of being more than social gatherings of friends by the end of 1955.

The only occasion on which the remnants of Sydney's two fan groups met again was a conference held towards the end of 1955 to discuss sending a delegation to the next convention which was to be held in Melbourne towards the end of 1956 and a joint Sydney and Melbourne conference that had previously been agreed to be held in Albury to fill in the long gap between the 1955 and 1956 conventions. Instead it was held in Canberra to support the small science fiction group there and local fan Geoff Bennet helped with the arrangements.

Sydney fans at the Canberra SF Conference. LtoR Doug Nicholson, Bill Hubble, Pat Burke and Mike Baldwin (*Extant* 2)

The Canberra Conference, called Can-Con, was a quiet affair attended by a small group of fans over the Easter long weekend of 1956.[32] Geoff and Betty Bennet's place was the centre of activities for the weekend which involved little programming and plenty of time for socialising. The group gathered at the Bennet's for a drink before going to dinner on Friday night, and on Saturday they gathered again at the Bennet's to talk and listen to Molesworth's tape recorder. The afternoon was given over to sightseeing and the evening to socialising which, for the Thursday Night Groupers, involved trying to find somewhere to get a drink. Sunday morning was dedicated to, as Crozier put it, 'going to church or repenting'. In the afternoon the group visited Mt Stromlo, Australia's major astronomical observatory, but it was closed. In the evening they watched films at the Bennet's place, and then it was time to head for home. The event was marred by rain and Sydney and Melbourne fans' inability to successfully navigate the Canberra road system (which has confused and dismayed many visitors before and since) so they got lost trying to find places to meet and sights to visit. Most fans seem to have enjoyed themselves, but there was no mention of plans for a future conference.[33]

---

[32] The attendees were: From Sydney, Pat Burke, Kevin Dillon, Vol and Laura Molesworth, Fred Frederickson, Mike Baldwin, Doug Nicholson, Bill Hubble and Lloyd Fisher. From Melbourne, Barry Salgram, Ian Crozier, Graham Lyell, Don Latimer, Bob and Molly McCubbin, Val Morton, Keith McLelland, Mervyn Binns and Jack Keating. From Canberra, Geoff Burnett, Ken Jones and Arthur Porter. *Etherline* 68.

[33] *Etherline* 68 and *Extant* 2.

At the Canberra SF Conference. LtoR Loyd Fisher, unknown, Don Latimer.
Merv Binns squatting.
(Merv Binns collection)

On steps in front of the Australian War Memorial, Canberra. LtoR Pat Burke, Bill Hubble, Don Latimer, Graham Lyell and Lloyd Fisher. Above, unknown.
(Merv Binns collection)

Molesworth's failure to lure the Thursday Night Group renegades back to the Society, falling attendances and lack of funds after the convention, made it inevitable that the Society was forced to leave its clubroom. This happened on 2 June 1955 and the library was moved to Alan South's home where it was still available to members. By the end of 1955 the Society had only nine members, borrowing from the library was slight and there were no more formal meetings.

The Thursday Night Group also suffered declining attendance after the convention but continued to meet because Cohen subsidised the weekly gatherings. Some of the regulars became less regular because they disagreed with Cohen's way of running the meetings but, with the virtual disappearance of the Society, the Thursday Night Group became the only visible presence of science fiction fandom in Sydney. After the convention the North Shore Futurians continued only as a library which Sherry Bohman laboured to keep going but by October 1955 Cohen had bought it and ran it as a commercial library in conjunction with Blue Centaur Books.

The Thursday Night Group continued partly though Cohen's support of the gathering at the Bridge Club and partly because some surviving Sydney fans used it as a regular meeting place. Some shared a meal at the Tai Ping restaurant, then a few drinks at a nearby pub such as the Occidental or the Tudor, and then went on to the Bridge Club. Sometimes some of them did not make it as far as the Bridge Club. The Thursday Night Group Christmas Party in 1955 began at the Occidental at 5.30 and then progressed to the Tai Ping at 7 before going on to the Bridge Club.

At Can-Con Mike Baldwin and Bill Hubble introduced their new fanzine, *Extant*. There is nothing quite like *Extant* in the history of Australian fanzine publishing. It was brash and bold, printed on one side of unfolded foolscap with hand drawn illos and a disregard for appearance that made the first issue of Harding and Jenssen's *Perhaps* look like a professional magazine. It might have set a new trend in Australian fandom and would have outraged many fans with its freewheeling appearance and contents, but by then there were few fans in Sydney left to outrage. In Melbourne Bob McCubbin reviewed it in *Etherline* but could make little sense of it and labelled it a crudzine.[34] When the second issue was published Baldwin alone was the editor and the third issue was published for the Melbourne convention in December 1956.

Extant's first issue featured a transcript of the first third of the business session of the 1955 convention but, although more was promised in following issues, no more appeared. Baldwin became active in the Thursday Night Group and some of the group contributed including Royce Williams, Doug Nicholson and Pat Burke. There was little encouragement to continue and in

---

[34] *Etherline* 68.

the editorial to the fourth issue, prepared in 1958 but not published until 1975, Baldwin apologised for being eleven months late but explained that 'a considerable amount of nothing had happened in Australian fan circles'. Apart from a few issues of *Etherline* there had been no conventions, no magazines, 'no nothing'. 'Fandom is just dead, and that appears that'.[35]

One other fanzine was published in Sydney during this period, *MC²* edited by Peter Jefferson and Roger Sebel. The first issue followed the Sydney model by being folded foolscap but broke with tradition by having an excellent cover and, following the overseas model of a general circulation fanzine, contained a wide range of material from overseas and local contributors including fiction, reviews and commentary. It was intended for an international audience with a print run of 250. When the second issue appeared in 1958 only Jefferson was editor, it was less adventurous and appeared to be assembled randomly, aimed at collectors with many pages of lists of books for sale mixed in with some reviews, some fiction and some editorial comment. There was no third issue. *Scansion* ran out of steam and ceased publication after December 1955. Graham Stone published sixteen issues of *SF News* between 1955 and 1959 with increasing irregularity.

The toxic atmosphere of Sydney fandom had turned most fans away from it and some dedicated themselves to developing their careers. Arthur Haddon, for example, lost the desire to be involved with fans and fandom and developed his career as an industrial chemist. Vol Molesworth took a position teaching philosophy at the University of New South Wales and published two books on logic. Nick Solnsteff and John Earls went overseas to develop their academic careers and others found their way back to academic studies or other careers. Mike Baldwin wrote a story titled 'God in the Marijuana Patch' that was published in a university magazine, which got it banned and Baldwin prosecuted for blasphemy.

Many Sydney fans, ranging across the spectrum from Graham Stone to Doug Nicholson became more involved in the Sydney Push, a left-leaning subculture with strong links to Sydney University. It was a heavy drinking, free thinking loose grouping that was the most stimulating intellectual environment and counter-culture in Australia during the 1950s. Its active participants ranged from university lecturers who gave the movement some of its more theoretical ideals to manual labourers who gave it a strong physical character. Links between Sydney fandom and the Push had been created through pubs and coffee lounges where both groups met, such the Lincoln Coffee Lounge which had been an early hang out for fans and was an early meeting place for artists and writers, university students, lecturers and bohemians. Most fans found themselves comfortable in this environment

---

[35] *Extant* 1, 2, 3 & 4. Issue 4 was never completed but the cut stencils were saved by John Foyster and published in time for Aussiecon in 1975.

which did not limit thinking to mundane norms and was, as a bonus, a happy source of illicit drugs and free love for those who desired them.

Through the rest of the 1950s a small group of friends continued their interest in science fiction and fandom centred around the regular gatherings at the Bridge Club on Thursday nights that Cohen continued to subsidise. Around May 1960 Cohen stopped opening for business at the Bridge Club, probably because the embargo on importing American publications into Australia had ended in 1959 so there was no longer much demand for specialist dealers such as Blue Centaur Books. As a social replacement remaining Sydney fans commenced meeting as a Tuesday Night Group on 3 May 1960 which was attended by nine who had an enjoyable time reminiscing about the heyday of the Thursday Night Group.

In May 1960 Pat Burke revived *Scansion* with the help of other fans and contributions from old timers including Lex Banning, Mike Baldwin, Royce Williams and Doug Nicholson. He wrote that talking about the old days had led to the burst of enthusiasm so they were trying to get things going again. Burke wanted the new *Scansion* to be a venue for discussing science fiction critically with literate discussion free of fannish jargon, so this version of *Scansion* would be a more mature and thoughtful fanzine. It was still a product of the old Sydney style with serious intentions and a simple and functional layout devoid of illustrations.[36]

In the second and final issue of *Scansion*, published a month later, Burke said the fanzine was an experiment with a limited life span, that it was not terribly interested in the inanities of the usual run of the mill fan magazines and that he would publish neither fan fiction nor letters which were almost invariably a waste of time. In opposition to Burke's rejection of fannish jargon a strong response came from a new Sydney fan, John Baxter, who had discovered the Thursday Night Group gatherings after the events of 1955. His long letter in that issue of *Scansion* criticised Burke for being out of touch with contemporary fandom and for continuing the Sydney tradition of mud-slinging, that was so much a thing of the past.[37]

Unlike Burke, Baxter was in touch with the zeitgeist of international science fiction fandom at the beginning of the 1960s. He had already published six issues of his own fanzine and begun to build a reputation in international fandom (which is the beginning of a new story). There was no third issue of Burke's *Scansion* which was almost the final creation of a fandom that had commenced in Sydney before the war. That fandom had become inward looking and self-obsessed so it had consumed itself and, finally, died from exhaustion and a lack of new ideas and inspiration.

---

[36] *Scansion* 3/1.
[37] *Scansion* 3/2.

CHAPTER 9
1953-1957

By 1953 there were science fiction fan groups in most Australian capital cities. Sydney had the largest and most active groups, followed perhaps by Melbourne. There were also groups in Canberra, Adelaide and Brisbane, and some science fiction readers knew each other in Hobart and Perth.

The size of Australian fandom matched the size of the country's general population and was very small in comparison with fandoms in Britain and North America. The country was large in area but its European population was small, only 8.8 million in 1953, and the populations of the cities in which fan groups formed were also relatively small. Sydney was the largest city with a population of 1.86 million in 1954, Melbourne had 1.5 million, Brisbane 502 000, Adelaide 483 000, Perth 348 000, Hobart 95 000 and Canberra only 28 000 residents.[1]

Australia's fan groups were isolated because travel between cities was limited and expensive. Flying was very expensive, train travel was more expensive than many people could afford and car ownership was limited and interstate roads poor. Telephone calls were costly and not easily made so mail was the main way in which Australia's science fiction fans and fan groups communicated with each other and the rest of the science fiction world. Stone's Australian SF Society had been created to help overcome this isolation by creating a national network but this did not actively encourage communication between the Society's members.

Science fiction was relatively scarce in Australia due to the embargo on American science fiction and very limited local publication. Several publishers tried reprinting overseas science fiction in magazines including *Science Fiction Monthly*, *American Science Fiction*, *Popular SF*, *Future SF*, *Science Fiction Library*, the *Satellite Series* and an Australian edition of *Fantasy & Science Fiction*. But, although some of these magazines broke even, they did not last long because there was not enough profit in them to make them worth the publishers' effort.[2]

---

[1] *Commonwealth of Australia Yearbook* 1955, p.308.

[2] The rise and fall of several attempts to publish science fiction in Australia was faithfully reported on by Graham Stone and Roger Dard in the American newszine *Fantasy Times* (later *Science Fiction Times*) up until the end of the 1950s. *Fantasy Times*, 216, 219, 222, 241, 243, 245, 256, 261, 263, 265, 267, 282, 293A, 294, 301, 305A. Also *SF News* 12, 14 & 23 and

The little science fiction available to the Australian public was British. There were British books, British magazines including *New Worlds* and *Science Fantasy* and British reprints of American prozines such as *Astounding* and *Galaxy*. To make sure they got everything that was available enthusiastic readers and collectors had regular rounds of bookshops, newsstands and second-hand shops to find as much science fiction as they could. In Sydney the best source of science fiction was the Thursday Night Group and the Futurian Society's library. In Melbourne most keen readers eventually found their ways to McGills Newsagency in Elizabeth Street where Mervyn Binns built up a small specialist science fiction section and promoted the Melbourne SF Group. Towards the end of the 1950s he had built up a good following and was selling up to 100 copies of each issue of the British reprint *Astounding*.

Some very keen Australians found ways of importing their own science fiction from international businesses such as Operation Fantast in Britain (which became Fantast Medway in 1955) That was one of the sources of science fiction that Cohen used to stock his Blue Centaur table at the Thursday Night Group meetings. Binns also imported science fiction from overseas dealers and sold it to personal clients, members of the Melbourne SF Group, and also through McGills to help add variety to the shop's offerings.

Australia's strict censorship regulations also affected the flow of science fiction. Inspectors looked for anything that might be of a questionable moral or anti-social nature, such as a great deal of slightly sexual or crime fiction, but the regulations were not enforced uniformly across the States so material that was confiscated in Western Australia was often allowed into Queensland. In the other States official attitudes fluctuated so the flow of overseas publications was often uncertain.

Isolation and scarcity forced Australian fans to focus on collecting and building libraries. It was a serious pastime because a good collector had to know what they already had, what they wanted and how and where to get it. This meant creating lists, knowing what had been published and what was being published. It was also good to know other collectors who could help with information about sources of science fiction and had duplicates they could trade or sell. However, many readers lacked the resources, time or inclination to become serious collectors so the central feature of all Australian fan groups were their libraries so members had more science fiction to read and to attract new members.

Canberra fan Geoff Bennet visited groups in Melbourne and Sydney around October 1953 seeking their advice about forming a science fiction club in Canberra. Melbourne fans offered him encouragement but

---

Etherline 56.

Molesworth in Sydney aggressively pushed the idea of establishing Futurian Societies all over Australia and Bennett took his advice.

Five people attended the first meeting of the Futurian Society of Canberra on 8 November 1953.[3] Their first priority was setting up a library which started with donations from several members, Sydney well-wishers and a loan of 20 books and prozines from the Sydney Futurians. The annual membership fee was 2/6 (to be increased as the library grew), with a borrowing fee of 6d per book and 3d for magazines. A year later they had built up a library of over 200 items.

The Canberra Futurians expected their new club would grow because an estimated 300 to 350 science fiction books and magazines were sold in Canberra each month. To help them grow the Australian SF Society offered to print slips promoting the club to be put into the books and magazines sold locally. However, only one new member, Arthur Porter, had joined the club by its fourth meeting in April 1954 and he was immediately appointed the club's Secretary. (Porter thought the Canberra Futurian Society failed to grow because it modelled itself on the Sydney Futurians. When he reported to the 1954 convention, by tape recording, he said that Bennett had seen both extremes of how clubs could be organised when he visited Melbourne and Sydney and had chosen the wrong extreme, judging by the response to their promotion.[4])

It is more likely, however, that the Futurian Society of Canberra never had more than seven members because Canberra was not fertile ground for a science fiction club in the 1950s.[5] Although the city had been founded soon after Federation it had barely been developed before the 1950s due to depression and war. It was the centre of the Commonwealth government and public service and a large proportion of the city's residents were migrants, either single and unattached career public servants who mostly lived in hostels, or newly married couples raising families in Canberra's new suburbs. The hostels developed their own self-contained social lives and raising new families in new suburbs left little time for active involvement in a science fiction club. Besides, being known as a fan of that 'crazy Speed Gordon stuff' would not have been helpful to building a Public Service career in the 1950s because of public attitudes to the genre.

Despite this the Canberra Futurians organised special events to attract interest. One was a couple of visits to the Mount Stromlo astronomical observatory in 1954, on one occasion for a lecture by a visiting expert on

---

[3] The office bearers were Geoffrey R Bennett, Director, and Peter Jones, Secretary/Treasurer.

[4] *Etherline* 28.

[5] There were four members and three apologies at the meeting on 2 May 1954. *Etherline* 29.

Mars and the other for an astronomical tour of the solar system and galaxy — including viewing the rings and moons of Saturn.

The group attracted more interest with a series of monthly film showings using a borrowed 16 mm projector and films from the Film Division of the National Library and other sources including the US Information Service and the South African High Commission. There were no science fiction films to show but there were films on scientific and technical subjects and, in 1954 before television was introduced in Australia, watching any movies outside the big commercial theatres was a novelty. Sixteen people attended the first film night on 14 May 1954 when the most popular film was about the basics of lubrication. Twenty three people attended the second film night on 18 June where the highlight was a colour film on the Mt Palomar observatory. On 23 July sixteen attended a showing which included the science fiction classic *Metropolis*.[6]

Monthly film nights continued well into 1955 with programs selected by group members and shown in members' homes. Colour films and travelogues on subjects including the Great Barrier Reef and the Kruger National Park in South Africa were particularly appreciated but the purpose for which the Futurian Society of Canberra had been formed, the promotion of science fiction, was no longer the group's main activity.

Adelaide, with its larger and more settled population, developed a larger and more active science fiction group. There was no organised group at the beginning of 1953 but Ian Moyle, who had a good science fiction collection, allowed Adelaide enthusiasts to borrow from his collection and held some gatherings at his home.

The Adelaide SF Society was formed around July 1953 when Mrs Joyce (Joyce Joyce, but rarely referred to as anyone other than Mrs Joyce) invited every science fiction reader she knew to her home to discuss setting up a library as the nucleus of a science fiction club. It had twenty members by October 1953, had over 400 items in the library and was 'doing a brisk trade'.[7] The Society held monthly meetings at Joyce's home and later met every second Sunday evening with the library open in the afternoon from 3–5 and during club meetings. Average attendance was 10 to 12 and the meetings also became quite social events.

By the end of 1953 the club's library had grown to 672 items that included 72 hard covers, 156 paperbacks and 103 American magazines. It had been boosted by a donation of books from Operation Fantast but had also sent some of its duplicates to help boost the Canberra Futurian's library. In late 1953 the Adelaide group was offered a collection of 230 pre-war American

---

[6] These were organised by a subcommittee comprising, initially comprising Arthur Porter, Geoff Bennett and David Kerr.

[7] *NSFS Notesheet* 6, *Vertical Horizons* 5, *Etherline* 17.

prozines and immediately raised £50 towards buying them. More money was raised by holding quizzes that became a regular feature of meetings, along with other social activities including chess.

The Adelaide group formally adopted a modified version of the constitution of the Futurian Society of Canberra in May 1954, elected office bearers and began holding formal business meetings. The group didn't seem to find its rules very onerous and no dissension seems to have arisen in the group because of them. The regular meetings began with a short formal session that gave way to informal conversation, so the Adelaide group remained mainly informal and social.[8] When the group celebrated the first year of its library's operation at the beginning of August 1954, with a birthday cake adorned with a space ship, it was close to being the single largest fan organisation in Australia with 35 members and 1136 items in its library.

Some group members became interested in fan publishing in April 1954 and started a club project to make a duplicator, starting with an old gramophone handle. It was nearing completion by June but never finished because the group's first priority was its library so, in July 1954, they instead formed a work party to help maintain it.

The collection had reached 1620 items by July 1955 when the group celebrated its second anniversary.[9] It had grown to 2113 items a year later when the club celebrated the its third anniversary with another party that concluded with a sumptuous supper including a birthday cake decorated with one rocket-ship, three candles and four spacemen. Discussion turned to how to look after their library so the group began building a desk-mobile in which it could keep library materials and the supplies needed to repair books.

When group numbers began to decline as old members dropped away the group recruited more members. On one occasion they printed flyers to insert into books and magazines and another time the group placed an advertisement in one of the local newspapers to attract new members.

Many group members became good friends. They enjoyed each other's company at the regular meetings and occasional parties where they felt free to talk about science fiction away from the censure of the mundane world. Members who had not been seen for a few months were welcomed back gladly and news of illnesses, engagements, births and accidents made the social rounds. Perhaps to encourage the social atmosphere of meetings Mrs

---

[8] The initial executive of the Adelaide group was: Ron Gum, President, J Johnson, Vice-President, Mrs Joyce Secretary, Treasurer & Librarian, M Downes Financial Officer, and D Walsh and O D Denton assistant librarians. Molesworth, Chapter 5.

[9] Office bearers elected at the July 1955 AGM were Norm Kemp, President; Dennis Walsh, Vice President; Mrs Joyce Secretary; R Kemp Treasurer; Hal Nicholson and Dennis Walsh, Librarians; Mrs Joyce and R Kemp Assistant Librarians and Margaret Finch Assistant Secretary. *Etherline* 53.

Joyce allowed music to be played on her radiogram from mid-1956. Drinking was forbidden at meetings but allowed on special occasions such as birthday parties and, during the group's third anniversary party in 1956, two bottles per head were drunk, after which members 'straggled off home'.[10]

A similar group came together in Brisbane, focused around a library and meetings in the home where the library was kept, the Brisbane Science Fiction Group. They began putting together the library in early 1953 which was supervised by a trust and managed by Betty Tafe. After early meetings at Frank Bryning's place the expanding group decided to meet weekly in a coffee lounge in the city centre, as fans in Sydney did.[11]

By the beginning of 1954 there were seldom more than six at the weekly gatherings and about fifteen people who attended occasionally. There were nine people at the July 1954 meeting, including regulars, Frank Bryning, John Gregor, Bill Veney, Betty Tafe, her husband George and his brother Tom. At that meeting Gregor distributed copies of *Etherline* and *Perhaps* and Betty Tafe spread some of the library's books on a table. The informal discussion began with the prozines, Australian fandom — with particular regard to Sydney — and ranged over many subjects including politics, flying saucers and, finally, Dianetics.

By September 1954 the group had identified forty-one science fiction enthusiasts in Queensland and fifteen attended the group's meeting that month. Fanzines from the south, including *Etherline*, *Question Mark* and *Scansion*, were distributed and the perplexing situation in Sydney was discussed with everyone agreeing that the Brisbane group had to remain strictly impartial. The meeting marked a turning point for the Group when Bill Veney announced he would be returning to Sydney and John Gregor announced he would be moving to Cairns. Gregor had become an important member of the group and served as the Australian agent for the American National Fantasy Fan Federation and Melbourne's AFPA. Betty and George Tafe took over the APFA agency in Brisbane and, also at that meeting, the group decided that following meetings would be held at the Tafe home in Chester Street, Teneriffe, so members would have full access to the group's library during the meetings.[12]

---

[10] *Etherline* 46, 48, 51, 53, 72, 75.

[11] Regulars included Frank Bryning, Bill Veney (after he moved from Sydney to Brisbane), John Gregor (who had published Australia's first fanzine under the name John Deverne), Harry Brook (who was in the Army and stationed near Brisbane) and Charles Mustchin (who lived down the coast in Coolangatta where he had a large collection, but frequently visited Brisbane).

[12] Present at that meeting were: Dick Milhans, Rick Day, Frank Bryning, Bill Veney, Tony Edwards, John Adams, Fred Drennan, Reg Urquhart and wife, Arthur Burrows, Betty Tafe, George Tafe, John Gregor, Iris Girvan and John Gurney. *Etherline* 36.

Science fiction was relatively abundant in Brisbane. The Queensland customs authorities were very lenient so there was almost no limit to what the group could import. One member, John Adams, was from the United States, (he had met John W Campbell and other famous science fiction personalities) and got some of his science fiction direct from home. Another occasional member, Iris Girvan, looked after the book section of a large city bookshop and always displayed science fiction prominently. This relative abundance, and the relaxed Brisbane lifestyle, meant Queensland fans did not feel the same need to form as tightly focused club or undertake other fan activity such as fanzine production. Rather they gathered at the Tafe's place on the first Thursday of each month to use the club library, enjoy the company of other science fiction readers and the freedom to discuss the genre in a friendly and unguarded atmosphere.

By the end of 1954 fan activity in Brisbane was almost exclusively the monthly meetings at the Tafe's home. There were usually ten or a dozen visitors and there was no formal program. Members used the library, Betty distributed copies of fanzines such as *Etherline*, there was some discussion and chat, George Tafe and John Gurney usually played chess and the evening wound up well with Betty's welcome supper of tea and cake, often laced liberally with rum. Occasionally Chas Mustchin visited from Coolangatta and, at the November 1954 meeting, a letter from Harry Brook, who was serving in the Australian Army in Japan, entertained the group. In February 1955 half a dozen group members traveled down to Coolangatta to visit Mustchin, be awed by his library and borrow some of his books and prozines. Bob Smith visited in May 1956. He had served with the Australian Army in Japan where he had recently met Harry Brook.

The highlight of 1955 was the visit of Arthur C Clarke and his partner Mike Wilson who came to Australia to make a movie and write a book about scuba diving on the Great Barrier Reef. The ship bringing them to Australia called in first at Melbourne in mid-December 1954 where the Melbourne Group welcomed them with an afternoon at Bob McCubbin's place, dinner the following night and a farewell drink on the ship before it sailed for Sydney.[13]

In Sydney Clarke visited the Futurian Society's clubroom in Taylor Square at the end of December 1954 and he was Guest of Honour at the 1955 science fiction convention at the end of March. Sydney fans wrote almost nothing about his visit, perhaps he already knew about their feuding and avoided it or perhaps they were too immersed in it to pay much interest to his visit. Clarke and Wilson spent their time in Sydney organising their expedition to the Great Barrier Reef without making any serious impression on Sydney fandom.

---

[13] At the dinner were Arthur Clarke, Mike Wilson, Bob McCubbin, Ian Crozier, Tony Santos, Merv Binns, Jack Keating, Don Latimer and Bill Tyrrell. *Etherline* 43.

Arthur C Clark in Coolangatta, 1955
(*Etherline* 49)

Clarke made a much greater impression in Brisbane. Before his arrival Frank Bryning had already been corresponding with him about the visit and the group began preparing to meet him. After the Sydney convention Clarke and Wilson drove north in a car laden with diving gear, photographic equipment and science fiction.

First they stayed in a flat that Mustchin had newly completed under his house in Coolangatta and Bryning drove down to meet them. They had planned to try out their gear by diving in the outlet of the Tweed River but heavy rains kept them inside for much of their stay where they fossicked through Mustkin's prozine collection and read letters they found in them written by people they knew. One evening Clarke gave a show of his colour films and slides to the local branch of the returned servicemen's league. They eventually managed a little diving and then drove north to Brisbane where Clarke and Wilson made further preparations for their stay on the Great Barrier Reef.

They were welcomed to Brisbane at a dinner and then a meeting of the Brisbane Group which was combined with a meeting of the Underwater Research Group and other guests at the Tafe's home. There they showed slides and colour film of underwater phenomena and a surf carnival they had filmed at Manly, and the meeting concluded with coffee and cake served by Betty and the other women.

Clarke and Wilson stayed around Brisbane for another couple of weeks, going down to Coolangatta for some more diving and making other arrangements including getting typed the manuscript of Clarke's newly completed novel, *The Stars and the City*. Then they went north to the Reef.

They visited Brisbane for a week in July when they attended the monthly Group meeting and returned to Brisbane at the end of August where they attended George & Betty's fourth wedding anniversary party. A few days later they gave a presentation to a gathering of 130 people organised by the Science Fiction Group, the Underwater Research Group, the Queensland Spear Fisherman's Club and the Wide Men's Club of the YMCA. They talked about their adventure and showed some slides and film from their expedition to the Great Barrier Reef. Finally a small group from the science fiction and Underwater Research groups shared supper with them before they departed.

Clarke's visit to Australia, and Heinlein's brief visit to Sydney, were the only exposure Australians had to well-known science fiction writers. A handful of local fans including Frank Bryning and Norma Hemming, began selling stories but were already known as friends in science fiction circles. The only other author many Australian fans had met personally was A Bertram Chandler. Chandler (known locally as Bert) had served as First Officer on a Savil Shaw liner sailing between Britain and Australia and visited club meetings around the coast when they coincided with his visits to port. He apparently relocated to Sydney in early 1956 with the intention of making writing a full-time career but, instead, continued his maritime career as an officer and Captain for several lines, culminating as a Captain for the Union Steamship Company of New Zealand which sailed between Australia and New Zealand and to some Australian ports. He also continued his writing career and became a well-known and welcomed visitor to the groups at the ports he visited.

After the Clarke and Wilson visit the life of the Brisbane Group returned to its quiet monthly existence. Clarke's presence in Brisbane had attracted a columnist for the Courier-Mail newspaper, Keith Dunstan, to visit the group and he wrote a gratifying half page about them that appeared in print a few days later. Otherwise the group continued its pleasant monthly meetings, enlivened by a card and a letter from Clarke. Meetings began with library business and the distribution of the latest issues of *Etherline*, followed by general conversation that was brought to a pleasant conclusion by Betty Tafe's customary tea, coffee and cake.[14]

The success of the Adelaide and Brisbane groups depended on the hospitality of their hosts who also managed the club's libraries. When there was nobody to fill that role the group failed. In the Hunter Valley region Ted Butt formed the Hunter River Futurian Society which had five members and a library of 165 prozines and books by September 1954. However, when Butt moved back to Sydney in October the small group disappeared.

A small group formed in Perth around mid-1953 which called itself the Perth Science Fiction Group. It had five members led by Roger Dard and Ralph Harding who edited the group's newsletter, *Perth Fan News*.[15] It was a very loose group of science fiction readers and collectors and the contact was so tenuous that when Harding died Dard only learned about it in a letter from Stone in Sydney. When John Park, another member of this loose group, died Dard helped dispose of his large collection of *Astounding*s and other pulp magazines by sending it to Stone in Sydney.

Due to his widespread correspondence and contributions to overseas fanzines Dard was the only Western Australian fan well known to the rest of the science fiction world and was perhaps also the best known Australian fan overseas. He became a regular correspondent to the widely circulated

---

[14] Entertaining reports of meetings written by 'Warrigo' convey the feeling of a small and friendly group who attend meetings as much for the company of friends as for the use of the library. *Etherline* 64, 66, 68, 69, 70, 72, 74, 75.

[15] The only report I have found of this group is in Lee Harding's *Wastebasket* 3. The group members were reported as Roger Dard, Ralph Harding, John Park, S M Michelaides and Jack Thomas. Their club fanzine, *Perth Fan News*, is reported as a three page mimeod clubzine edited by Harding. I know of no copy of this fanzine today. *Wastebasket* 3.

Fantasy Times, reporting on the publication of science fiction in Australia until the end of the 1950s, often with bibliographic details.

Dard published a single issue of the fanzine *Star Rover* in November 1950. It was an undecorated twelve page folded foolscap fanzine which showed his immersion in American fandom with a page of well-informed comment on overseas fanzines. A page of Dard's 'wants' suggested the scope of his collection. He was looking for only twelve numbers from eight prozine titles of which the earliest were four issues of *Astounding* from September 1930 to March 1935.[16]

By 1953 Dard was beginning to distance himself from organised fandom, partly as a result of his fights with the Western Australian customs officials about the material he wanted to import, partly his disenchantment with the state of fandom in the eastern states but mainly because of the pressure of personal business. He said he wanted to spend the spare time he had looking after his collection but he did maintain contact with some old fans he knew including Stone and Tuck.

Don Tuck had been active in Australian fandom before the war and moved to Melbourne at the end of the 1941 where he was fully employed in war work. He returned to Tasmania around 1952 and became aware of several other science fiction readers in Tasmania; Frank Hasler, Eric Rayner, John Morrisby and Roy Gregory. They met occasionally in each other's homes for a pleasant evening's chat about science fiction but they were readers and collectors who showed little interest in forming a club.

Like many fans of his generation, Tuck became primarily a collector. When he traveled to the mainland he made contact with a few old science fiction friends and collectors and visited shops where he hoped to pick up more items for his collection. At home he had, as did most fans did during this period, a regular beat of shops where he might pick up second-hand items to add to his collection.

Tuck's collecting led to an interest in bibliography. In mid-1951 he began listing the items in his collection in a note book which soon expanded into a large folder where he devised a way of making amendments to existing entries. With Dard's encouragement he decided to expand his index and, with the help of overseas fans including Tom Cockcroft in New Zealand and Howard Devore in the United States, the project continued until he had a draft which he circulated to interested fans in the first few months of 1953. He began cutting stencils for a publication in mid-June that year, about three stencils a night on the two spare nights he had each week, each taking about seventy minutes. They were then run off in the office where Tuck worked

---

[16] *Star Ranger* 1, *Etherline* 16.

with the assistance of the office boy, and the complete 154 page *A Handbook of Science Fiction & Fantasy* was ready for distribution in March 1954.[17]

The Tuck Handbook was received enthusiastically with reviews of high praise in the main prozines. It sold well and cemented Tuck's reputation as perhaps the world's foremost bibliographer of science fiction and fantasy. He continued with his research and publishing that included a regular author listing in every issue of *Etherline* following the first one in November 1954. There was also the twenty-eight page *A Checklist of Anthologies* published in May 1959. That year he also published the second edition of his *Handbook*, this time in two volumes of 400 pages which covered everything except comic books (only because he did not have enough data on them). It again received enthusiastic reviews in the leading prozines.

Tuck's bibliographic work and his *Handbook* were recognised by a special Worldcon award at Chicon II in 1962 but Tuck had almost completely isolated himself from the rest of Australian fandom by then. His interest was in bibliography, not in science fiction fandom so that, apart from his contributions to *Etherline* and a couple of Harding fanzines, he had little contact with most Australian fans.

The Adelaide group celebrated its fourth anniversary at Mrs Joyce's home with a good attendance and a cake decorated to celebrate space opera with a Martian giant, earthmen and a damsel in distress. The club's library had grown to over 2550 items of which 443 were hardcover books. The Brisbane group also continued to hold monthly meetings at the Tafe's home with activities including borrowing from the group library, general discussion and supper. In June 1957, for example, nine fans gathered and discussed matters such as sunken cities and psi, followed by a coffee and cake supper served by the women.

By around the middle of the 1950s each of Australia's fan groups, with the exception of Melbourne, had become a self-contained small social group meeting in members' homes to use their libraries and enjoy each other's company where they could socialise and talk freely about science fiction. However, these small social groups did not engage actively with other groups or publish fanzines to engage with fandom outside their own circles. There may have been some correspondence between individuals but the only way in which fans across the rest of Australia and the science fiction world knew about their activities was through the reports published in the pages of *Etherline*, edited by Ian Crozier in Melbourne. Over time these reports became fewer and shorter and had all but ceased by the end of 1956. The groups may have continued to meet for months or years to come, but they left no record to tell us how they fared and what was their fate.

---

[17] Tuck wrote a description of his process which was published in *Antipodes* 2.

CHAPTER 10
1953-1956, Melbourne

The Melbourne SF Group was probably about the same size as the groups in Adelaide and Brisbane in 1953. It had, however, five advantages the other groups lacked; Bob McCubbin, Mervyn Binns, Ian Crozier, a separate clubroom in the city centre and the AFPA duplicator.

Bob McCubbin was a resilient and likeable school teacher whose abilities kept the club running and allowed Binns and Crozier to get on with the things that interested them most. He received early help from pre-war fans Marshall McLennan and Warwick Hockley who did not, however, join the new group. In early 1953 he tried to reduce his activities in the group but the younger members persuaded him to stay because he had the skills for organisation they lacked. Although the group had no formal structure McCubbin became its defacto leader and took charge of most of its formal activities including collecting money for the rent, liaising with outside organisations and chairing the informal session at most regular meetings at which members discussed Group business. By September 1953, and after the reorganisation of AFPA, McCubbin probably felt the group had a future and opened a bank account in its name.

Bob McCubbin
(*Australasian Post*, 8 October 1953)

McCubbin was the prominent member of the Group so when a journalist for the *Australisian Post* wanted to write an article about science fiction in September 1953 he interviewed him. The writer concentrated excessively on the theme of BEMs (Bug Eyed Monsters) but the article was light hearted and portrayed fans as the protectors of the world against monsters, particularly in science fiction.[1] It painted McCubbin as a slightly odd character with an obsession with BEMs, which did not please Don Tuck who complained

---

[1] *Australasian Post*, 8 October 1953.

that now most of his friends thought he was batty because of the emphasis on BEMs. Melbourne Group members were pleased with the publicity the article brought them with a few enquiries from science fiction readers.

Merv Binns was key to the group's success. He was naturally cheerful and optimistic and dedicated himself wholeheartedly to supporting science fiction and the Group. Among other things he cranked the AFPA duplicator to publish fanzines and on it he printed flyers promoting the Group that he put into the science fiction books and magazines where he worked at McGills Newsagency. McGills was a Melbourne institution, a dim and narrow shop in busy Elizabeth Street opposite the GPO. There Binns built up a selection of science fiction that made McGills the main source of science fiction in Melbourne.

Binns main interests were in collecting and building up the Group's library. He had little direct contact with fans outside Melbourne though he attended the fourth convention in Sydney. His interest meant that, unlike other book sellers in Melbourne at the time, he knew the science fiction field well and knew what would attract customers. The main Australian distributor, Gordon and Gotch, imported the British Reprint Editions of American prozines but not the British magazines *New Worlds* and *Science Fantasy*, so he imported and sold them in McGills. McGills also handled second-hand books and magazines that sometimes included science fiction which Binns

Merv Binns and the AFPA Roneo 500 (probably in his parents converted garage)
(Merv Binns collection)

sold over the counter, bought for the Group's library or for his own collection. McGill's management knew about Binns' activities but also knew science fiction sold well so they were happy with the arrangement.

Also over the counter at McGills Binns sold the fanzine *Etherline* that he published in partnership with Ian Crozier. Crozier was the editor and Binns the publisher, running off all the copies of every issue on the AFPA duplicator.

Ian Crozier discovered fandom through Roger Dard and Operation Fantast and soon became involved in the Melbourne Group's activities.

Ian Crozier at the Canberra SF Conference (Merv Binns collection)

He was likeable, friendly, very hospitable and worked as a customs agent from an office in Richmond. Crozier's strong business interests and ethos led him to propose that AFPA should buy the expensive Roneo 500 duplicator and organise how to pay for it. His attitudes were generally conservative and right-leaning but when the American fan Harlan Ellison was attacked by American right-wing fans for his inclusive views on race Crozier wrote supporting him. He didn't mind saying what he thought and his criticism of the 1953 convention in Sydney was forthright while his criticism of Stone's 'No convention in '55' campaign made Stone believe Crozier was largely responsible for Melbourne fandom's hostility to Sydney.

Unlike most Group members Crozier was business minded so, while Harding, Jenssen and Mathews saw fanzine publishing as a creative act to promote science fiction, Crozier saw it as a small business opportunity. His idea was to establish a semi-professional publishing business selling to science fiction fans by subscription or through retail outlets such as McGills in Melbourne, Blue Centaur in Sydney and the fan groups in Adelaide and Brisbane. (This basic disagreement over the purpose of fan publishing had led to the conflict between Harding and Crozier and Harding's departure from the group (see chapter 6).)

After Harding and Crozier fell out Crozier built up his own contact with Australian and overseas fans as sources of news for *Etherline*. He assembled the contents for *Etherline* and cut the stencils, and Mervyn Binns ran off the issues on the AFPA Roneo. Crozier worked hard to make *Etherline* look as professional as possible with the folded foolscap format and neatly laid out and clearly typed pages. He made extensive use of electro stencils, with the gradual introduction of elaborate headings and interior artwork and fillos, most provided by Dick Jenssen, Keith McLelland and Don Latimer. As his confidence and Binns' experience with the Roneo grew they used more frequently the red ink drum they had bought with the Roneo.

The size of issues generally ranged from 16 to 32 pages, depending on the material available. From late 1953 Crozier used partly pre-printed covers bearing the title but blank spaces which he filled with a piece of electrostencilled art and text promoting the contents. To help *Etherline* look more professional Crozier typed the stencils with right hand justification, which required the laborious process of typing and then retyping each page of text. With the 36th issue, in September 1954, Crozier began using a typewriter with a smaller type face to improve the magazine's appearance even more. When he introduced the pre-printed covers Crozier announced that they intended *Etherline* would eventually be professionally printed, but that never happened.

Etherline's contents were usually informative and useful for science fiction readers and collectors but usually not lively. Nicholson said *Etherline* was educated but dull and Mike Baldwin jokingly referred to it as a trade journal rather than a fanzine.[2] Issues usually contained news of forthcoming books and prozines, short reviews of books, magazines, movies and, occasionally, fanzines. There was news of overseas science fiction activities and occasional reports from Australian fan groups. Crozier built links with a number of overseas correspondents, including Forry Ackerman, and published material by them in *Etherline*. There was always a page advertisement for McGills and usually advertisements for Operation Fantast, Blue Centaur and the Melbourne Group. Kevin Wheelahan occasionally advertised his radio repair business and Don Latimer regularly advertised his book binding service with the slogan 'Don Latimer is bound to please'. *Etherline's* Trading Bureau was another regular and popular feature which listed the wants and disposals of many Australian collectors. From the 39th issue in November 1954 Don Tuck's bibliographic 'Author Listings' also became a regular feature.

Crozier maintained an almost unbroken regular fortnightly schedule right through to 1956. Before long *Etherline* had established itself as Australia's leading fanzine, mainly because of its regularity and its content of news about science fiction which matched the taste of most Australian fans at that time. Don Tuck wrote that *Etherline* gave him information of what science fiction was available, Veney congratulated Crozier on editing what was, without question, the outstanding Australian fanzine and Molesworth wrote that *Etherline* had established itself 'as the news magazine of Australian

---

[2] Interview with Doug Nicholson, *Extant* 3.

fandom'.³ It received positive reviews in overseas prozines and in November 1955 the fanzine reviewer of *Amazing Stories* wrote that '*Etherline* must be as valuable to Australian sf fans as *Fantasy Times* is to those of the US, ...'⁴

Despite this praise *Etherline* was probably never the success that Crozier hoped for it. Binns, who duplicated every issue, later recalled that the print run was probably fifty or less. Most copies were sent out by mail, Cohen sold them for six pence at the Thursday Night Group meetings and Binns sold them at McGills, but no more than a dozen copies of each issue.⁵

Crozier also launched a fiction fanzine with, at first, a question mark on the cover that was usually referred to as *Question Mark*. It was in the planning stages before Harding was expelled from AFPA and two new members, Bruce Heron and Kevin Wheelahan, were introduced to publish it as associated editors. The first issue was published in August 1953 and the second and third issues had appeared by the end of the year.

Crozier reported that the sales figures in Melbourne bookshops were really phenomenal and optimistically offered a special subscription rate of 24/- for 26 issues of *Etherline* and 12 issues of *Question Mark*. His enthusiasm continued when he reported that, after its first week, the sales figures for the third issue were almost double the first fortnight's figures on the previous issue. He said they intended to improve the magazine in both contents and appearance, but there were only three further issues. Bruce Heron was probably only involved in the first issue and in July 1954 Crozier announced that Wheelahan was studying Arts at University and did not have much time for fandom so *Question Mark* was put on a quarterly schedule. A few months later in March 1955 Crozier announced that the sixth issue would be the final one due to pressure of work, poor reception and lack of material. Despite Crozier's early hopes *Question Mark* was a failure and in McCubbin's interview in *Post* he said *Question Mark's* price was 1/-, but they gave away most copies.⁶

Crozier appears to have given up hope of running AFPA as a semi-professional business by the end of 1954 and announced that *Etherline* would be published by AFPA for the Melbourne Group in the future.⁷ The AFPA duplicator then became virtually the Group's duplicator.

Collecting and reading science fiction were the Group's central activities. American prozines were most prized and when somebody arrived at a Club meeting with some to sell they went quickly. Members also made good use of mail order services from overseas. It seems that before June 1954 most

---

³ *Etherline* 18, *Scansion* 22 and *Mumblings from Munchkinland* 33.
⁴ *Mumblings from Munchkinland* 30.
⁵ Interview with Merv Binns.
⁶ *Australasian Post*, 8 October 1953.
⁷ *Etherline* 41 & 42.

parcels of books and magazines ordered by Melbourne Group members passed through customs unopened but, after an unscrupulous dealer imported suspect items, customs began opening parcels. However, nothing was lost to Group members and, for a while, *Etherline* kept track of imported parcels. In June Crozier landed nine parcels and McCubbin two. Another nine parcels passed through Customs without trouble a couple of weeks later and by September parcels of American prozines were coming in regularly with nine arriving in one week, and another twenty or thirty on the way.

The Group's library was its most important asset and a great attraction for new members. It consisted of novels, pocket books and prozines donated by Melbourne, country and interstate fans with special help from the Sydney Futurians. The Club also funded some purchases, it had £12/16/5 in November 1954 after it had advanced £4/4/- to the library. As the Franklin's lending library wound down many of its bound pulp magazines that had so entranced Harding and Jenssen found their way into the Group's library. Binns was its custodian by September 1953 and as the library grew so did the work that Binns put into keeping the card index up to date so two volunteer assistant librarians, Val Morton and Neil Merriless, began helping him. By May 1954 a Library Committee had been appointed to manage the library but most of the work still fell on Binns.

By the middle of 1957 the library had outgrown the storage space available for it so the British Reprint Edition prozines and pocketbooks were moved to Binns' garage in Preston. So members could find out what was available work began on producing a catalogue they could use to order books from the library. This was also very useful for members who were unable to attend group meetings and borrowed from the library by mail.

Club members also sold or traded science fiction. There were auctions at most Group meetings or, if not an auction, some trading between the members. With Race Mathews slowly selling most of his collection and Dick Jenssen refining his so there was often some choice items on offer. The Group took a small commission from sales and the Club's library sometimes entered the bidding for items it didn't already have, probably using money raised from the commissions.

The Melbourne Group met every Thursday evening in the Oddfellows Hall, and then continued at a nearby coffee house. Meetings were informal and fell into a general rhythm that included a short 'business' meeting led by McCubbin. By about September 1953 chess matches had become popular but most meetings were spent in general chat and discussion about whatever interested members.

There was a bunch of regulars and a steady stream of newcomers whom McCubbin introduced to the Group, most recruited by Binns from McGills,.

Many were readers and collectors who attended meetings occasionally to borrow from the library or buy and sell books and magazines. By April 1954 the Melbourne Group had details of 97 people interested in science fiction but most were not regulars at the club.

Occasional interstate visitors included Doug Nicholson, Bluey Glick, Loralie Giles and Bert Chandler from Sydney, John O'Shaugnessy from Albury, Geoff Bennett from Canberra, Ted Butt and Eric Rayner from Tasmania, and John Gurney, Frank Bryning and Harry Brook from Queensland. In April 1956 the Group welcomed Sergeant Bob Smith to Melbourne after his return from service with the Army in Japan. In mid-1956 Wynne Whiteford also joined the Group, a new Australian author who had sold his first story to *Science Fiction Monthly*.

In addition to Thursday evening meetings the Group also held fairly frequent social evening in member's homes. Fifteen fans enjoyed a highly successful auction and much conversation, stimulated by food and drink, on 23 October 1953.[8] In November they gathered for a barbeque at the Binns' home and in December gathered again at the Crozier place. In March 1954 they held a quiet lightning chess tournament starting with ten players and concluding when Dick Jenssen defeated Jack Keating in the final.[9] In June 1954 they gathered at Val Morton's home to drool over his collection of comics and records, hold an auction, play chess and enjoy supper. In December a typical Melbourne downpour limited the gathering to eight who were the guests of Mrs Williams for chess and chatter, gossip and grog. Another gathering at the Crozier place in January 1955 continued until one in the morning for chess, chatter, a Binns quiz which was won by Tony Santos and a lightning chess tournament won by Don Latimer.

There were also two special gatherings. One was for the wedding of Sydney refugees, Loralie Giles and Bluey Glick on 12 January 1955. The second was Merv Binns 21st birthday party on 8 July 1955. It began with a big party at a nearby hall that included dancing and games. Then friends, family and fans adjourned to the Binns' home for a second supper laid on by Mrs Binns. Merv's parents gave him a tape recorder which they played with until 2.30 in the morning with a singing session.[10]

Average attendance at the Melbourne Group's Thursday night meetings was usually around ten, sometimes it was as low as half a dozen and occasionally as many as fourteen or fifteen, when the room was crowded. The

---

[8] People there were Mr & Mrs Santos, Mr & Mrs Latimer, Mr, Mrs & Miss Walker, Race Mathews, Geraldine McKeown, Kevin Wheelahan, Merv Binns, Keith McLellan, Harry Brook, Bob McCubbin and Ian Crozier, *Etherline* 16.

[9] The contestants were McLelland, Wheelahan, Crozier, Binns, Keating, Latimer, McCubbin, Walker, Jenssen and Bicknell. *Etherline* 25.

[10] *Etherline* 43 & 53.

club's library, which was stored in a cupboard in the hall outside their room, continued to grow and storage became a problem so the Club's thoughts turned to moving somewhere larger towards the end of 1953. By this time the AFPA duplicator and other science fiction paraphernalia was probably in the Binns garage in Preston so he suggested that it could be converted into the clubroom which would give members good access to the library and where they could hold fortnightly meetings. But the garage in Preston was 11 kilometers north of central Melbourne and the Club's general consensus was that it was too far from the city. There were also no nearby coffee lounges for the Group's customary after meeting gathering. To find a new clubroom they placed an advertisement in a newspaper, but nothing came of it.

Pressure to move came again in March 1954 when the rental for the room in the Oddfellows basement was increased to 17/6 a week because, so the Group was told, of increases in the cost of lighting and heating. 'What heating?' they asked. Other reasons for moving including activities upstairs such as dancing and boxing disrupting Club meetings. In May the MSFC arrived for its weekly meeting to find three telephones had been installed in their room, making them curious about what else went on there. Again the Group searched for a new home with requests placed in newspapers and on the radio and again no new home could be found.

In May it seemed they had found a room, but it turned out to be unsuitable. In June McCubbin spent a day leaving his name with eleven estate agents, but could find no suitable accommodation for the Group. In September 1954 the Melbourne Group was told they now had to vacate the room by 10.30 in the evening, giving them more encouragement to find a new home. At a meeting in February 1955 one member offered the Group the use of the front room of his home near St Kilda station but it was considered not as central as their current location.

By July 1955 the Melbourne Group had found a new home, at 168 Lennox Street in Richmond, near the corner of Bridge Road and upstairs from the office where Crozier worked. The Group had to do some work to make the room useable but they moved in in October. Their first meeting was crowded, owing to the unusually good attendance, but the library was now on display and coffee and biscuits were provided free of charge. It seemed that already this new room might be too small but, as attendance levels settled, Thursday evenings were less crowded and members enjoyed the extra space.

In the years before television watching almost any movie outside the commercial theatres was a novelty and showing them became an important part of the Group's activities, Dan Bicknell was projectionist when movies were occasionally shown in the Oddfellows Hall and at the Group's social gatherings. They borrowed films from the State Film Library, and other sources, so the Melbourne Group had to affiliate with the Film Exhibitor's Association and had to form a separate Film Group.[11] There were almost no science fiction or fantasy movies on 16 mm film available for private showings and the ones that were available were second rate at best. Movies about space, astronomy, science and technology were popular but they would watch almost anything so one evening they watched movies about northern Australia and the solar system and comets.

Melbourne fans probably spent more time discussing the state of fandom in Sydney than Sydney fans spent talking about Melbourne fandom because there was so little conflict in Melbourne to discuss. If there were any disagreement it was managed and kept away from the public gaze. A handful of Melbourne fans attended the conventions in Sydney where they experienced first hand the conflict in Sydney fandom but Melbourne fans probably didn't understand the depth of the Sydney problem because there was then so little contact between Sydney and Melbourne fans. There were few fan publications coming from Sydney after 1954 so Melbourne fans had to subsist on a diet of rumours and reading between the lines to understand what was happening there. All Dick Jenssen knew about Sydney fans was that they were 'a back-stabbing bunch and that nasty things happened there'. Lee Harding thought Sydney fans were a stuffy lot who took their science fiction very seriously. He knew that Sydney fans didn't like Melbourne fans very much and Melbourne fans 'didn't give a hoot' about them.[12]

If they concerned themselves with it, Melbourne fans might have taken the side of the Sydney Thursday Night Group, partly because they shared a similar informal attitude to fan organisation and partly because Stone had already alienated many Melbourne fans. Stone did not help the situation when he published his 'No Convention in 55' report which puzzled Melbourne fans who thought he was trying to make trouble. 'Graham, I hope this is not a sabotage attempt!' Crozier wrote in *Etherline*.[13]

On the other hand, when copies of *Scansion* circulated in Melbourne in February 1955 Nicholson was congratulated for his sane and balanced appeal for tolerance between the Sydney groups. *Etherline* also published several reports of Thursday Night Group meetings but none from the Futurians, probably because it did not receive any.

Melbourne fans briefly considered offering to hold the Australian convention in 1955 but then decided they would rather link their convention to the Olympic Games that were to be held in Melbourne in 1956. (This change of

---

[11] The officers of the Film Group were: Eric La Motte the organiser, Bob McCubbin the treasurer and Bruce Heron, Tony Santos and Don Latimer the committee of management.

[12] Interviews with Dick Jenssen and Lee Harding.

[13] *Etherline* 33.

heart may have led Stone to think the Thursday Night Group had talked Melbourne fans into withdrawing their 1955 offer so the North Shore Futurians could host it instead, leading to his animosity towards the 1955 convention and Melbourne fans.) Bob McCubbin announced that Melbourne wanted to hold the 1956 convention at the 1954 convention business session, the meeting agreed and it was formalised at the 1955 convention.

The Melbourne Group's convention committee met for the first time on Sunday 6 June 1954 at McCubbin's place. It included McCubbin, Crozier, Binns and Keating who appointed an Interstate Advisory Committee including Arthur Haddon in Sydney and Don Tuck in Hobart.[14] The name for the convention was obvious: 'Olympicon'.

Olympicon program book cover (Merv Binns collection)

The Olympicon committee hoped to hold the convention over a long weekend during the Games but the only available long weekend coincided with the Games' opening so they settled on the weekend of the closing ceremony, 8 and 9 December 1956. They planned to host the best convention so far staged in Australia and looked for a suitable venue that was within their budget. The Oddfellows Hall was already booked and not available but, after a frustrating search, the Richmond City Council agreed in March 1955 to hire them facilities at the Richmond Town Hall. It was just what they were looking for. The hall was well lit and ventilated, equipped with power points and good quality theatre style seating. They had sole use of the western entrance, the upstairs hall, all conveniences and a small but well-furnished kitchen.

The Olympicon committee's main challenge was in raising money to pay for the event. They began in mid-1954 by passing the hat around and had raised £13/6 by August.[15] Support came from Westercon 8, held in San Francisco that year, which sent a shipment of prozines that were auctioned to raise money for the convention. After the 1955 Sydney convention the Olympicon committee began collecting subscriptions of 10/- (US$1.00 and

---

[14] The committee comprised Bob McCubbin (Organiser, Chairman & Treasurer), Ian Crozier (Overseas and Interstate Publicity), Merv Binns (Displays & Victorian Publicity), Jack Keating (Auctioneer and Sound & Lighting), Eric La Motte (Films) and R Parlanti (Social Organiser) *Etherline* 30. The Interstate Advisory Committee included Arthur Haddon (New South Wales). Rick Day (Queensland), N J Shalders (South Australia), Don Tuck (Tasmania) but had received no reply from Western Australia. *Etherline* 51.

[15] This equates to $1.35 in decimal currency which was worth about $24.50 in 2021 value.

7/6 Sterling) which entitled all members — attending or supporting — to a membership badge, souvenir booklet and convention report. Within a couple of months they had ten members including three from the United States and one from Korea. To help boost the convention's finances the weekly Group meeting fee was increased from 2/- to 2/6 in April 1955. The biggest boost to the conventions finances was £26/8/3 passed on to it from the 1955 convention so the committee had raised £49/18/3 by July 1956.

Organising Olympicon drained the resources and energy of the small group. During 1956 other activities such as publishing *Etherline* began to suffer and it became irregular. By September some of the Melbourne Group were busy preparing for the play Norman Hemming had written for the convention with set building and rehearsals directed by Barry Salgram. Others were busy preparing the auction and Binns began preparing the convention's displays. They had sent requests to all the prozines for covers and interior art for the display but response was poor, apart from six covers and a some interior illustrations from *New Worlds*, and some original manuscripts.

The Melbourne Group planned to host the biggest and best convention ever held in Australia, an 'event to live in the memories of all those attending it'. The Olympic Games was the biggest international event so far held on Australia that would attract thousands of overseas visitors at a time when international visitors were rare in Melbourne.

Organizing the auction at the Fifth Australian SF Convention. LtoR Bary Salgram, Jack Keating, Ian Crozier and Tony Santos
(Merv Binns collection)

They had hoped that an association with the Olympic Games would attract some overseas spectators or athletes but none came.

Olympicon followed the format of previous Australian conventions. It began with registration and gathering on Saturday morning to look at the displays put together by Merv Binns and Keith McLelland. Next came the first part of the auction (which had only a small attendance with fair prices) and then the Guest of Honour, Frank Bryning and talks by Wynne Whiteford and the Melboune radio script writer Harvey Blanks.[16] More auction followed with brisk bidding but low prices and then a dinner and perfor-

---

[16] The texts of their talks can be found in *Etherline* 80.

AFPA display panel and attendees at the Fifth Australian SF Convention
(Merv Binns collection)

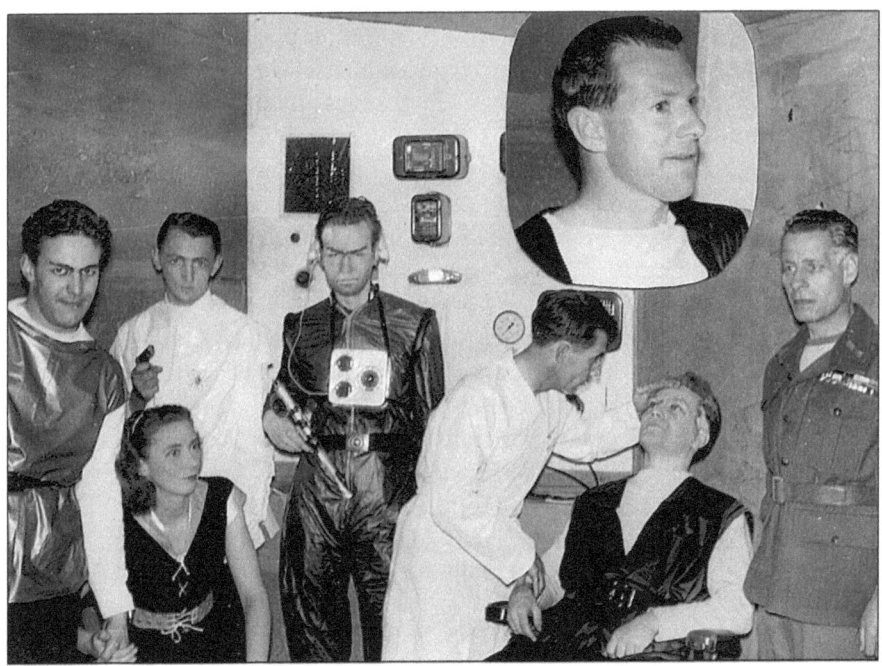
The cast of Nora Hemming's play at the Fifth Australian SF Convention. LtoR Barry Salgram, Norma Hemming, Graham Lyell, Jack Keating, Larry Jones, Brig Young and John McKerchner
(Merv Binns collection)

mance of Norma Hemming's play 'Balance of Power'. The auction continued on Sunday morning with the *New Worlds* covers bringing good prices.

The feature on Sunday afternoon was the Business Session, which lacked any of the drama of previous convention business sessions. The usual reports from science fiction groups around Australia was dismal. There were reports from the Melbourne and Adelaide groups, Tasmanian fans and a short comment from Frank Bryning that Brisbane fans were too busy with other things to do much. From the Futurian Society of Sydney, the Sydney Thursday Night Group, the Futurian Society of Canberra and fans in Western Australia there was nothing.

The only other issue discussed at the business session was the next Australian convention. When bids were invited none were received but, perhaps prepared for this eventuality, Barry Salgram proposed that the next convention be held in Melbourne over Easter 1958. Olympicon had been held very late in 1956, Easter was the best time for a convention and Easter 1957 was too close so it was best to hold the convention in 1958. Mike Baldwin from Sydney agreed, saying that in his opinion there was no responsible organisation in Sydney able to organise a convention.[17]

The convention concluded on Sunday evening with the showing of two movies with the final one, *The Five Thousand Fingers of Dr T*, watched by over 110. Finally McCubbin rose to thank all who had attended and those who had joined the convention but were unable to attend, especially the 24 Americans who had joined but had no expectation of attending. He said he trusted that those who had attended enjoyed themselves and hoped to see them again at the next convention.[18]

After the convention McCubbin wrote that it had been a social success but it had run the Melbourne Group into serious debt because it had been very poorly supported by other Australian fans and the attendance was almost entirely from Melbourne. Olympicon had 117 registered members, 87 from Victoria, 28 overseas members, 19 from New South Wales and the rest from other states. The lowest attendance had been 26 on Sunday, in the 30s on Saturday, 83 had seen the Hemming play and 112 (not all convention members) had watched the films on Sunday evening. The Melbourne Group had hoped for strong support from fans in Sydney but had received almost none and only a couple of Sydney fans attended.

Melbourne fans had put all their effort into holding the best possible convention they could for Australian fandom but only a handful from outside Melbourne had attended. Melbourne fans made little of this disap-

---

[17] *Etherline* 80.
[18] *Etherline* 48 & 80.

pointment but ten years later Binns wrote simply '... we were let down badly by the country and interstaters.'[19]

---

[19] The Australian *Science Fiction News*letter, April 1966.

CHAPTER 11
1957-1961, Melbourne

At some point during this period the Group was renamed the Melbourne Science Fiction Club (MSFC). This was apparently done because Binns felt the name 'group' did not sound as official as 'club' and started to call the group a club when they were looking for a new meeting room. Nobody seems to have noticed or cared about the change and it had no effect on the group's activities.[1]

Olympicon drained the club of its energy and enthusiasm of its energy and enthusiasm. The promised convention report appeared late as a large issue of *Etherline* including short comments on the convention sessions, transcriptions of the three Saturday talks, a few statistics and a few poorly reproduced photos. In that issue Crozier announced there would be a three months break before following issues, and when *Etherline* returned it was never on the frantic pre-Olympicon publishing schedule. They had published 80 issues between March 1953 and the beginning of 1957 and only a further 21 from after Olympicon to the final issue in late 1959. Those issues were larger, never smaller than 28 pages, but Crozier kept them full by introducing fiction and articles. The 100th issue was a large 64 pages containing fiction, news (from Forry Ackerman), book lists, book reviews and McCubbin fanzine reviews. The next issue promised a revival but was, in fact, the final one.

MSFC meetings continued much as before but were subdued. They began film nights early in 1957, charging 5/- admittance, but there were so few decent science fiction movies that they had to alternate them with movies of more general interest. Even so, after five showings of which only one was financially successful, further showings were cancelled in September 1957. By then there was additional competition after television started in Melbourne just before the opening of the Olympic Games. Early television sets were very expensive so few people had them at first and it became common for people to visit their friends who did and watch theirs. In early 1957 fans gathered at Val Morton's place to watch an episode of Disney's 'Man and The Moon' on his television set.

---

[1] Interview with Merv Binns.

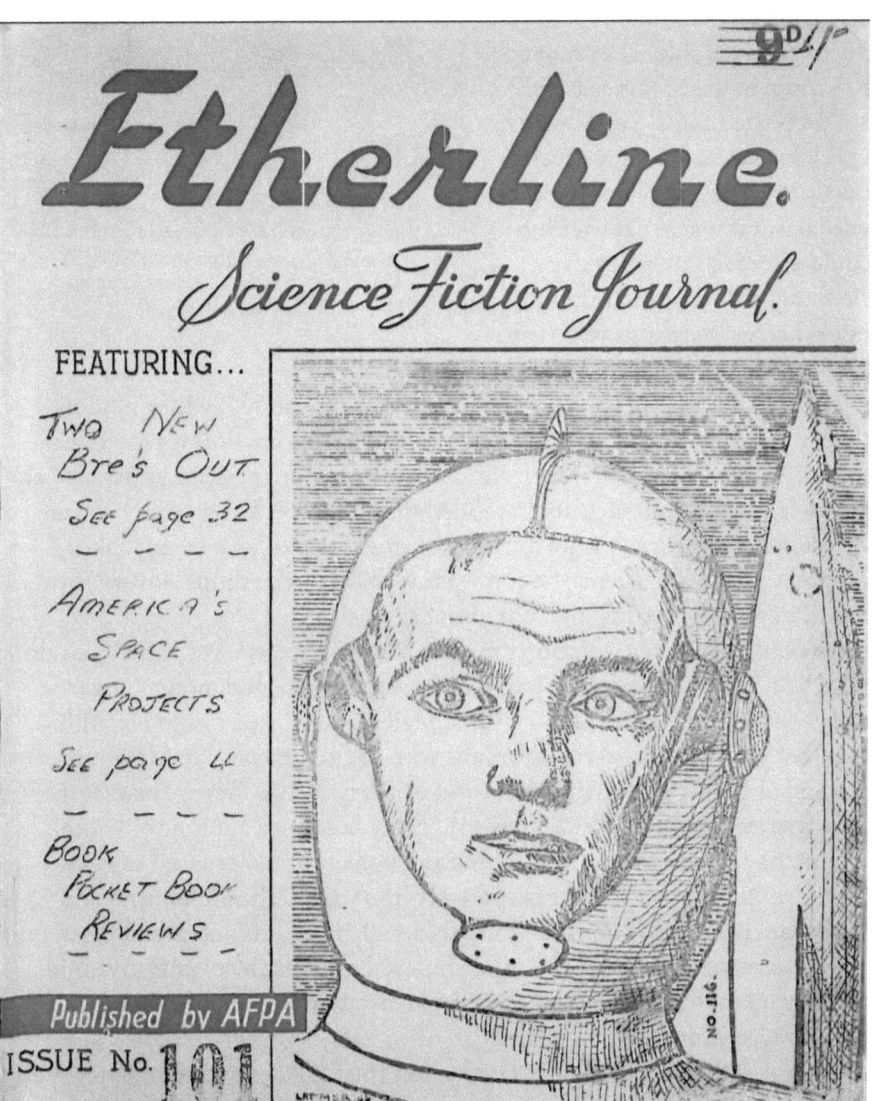

The 101st and final issue of *Etherline*
(Fanac.org)

The Club left its room above the office where Ian Crozier worked in April 1957, possibly because he had started a new job so the room was no longer available. They moved to a room in the St James Building at 506 Little Collins Street which was little larger but only accessible by lift. They were not happy with it but it was what the club could afford, so they began by cleaning, painting and building bookshelves. Meetings were held on Tuesday evenings, starting at 7.30.

Chess players and the library in the Melbourne SF Club's room in the St James Building
(Merv Binns collection)

Perhaps because of the way Melbourne fans felt about Sydney fandom, they mostly ignored what remained of Sydney fandom. When a Melbourne fan was planning to visit Sydney he asked McCubbin for the addresses of any active fans there and McCubbin replied that he didn't know of any. When Crozier had some spare time during a business trip to Sydney he looked around to see what science fiction was available in the shops — very little — but didn't bother telling any fans about his visit.

The only new science fiction group to form in Victoria was the Mountain District Science Fiction Club based in Upway in the Dandenong Ranges about twenty-five miles north west of Melbourne. It was formed by MSFC member Jack Bristow to cater for fans who could not travel to Melbourne. By the end of 1954 it had 22 members and a library of 200 items. The members took their wives and families to the monthly meetings at Bristow's home where they played darts, table tennis and hookey and discussed science fiction, followed by a supper prepared by the wives. The Melbourne and Mountain District groups maintained friendly relations and members of one group occasionally visited the other, but in the 1950s the twenty-five mile journey up to Bristow's home along a narrow, winding mountain road discouraged more frequent visits.

After the disappointment of Olympicon the MSFC expected much less of the convention they were committed to host in 1958. They booked the same venue, the Richmond Town Hall, but for only one day, Saturday 5 April 1958. They also arranged with the Mountain District group to hold a barbeque picnic in the Dandenong Ranges on the second day. They were less energetic in promotion and in seeking material for their displays and auction, and the catering was more modest with Mrs McCubbin making the cups of tea. By January 1958 the convention had over 60 members who had paid the 10/-

Display panels at the Sixth Australian SF Convention
(Merv Binns collection)

In Jack Bristow's garden at Upwey following the Sixth Australian SF Convention. LtoR Bob McCubbin, Larry Jones, Graham Lyell and Barry Salgram
(Merv Binns collection)

membership, five from Sydney but none from Adelaide or Brisbane.[2] By April the convention had 98 registered members but the attendance ranged from 30 on Saturday afternoon to 45 in the evening. The progam comprised addresses on Saturday afternoon and a full length science fiction film in the evening. Crozier wrote that he thought the event had been okay, there had been some problems but everyone present seemed to enjoy themselves immensely. The business session received reports from only the Melbourne and Brisbane groups and there was no mention of a further convention.

Sixth Australian SF Convention program book cover (Merv Binns collection)

Science fiction fandom in Australia had run out of energy and enthusiasm. Sydney had become a wasteland with only the remnant of the Thursday Night Group meeting and Graham Stone keeping the Sydney Futurian library open. There were also the libraries and social gatherings in Adelaide and Brisbane but their main contact with fandom was through *Etherline* and as it slowed so did their contact with the rest of fandom.

The energy had gone in Melbourne too but the science fiction Binns offered through McGills, and his promotion of the Melbourne Club, kept it supplied with new recruits as older members dropped off. Melbourne also had McCubbin and Crozier to give the group momentum, but they too had run out of energy and enthusiasm, particularly after the 1958 convention.

Bob McCubbin was appointed Deputy Principal at the Ferntree Gully North High School which made it difficult for him to attend meetings. He had given much to the group but began to take on more responsibilities in his teaching career. Crozier also began to drift away. He had other interests including motor racing, the Navy Reserve and he was also the secretary and treasurer of the Hawthorn Football Club Supporters Club. He married in 1958 and, earlier, had taken a position as representative for the steel maker, BHP, and had a circuit in South East Asia where he travelled for the company.

Of the old group only Binns remained, and he was determined to keep the Club going. After the 1958 convention there were about 12 regular members

---

[2] *Etherline* 85, 94 and *SF Times* 278.

at the weekly meetings and about 30 irregulars. Several members who helped him included Tony Santos, Dave Sofar, Cedric Rowley (who became the club's projectionist) Barry Salgram and Don Latimer. There were occasional new members attracted by the library which had close to 1500 items for them to borrow.

Binns built up contact with distributors in Britain, Canada and the United States who supplied him with the books and prozines not usually available in Australia and, although this was theoretically illegal, nobody stopped him. Some imports went into the club library, some into his own collection, some to a list of his personal clients, and some went onto the shelves at McGills to build up the science fiction offerings there. In agreement with the shop management he created a system of trades between the shop, the Club and himself so he could supply customers with what they wanted, either over the counter at McGills, through his personal mail order business or through the Club. McGills management were happy with this arrangement because science fiction sold well in their shop.[3]

To replace the failing *Etherline* Binns started publishing a newssheet he called the *Australian Science Fiction Newsletter*, not as a replacement for *Etherline* but as 'a means of keeping touch with the many friends we have made in the time the AFPA and *Etherline* have been in existence'.[4] It was irregular at best and an untidy combination of lists of books and prozines for sale, library catalogues, an occasional review and snippets of news, mainly about doings in Melbourne. Unlike the tidy and well-presented *Etherline*, the Binns newsletter was untidy, unorganised and unpredictable, but it was the only thing being published in Australia for general circulation to science fiction fans.

If Club meetings had any formality when McCubbin was in charge that disappeared with Binns and meetings became completely informal and unorganised. However, few seemed to mind. Newcomers might have been put off by the informality but some found the Club a little haven of safety and peace, as the group had been from the beginning, where they were free to talk openly about science fiction and felt free to be themselves.[5]

The Club moved again from its room in Little Collins Street, probably in early 1959, because it was in a gloomy part of the city and was a bit pricy for the club's treasury. They found a new home at Room 5 on the third floor of 25 McKillop Street, also in the city. It was smaller than their previous room but it was what they could afford, barely. It was so small that it was crowded when only a handful of members were there and about 20 people attended the first meeting there.[6] To add something new the group bought a dart

---

[3] Interview with Merv Binns.

[4] *Science Fiction News*letter 1.

[5] Interviews with Lee Harding, Bill Wright and Dick Jenssen.

[6] *Etherline* 101

board but the only place they could hang it was on the back of the door, which made entering risky if there was a darts match in progress.

Australian fandom had almost no presence overseas and when fans in the northern hemisphere thought of fandom down under they thought of New Zealand. Towards the end of the decade there were active fan groups in cities including Auckland and Wellington. Several New Zealand fans including Roger Horrocks, Bruce Burn and Mervyn Barrett were corresponding with overseas fans and writing to American and British fanzines. They were also producing fanzines that circulated and received favorable reviews overseas. In comparing Australian with New Zealand fanzines one reviewer wrote that 'there is an air of freshness blowing though it that is rather unusual for a fanzine from downunder'.[7]

By the end of the 1950s there may have been only two active fan groups in Australia, one in Melbourne and the other in nearby Ballarat where it was one of several groups hosted by the local astronomical society. Barry Salgram moved back to Ballarat permanently because of his father's health and another Club member, Joe Czinsky, already lived there. In 1959 McCubbin and McLelland went to visit the group and McCubbin gave a talk on Science Fiction and education. Later Binns went to visit the group and was impressed by the setup there and plans were made for a weekend visit. In 1960 they planned an exhibition in conjunction with the annual Begonia Festival to include displays, talks, films, a dinner and 'stargazing' at the Observatory.

The availability of science fiction in Australia changed dramatically from mid-1959 when the Commonwealth government lifted its embargo on the importation of American books and magazines. The material that had been scarce since 1940 soon became available in abundance with the American magazines such as *Astounding*, *Fantasy & Science Fiction*, *Galaxy* and *If* starting to appear on Australian newsstands in about September 1959. Gradually importers began bringing science fiction into the country so that the full range of American prozines was available by mid-1960. By the end of that year American books and magazines were flowing into Australia regularly, although the importation of American books was still prohibited under a British and American copyright agreement, in theory at least. Lifting the embargo also allowed American publishers to dump a lot of their back stock in Australia and Harding recalled seeing a large number of *Fantasy & Science Fiction* back issues appear unexpectedly in Melbourne's Technical Book Shop.

The end of the embargo may have been why Cohen stopped supporting Sydney's Thursday Night gatherings at the Bridge Club. That did not happen in Melbourne where McGills continued to be the main source of science

---

[7] Rick Sneary, *Science Fiction Parade* 5, 2nd Quarter 1957.

Merv Binns (slightly damaged) at work in McGills
(Merv Binns collection)

fiction, Binns continued to supply his personal list of customers and the Club continued its regular weekly meetings.

A bigger effect was the 1961 recession. The 1950s had been generally good years in Australia because the economy was partly protected by restriction on imports. In February 1960 the government lifted its restriction on imports generally which led to a balance of trade problem which led, in November 1960, to the government imposing a sharp increase in sales tax and restrictions on credit in an attempt to bring the Australian economy back into balance. This created a recession, an increase in unemployment and limited Australian's ability to spend.

Binns felt this directly because activity and attendance at the Club dropped and the majority of his regular customers could not afford to buy much. Some club members were forced to sell their collections to raise funds and, although he could advertise forthcoming books, Binns could not afford to import many of them. Selling books, which had become one of the club's main sources of revenue, had dried up and he wrote 'I am broke, the club is broke but if you are not broke please help us out by buying some of the items we have for sale'.[8] In an attempt to raise some more money Binns had the AFPA Roneo repaired and offered a printing service. The club planned to

---

[8] *Australian SF News* 7, July 1961.

revive film shows to raise more money, but the clubroom was too small and arranging a venue and ensuring the showings were profitable led to delays.

The club's position became even more precarious in September 1961 when it received notice to quit its room in McKillop Street. A special meeting early in October discussed the problem. If the club could find a new and larger place it could offer members more activities like regular film showings, chess tournaments and card nights which would enable it to grow. But if a suitable place could not be found the club would have to go into recess. Binns announced that the final meeting at McKillop Street would be held on 19 October and it would be open the following Saturday to clear all remaining sale items. Binns also hoped that any change would help to lift from his shoulders some of the responsibility for running the Club and put it on a stronger basis, financially and constitutionally.

In mid-October, when Binns threatened that the Club might have to go into recess, he might already have had in mind a solution to the problem. McGills had a three-storey bulk warehouse in Somerset Place, a lane running parallel to Elizabeth Street behind the shop, and the top floor was unoccupied. Binns persuaded McGills management to let the club occupy the top floor of the warehouse and it moved in to 19 Somerset Place in November 1961. It cost more to rent but the additional space offered the possibility for the club to expand its activities to attract more members to pay the increased rent.

Strictly speaking the Club should not have moved into Somerset Place because it was an unsafe fire trap. The only access was in an old hydraulic lift connecting the ground floor with the top level. It was a primitive goods lift which had only a floor and side walls but no front, back or top. To make it work somebody had to pull a cable in the lift to activate the hydraulic system and if the lift was at the top anybody wanting to go up had to yell for somebody to send the lift down to them. Don Latimer startled many members with a trick he played in the lift. When they called for the lift to be sent down he got in, started the lift and then held himself against the open wall while the lift went down. As the lift came up again the person in it suddenly found themselves with unexpected company.

The room was spacious by the club's standards, about 72 square metres, creating space for the library, the AFPA duplicator and a small kitchen. A mezzanine floor up a flight of stairs contained three toilet cubicles and a washbasin. Some theatre seats were found and installed and the club held its first film night before the end of 1961 which attracted 34 people. Before long a table tennis table was built at one end of the room and its popularity soon replaced other club activities such as darts. In the first few months attendance at club meetings averaged about 18, which was twice the attendance at the previous clubroom so Merv Binns felt positive about the future.

CHAPTER 12
Fork in the Track

Science fiction fandom in Australia was reborn from the early 1960s, having little to do with the fandoms that had previously existed. The story of this revitalisation will be told in the second part of this history.

However, while this revival occurred the traditions of the Futurian Society of Sydney were maintained by one science fiction enthusiast, Graham Stone. A history of science fiction fandom in Australia would be incomplete without a brief chapter about Stone's activities but, since he continued the traditions of earlier Australian fandom rather than engaged with the revived Australian fandom, it is appropriate to tell that story as a continuation of this part of the history.

As a historian I find Stone and his attitude and activities of interest in offering an alternative to the way in which science fiction and its fandom in Australia developed. Fans devised two words to describe their approaches towards their relationship with science fiction and its fandom. 'Sercon' was shorthand for 'serious and constructive' while 'fannish' related to the social aspects of fandom. These tendencies had been apparent in Sydney fandom in the 1950s with the division between the Futurian Society of Sydney and the 'Thursday Night Group'. Think of the difference as a continuum from two extremes with most fans located somewhere on that continuum with the Society heavily towards the sercon end of the spectrum and the Thursday Night Group more to the fannish or social end. The Melbourne SF Club, which was virtually all that remained of Australian fandom by the end of the 1950s, was somewhere between the two extremes.

When I came to fandom in Melbourne in the mid-1960s Stone's name was rarely spoken, but when it was it was to dismiss him as being bad tempered, stubborn, intolerant

Graham Stone
(photo courtesy of John Tipper)

and irrelevant to what science fiction and its fandom in Australia were and did, so I paid no attention to him or his activities. We met once, introduced to each other by John Baxter at a Word Festival in Canberra in the mid-1980s. He turned out not to be as I had expected, instead being mild-mannered, reticent and somewhat abrupt in his speech, which might have been because of our locations at the extreme opposite ends of the fannish spectrum.

Thirty years earlier in the mid-1950s Stone may have been everything that I was told about him and much more energetic and aggressive in his promotion of what he believed to be the correct way to understand and promote science fiction. He and Molesworth had become the dominant figures in the Futurian Society of Sydney and it had been left to him to lead the Society after Molesworth took a back seat. As the leader of the Futurians his undiplomatic and stubborn personality had done a great deal to fuel the dispute between Sydney's two fan groups which ultimately led to the collapse of both.

After the Sydney Futurians had abandoned their clubroom at Taylor Square and the Albion Futurians had degenerated into a social gathering all that remained of the Futurian Society of Sydney was its library. For a while it was located in Alan South's home and, when he could no longer accommodate it, Stone kept the library in his home for a while. Eventually he rented an office in the city at his own expense and kept the library there. By then it had over 5000 books and 1100 prozines. He opened it on Saturdays, gradually building up a group of more than 60 borrowers, some local to Sydney and others who borrowed books using the postal service. He enrolled those using the library as Associate members of the Society. He also had a duplicator in the office which he used to issue irregular newsletters and book lists.

Occasionally Stone attempted to do more than maintain the library. In January 1957 he announced that the Society would sponsor a conference which was 'not a circus, just a meeting to discuss science-fiction'.[1] In early 1959 he announced that he would be publishing books under the Lucian Book imprint, starting with a 1869 classic *The Brick Moon* and would publish books of a similar nature. It does not appear that either of these ideas came to fruition.

Stone worked for two science fiction magazines that were published in Australia briefly in the mid-1950s. In 1954 he worked in an advisory role for *Future Science Fiction* and *Popular Science Fiction* which printed mainly overseas written fiction but included stories by several local writers including Norma Hemming and Frank Bryning. Stone wrote short editorials on science fiction for four issues but the magazines folded after only six. A little later he did similar work for a new magazine, *Science Fiction Monthly*, with sixteen

---

[1] *Fantasy Times*, 263.

pages to fill with reviews and other material about science fiction. That magazine folded in February 1957 after eighteen issues, with Stone's contributions in the final seven.

Stone also regularly contributed news about science fiction in Australia to the American news fanzine, *Fantasy Times*. It was usually bibliographic information about what was being published in Australia but nothing about fan activities. It appears that in the aftermath of the 1954 convention, and the bitterness that led to the collapse of Sydney fandom, Stone resolved never to mention fans or fandom again in anything he wrote so there is no mention of fan activities or the two conventions held in Melbourne in anything he wrote, though the Australian SF Society was mentioned once or twice.

Despite his feelings about fandom Stone was still keen to promote science fiction, but in ways he thought were appropriate to the genre's importance. During the 1950s he published 24 issues of *Science Fiction News* which was intended for a general readership, not fans. It was deliberately impersonal in the style of Futurian fanzines of the period. Its purpose was to promote science fiction by providing interesting information about it to encourage the general public to accept and read it. It also celebrated the way in which the genre could be the harbinger of science in the future. When, for example, the first artificial satellite, Sputnik 1, was launched in 1958 the headline of the following issue of *Science Fiction News* was an impatient 'Off the Ground at Last'.[2]

Despite all his efforts it seems that Stone made little impression on the general public, the Society was not revived and publishing *Science Fiction News* seems to have drained him, personally and financially. In the 24th issue in August 1959 he made a personal statement that it had not been a commercial proposition and was published 'as a contribution to the cause'. He wrote that time, money and other pressure of work would make it difficult to meet a regular schedule in the future and it was the final issue.[3]

Typically for the Sydney Futurians, when something didn't seem to work they gave up on that and started something new. Perhaps Stone was inspired into taking a new approach by the formation of the International SF Society, a short-lived European based organisation that said it would collect and disseminate news about science fiction and be a conduit between science fiction fans and professionals. This was like the aims of Stone's Australian SF Society that had lain dormant for a few years. He announced that the Futurian Society of Sydney would represent the International SF Society in Australia as an affiliated group. Around September 1959, he sent out a circular announcing that the Futurian Society of Sydney had taken on the job of representing the ISFS in Australia and the Futurian Society would be taking

---

[2] *Science Fiction News* 19.

[3] *Science Fiction News* 24.

over the functions of the ASFS which would be retired to simplify arrangements.[4]

The twentieth anniversary of the first meeting of the Sydney Futurians occurred on 5 November 1959 and, to mark it, the Society's first meeting in four years was held in a Sydney cafe. Three people attended, Stone, Molesworth and Alan South. The meeting discussed the ISFS, approved of it and the FSS representing it as the Australian Branch Office. The meeting also endorsed Stone's activities and elected Molesworth as the Society's Director, South as its Treasurer and Stone as its Secretary and Librarian. Molesworth and Stone were also granted Life Membership in the Society. The meeting agreed that Stone would maintain the library which then had 68 members and associates, most of them Associate Members of the Society who lived outside Sydney and had no voting rights. They decided to revive Society meetings for members and associates in Sydney in 1960, approved publication of Stone's *Index to British Science Fiction Magazines* and publication of an irregular *Notes & Comments* for the members.[5]

Stone published the first issue of *Notes and Comments* around the end of 1959. It was an austere little fanzine, neatly published in a folded foolscap format with a card cover without illustrations. Stone told its readers that it would be published at least four or five times a year and be a fanzine of record devoted entirely to information and discussion relevant to science fiction. It would only present material of sufficient interest to be placed on permanent record, so there would be lots of reprints. Circulation would be limited to members and associates of the Society. Three more issues were published in the following three years. In addition Stone published over 35 issues of the *FSS Circular* for distribution to members from 1959.

Stone continued to run the Society almost single handed, with occasional help from Alan South and Kevin Dillon. Since the early 1950s he had been employed by the New South Wales Education Department working at the State Library and, in August 1963, he was offered a position as a Librarian Grade 1 in the Australian National Library in Canberra. To make arrangements for the Society's future another meeting was held, again attended by three people, Stone, South and Kevin Dillon. Dillon was elected a Society member, agreed to look after the office and library when Stone moved to Canberra and South was granted Life Membership.[6] (Molesworth was not present, probably because of his poor health. He died after a long illness at the age of 39 on 14 July 1964.)

After Stone moved to Canberra the organisation of the Futurian Society of Sydney collapsed and its library was dispersed to ten locations. Stone had

---

[4] *Mumblings from Munchkinland* 34.

[5] *Science Fiction Times* 331.

[6] *Mumblings from Munchkinland* 34.

hoped to use the FSS as the basis for a broader organisation but he now did it by creating the Australian Science Fiction Association (ASFA). As part of its constitution it could have branches where there were ten or more Association members and what was left of the Sydney Futurians appears to have been reconstituted as a branch of the ASFA. By the end of 1968 it was holding monthly meetings and its library was in two parts, some being kept by Laura Molesworth and some by Mike McGuinness. Meetings continued into the 1970s and were mainly film nights, although in 1971 the group planned to return to its original purpose of meeting to talk socially about science fiction.

The ASFA was formed, Stone wrote in the first issue of its journal, to 'provide a basis for communication among those interested in this unique intellectual movement'.[7] He wrote that the study of science fiction needed detailed information about the field to proceed effectively because students of the genre needed to know what material existed. He wrote that there did not yet exist a comprehensive list of science fiction books, the magazines had only been partly indexed and there had been little research into the isolated short stories and adaptions to other media. He hoped the Association would work on these problems because, although a lot of material had already been published, the field was open to more systematic research. The Association would also encourage and publish debate about science fiction. He wrote that although science fiction was designed for recreation the nature of the material made it of serious interest and the Association hoped to pursue the provision of information for that study.[8] Stone invited members of the Association to join him in this much needed research, there was so much to do that it had be to divided up and reviews and critical articles be written.

Central to the ASFA project was *The Journal of the Australian Science Fiction Association* which Stone published in about a dozen issues between September 1965 and 1970. Its tone was established in the first issue with a long bibliographical article by Don Tuck about Australian science fiction written during and after the war. Stone developed that direction with a tentative booklist of Australian science fiction in the second issue and all further issues comprised mainly bibliographic lists of various kinds and a large number of usually solid and reliable book reviews. The third issue, for example, comprised a bibliography of science fiction short stories published in 1964-65 and some reviews while the fourth contained a list of science fiction books published in 1964-65, an article on Australians in American magazines and more reviews. On rare occasions Stone included short notes about the activities of the Association and requests for more assistance with its bibliographic and reviewing work. The most animated discussion in its pages was commentary on the movie *2001: A Space Odyssey* which ranged

---

[7] *Journal of the Australian Science Fiction Association* 1/1.

[8] *Journal of the Australian Science Fiction Association* 1/1.

over three issues and showed the Association's members' general disdain for it and the kind of art it represented.

The *Journal* was a simple and unadorned fanzine (though Stone would never have called it that) in the style of *Notes and Comments* he had published while still in Sydney. There were no illustrations or other decorations apart from a sometimes very restrained graphic on the cover. There were no moments of excitement or expressions of joy or unhappiness. The Association existed to promote the study of science fiction in a sober fashion and that was how Stone produced the *Journal*. He dismissed a suggestion that the Association might adopt a more imaginative name for its journal with the comment; 'SF has had enough publications with foolish titles, and sensible ones are hard to find available.'[9] There was nothing in the Journal about fan activities, apart from a couple of notes about the Association, and the membership lists published in several issues showed that its membership grew from 54 in March 1966 to 57 in May 1968.

The *Journal* demonstrated that Stone's attitudes to science fiction and its fandom were stubborn and set in concrete that had been poured many years earlier. Perhaps reacting to the ridicule that fans had, and were still, subjected to, and the Futurian ethos that science fiction was a doorway to preparing for the future, Stone believed science fiction was serious, important and had to be treated seriously. Almost from the beginning he avoided publishing anything about fannish activities such as conventions or fanzines because they detracted from the solid and respectable middle-class image of science fiction he wanted to promote.

Stone believed fandom had gone off on the wrong track from the early days when its devotees began calling themselves 'fans' because that gave people the wrong idea so they would not take science fiction and its enthusiasts seriously. To him a 'fan' was somebody who went to a football match to drink beer and fight, not somebody who was seriously interested in a subject. He wrote that other groups of enthusiasts for things like stamps did not call themselves stamp fans and people who went to church did not call themselves god fans so serious science fiction enthusiasts should not call themselves fans either. 'Anyone who calls himself a "fan"', Stone wrote, 'is declaring "Pay no attention to me. I'm a dickhead."'[10]

Similarly, he considered the word fanzine a 'horrible neologism'. He said that using the word to describe the magazines that fans published was a way of excusing their inferior quality and content. He believed that any publication should be judged on its own merits and that it was a mistake to invent a

---

[9] *Journal of the Australian Science Fiction Association* 1/5.

[10] Additional note by Stone in Molesworth, *A history of Australian science fiction Fandom, 1935-1963*, Chapter 1.

special category in which normal standards could be ignored.[11] He had published *Science Fiction News* to this ideal even though it does not appear to have been very successful in the wider community.

Stone held these beliefs stubbornly. He was also prepared to be rude when criticising things he did not like or agree with, which made him unpopular with many people, in particular fans in Melbourne who had been subject to his vitriol in the first half of the 1950s. He may have had a temper and inclination to argue vigorously in public with those he disagreed with, leading to problems in Sydney fandom. In print he was more restrained, most of the time. However, his language was sometimes undisguised and inflammatory when, for example, he began a notice about the publication of a few books in the Australian 'Satellite Series' in the American *Science Fiction Times*: 'Each successive turkey perpetrated by Australian pulp publishers ...'[12]

Years later Stone summarised his general approach. He never said anything discreditable to science fiction, never responded to attacks, never acknowledged arguments he didn't endorse and never objected to errors or challenged false statements of fact. He acknowledged that there were weaknesses in this approach so it was easy to see that he did a lot of things the wrong way but, he added, everyone made mistakes.[13]

The occasional notes Stone wrote for the *Journal* reflected his policy of not saying anything negative about science fiction and not becoming involved in criticism or attacks. From about 1955 there is no mention of the activities of fans in Melbourne in its pages, not of the two conventions held in Melbourne in the 1950s or that city's long running fanzine, *Etherline*. This attitude continued into the 1960s as Australian fandom was revived, centred around fans in Melbourne and the Melbourne Science Fiction Club. Stone mentioned none of this, not even a World Science Fiction Convention in Melbourne, in his publications.

That other track of Australian science fiction fandom which had forked off from Stone's noticed him briefly in 1968. John Bangsund wrote in an editorial in the April 1968 issue of *Australian Science Fiction Review* that he and his friends had discussed the idea of a national science fiction organisation to do things like organise conventions. They distributed a proposal to form an Australian Science Fiction Society and discussed it at the convention held in Melbourne over Easter 1968. Then they discovered that such an organisation, the Australian Science Fiction Association, already existed but that it was under Stone's control and he would do none of the things they thought it should. Bangsund wrote: 'He despises everything fannish, and exercises such autocratic control over his Association that any attempt on the part of

---

[11] Ibid.

[12] *Science Fiction Times* 301.

[13] *Mumblings from Munchkinland* 24.

its members to hold an election or to conduct any other activity than compiling bibliographies would be laughable'. Bangsund noted that *ASFR*, which had gained an international reputation as an arena for serious discussion of science fiction, had not been mentioned once in the pages of the *Journal* and that, so far as Stone was concerned, fans 'were on the wrong wavelength'.[14]

Later in the year Bangsund wrote that he had been in correspondence with Stone and had discussed him with others who knew him. He had reached the conclusion that Stone 'acted like a dictator, believes that everyone is against him or his interests and has the knack (odious in his case) of totally ignoring any person he wishes to.'[15] Bangsund demanded a response to his questions and accusations but Stone, as always, made no response in the Association's publications and Stone and the other branch of Australian fandom continued to follow their distinct and separate tracks.

Although Stone chose to ignore the rest of Australian fandom, in print at least, it is likely he noticed what was happening: the blossoming of a fanzine culture, the establishment of new science fiction clubs, a couple of conventions with more in the planning and the growing reputation of Australian science fiction fandom overseas. His *Journal* had begun with a promised bi-monthly schedule but Stone had published only four issue in 1966, one in 1967, four in 1968 and one in 1969. He knew this was highly unsatisfactory and that many Association members looked for a more frequent and regular contact so, to increase the Association's presence, he launched a new ASFA publication in January 1969. He revived his previous title, *Science Fiction News* which would be, he said, a monthly record of the science fiction field and a guide to what was being published.[16] Like the previous *Journal* its title was simple and, he commented, did not try to impress with a fanciful wit or profundity or 'express contempt for the serious reader of SF by deliberate absurdity'.[17] Its meat and potatoes were the same as had filled the pages of the *Journal*, bibliographic material, reviews and occasional comments on other science fiction focused matters. It was a simple fanzine, folded sheets of yellow paper in the traditional style, uncluttered by illustrations and other adornments, unrelentingly serious and almost entirely humourless.

To the outside observer the Association and *SF News* were the same thing and the material in that magazine reflected what, Stone wrote, were the purposes of the Association. His statement of purpose varied slightly in emphasis from time to time but was fundamentally that the Association existed to bring together people interested in science fiction and to promote the study of the field by compiling bibliographic and other information and

---

[14] *Australian Science Fiction Review* 15.

[15] *The New Millennial Harbinger* 3.

[16] *Science Fiction News* (Second series) 1 & 16.

[17] *Science Fiction News* (Second series) 50.

disseminating it.[18] Stone asked for volunteers in the process of collecting the information and prepared guidelines on how bibliographic information should be recorded. Several extensive bibliographies were published in *SF News* and Stone also had a few capable reviewers who provided him with more content for it. He said that the Association was not concerned with the 'casual reader' but for anyone seriously interested in the appreciation and study of the field and that the Association existed to help them keep abreast of what was happening with a regular coverage of the field.[19]

In addition to its steady diet of current book listings, reviews, other bibliographical and historical material, *SF News* occasionally included comments about the events of the time. The first landing on the Moon in July 1969 inspired a note about what it had been like for fans in 1939, knowing that such an event was likely and that the world would be quite different in the future. He concluded; 'It is our privilege to cherish the memory of it'.[20] In November 1969 he noted that there had been an informal Sydney Futurian reunion on 29 November to mark the fortieth anniversary of its formation in 1939. The only original Sydney Futurian to attend was Bill Veney and Bert Castellair rang the meeting with an apology. Veney recalled the days when the youthful group, interested in what was then a highly esoteric literature, decided to look for a way of helping themselves to enjoy it better, and adopted the name Futurian to show their support for one side of a controversy at the time in American science fiction activities.[21]

In 1969 and 1970 Stone noted the arrival and death of another attempt to publish a science fiction magazine in Australia, *Vision of Tomorrow*. To Stone its contents were sometimes on the positive side of adequate but he wrote that it needed better editing and distribution. It was, he wrote, at last a serious attempt to publish a satisfactory sf magazine in Australia.[22] (See Part 2 of this history).

For the most part Stone maintained his policy of being positive about science fiction although many of the reviews condemned books the reviewers didn't like. However, he was scornful of science fiction published in Australia for not meeting his required standards. His review of John Baxter's *Second Pacific Book of Australian SF* was titled 'Like a Hole in the Head' and he described the collection as 'contemptible'. 'Despite all appearance of desperation in scraping the barrel, this offering is on the whole no worse than the previous insult to the intelligence'.[23] When Horwitz published four books in

---

[18] *Science Fiction News* (Second series) March 1969, June 1969 and January 1971.
[19] *Science Fiction News* (Second series) 13.
[20] *Science Fiction News* (Second series) July 1969.
[21] *Science Fiction News* (Second series) November 1969.
[22] *Science Fiction News* (Second series) September 1969 & September 1970.
[23] *Science Fiction News* (Second series) 32.

```
/////////////////////////////////////

    S C I E N C E    F I C T I O N

              N E W S

/////////////////////////////////////
```
                                                No. 48

REVIEWS

COMMUNE 2000 A.D., by Mack Reynolds. Bantam PB. 95¢

Reynolds has written several novels on the basic theme of a society with Universal Guaranteed Income -- negative income tax -- in which the dissatisfied go off to live in special interest towns ("Communes", though they don't sound much like communes to me). Here he treads the same ground again. The basic idea is suspect, because artificial utopias have seldom worked in history. The lectures -- oops, sorry, discussions between the characters -- which are meant to tell us how and why the commune movement grew up did nothing to convince me, but I confess that I soon started to skip over them. These lectures are interspersed with some quite funny set scenes (Reynolds doesn't intend them to be funny). Oh, yes, I forgot, there was a plot in there somewhere, I think. But not much of it.

I found this a hard book to read, for several reasons. Some of them are outlined above. Another is Reynolds' view of future slang -- he postulates a new set of words, which is okay, but there are so few of them and every character uses them all the time. Conversation today isn't so tedious as it apparently will be in twenty-six years. In general the writing is pedestrian, and padded.

Three frightening things. First, Reynolds has written much better books than this -- not only fresher and better plotted, but better written. This reads like a first draft, and it's bad when authors are paid for first drafts. Second, the book is labelled "A Frederik Pohl Selection", and apparently Bantam intend to put this label on the cream of their crop only. And third, the book has been moderate-

1970 he described the novel by David Rome as '... a book with absolutely nothing to recommend it' and, of the Lin Carter reprint, he wrote that it was impossible to welcome the book because it would only encourage 'more of the same kind of garbage' if it sold well.[24] When an Adelaide publisher issued what were probably six reprinted novels Stone wrote 'A less distinguished company is not to be wished for. None is worth reviewing'. He concluded with a general comment about science fiction published in Australia. 'Considering how poor a prospect publishing SF in Australia is at best, it is hard to imagine the reasoning behind choosing such feeble material'.[25]

By 1974 Stone had published 47 issues of *SF News*. At the National Library of Australia he worked in the Bibliographic section where he greatly enjoyed cataloguing films. He later joined Film Collection and Services to collect, catalogue and preserve the nation's movies. He loved his work and, as a member of staff, he had access to publications held in the Library. This allowed him to complete two editions of his *Australian Science Fiction Index 1939-1962, Index to British Science Fiction Magazines 1934-1953* and *Australian Science Fiction Book Reviews 1969-1972*. He was content, committed to his family, work and sf interests. In 1972 he was promoted with responsibility of the overall operation of the National Library's film activities which included a lending service making around 15 000 films available across the country. In 1973 he applied for another promotion but was unsuccessful. Showing his stubborn character and belief in his own rightness he refused to accept his failure, appealed against it and, when that failed, he resigned from the Library and returned to Sydney.

Stone was unhappy with life when he prepared the 48th issue of *Science Fiction News*, around late 1974 or early 1975. Uncharacteristically he allowed himself over two pages of reflection about his new situation and that of the Association. Still standing in opposition to the fannish standards he rejected he declined to write about his personal problems and, implying criticism of that form of fannish writing, wrote: 'SF suffers from far too much cult of the personality, and if you want to read what a lot of rather uninteresting characters have to say about themselves there are always plenty of other places for just that.'[26] A paragraph later he expressed his disappointment with the track he thought science fiction had taken.

> It seems worth remarking that these days my enthusiasm for SF is not quite what it used to be. Having been actively interested most of the time since 1940, obviously neither the field nor I have stood still. The basic problems today are not promoting SF, getting abysmal standards raised a

---

[24] *Science Fiction News* (Second series) 23.
[25] *Science Fiction News* (Second series) 38.
[26] *Science Fiction News* (Second series) 48.

> little and helping serious readers develop their taste — they are more trying to preserve a fading tradition, sorting out the acceptable from the garbage and saving the field from the carpetbagging charlatans, parasites and meatballs. If it can still be saved, which I am beginning to doubt.[27]

Despite his disillusionment with the state of science fiction he said he planned to continue with the work of the Association and to continue publishing *SF News*. But his attitudes remained rooted in his first exposure to science fiction fandom and the Society in 1940. In the two and a half decades that followed the nature of science fiction and the character of its fandom in Australia had changed, and changed significantly, but he had stubbornly refused to change with them. The work of research and recording that he had done, and continued to do, might have made an important contribution to the development of Australian science fiction and fandom. Sadly his stubborn refusal to change with changing times and his refusal to engage with the new Australian fandom alienated it and made Graham Stone and his work largely irrelevant to what happened in Australian science fiction and its fandom after about 1960.

---

[27] Ibid.

CHRONOLOGY

1926
April — *Amazing Stories*, first issue published, first science fiction prozine

1927
October — First Australian letter of comment published in a prozine, written by John Cooke

1935
15-Aug — Sydney Chapter of the Science Fiction League chartered

1937
'Spacehounds' circulated at the Randwick Intermediate High School by Bill Veney and Bert Castellari

1938
Junior Australian SF Correspondence Club (JASFCC) established informally
May — Australian Government imposed restriction on importation of some foreign literature on moral grounds

1939
early — Junior Science Club formed by Vol Molesworth and Ken Jefferys
January — Harry Warner Jnr sent a copy of *Spaceways* to Bert Castellari
26-Feb — Inaugural meeting held of the JASFCC
March — *Science Fiction Review*, sole issue published by John Deverne
May — *Australian Fan News*, sole issue published by Bill Veney, Eric Russell and Bert Castellari for the JASFCC
1-Sep — World War 2 commenced
October — *Ultra*, first issue published by Eric & Ted Russell
October — Meeting held to discuss formation of a SF club in Sydney
5-Nov — Futurian Society of Sydney (FSS), inaugural meeting
December — *Luna*, first issue published by Vol Molesworth

1940

early	Correspondence began with British fandom
January	*Futurian Observer*, first issue published by Bill Veney and Bert Castellari
April	*Cosmos*, first issue published by Vol Molesworth
1-Apr	Australian Government imposed embargo on importation of all fiction magazines from non-sterling countries
June	David Evans appointed to 'referee' FSS meetings
June	1940 *Austra-Fantasy*, first issue published by Warwick Hockley and Keith Taylor
28-Jul	Futurian Association of Australia (FFA) established by a meeting of Sydney fans
August	*Zeus*, first issue published by a collective of Sydney fans
August	*Hermes*, sole issue published in Sydney
September	Vol Molesworth hospitalized with diabetes
September	David Evans elected FSS Director
23-Sep	FSS suspended
October	British reprint editions of American prozines began arriving in Australia
November	*Melbourne Bulletin*, first issue published by Warwick Hockley
November	Graham Stone first met Sydney fans
6-Dec	First Sydney SF Conference

1941

January	*FFA Bulletin*, sole issue published by Eric Russell
21-Jan	FSS, first meeting on revived
February	*Futurian Observer*, Bill Veney left and Ron Levy took his place
March	*Telefan*, sole issue published by Vol Molesworth
March	David Evans attempted to collect stories for a SF anthology
April	*Profan*, first issue published by Don Tuck and others in Hobart
April	*Spaceward* first issue published by Vol Molesworth for the FFA
13-Apr	Second Sydney SF Conference
August	Arthur Duncan joined the FSS
12-Aug	*Science and Fantasy Fan Reporter* first issue published by Colin Roden and others
9-Nov	FSS second anniversary meeting, Molesworth called for a Court of Inquiry
5-Dec	Don Tuck relocated to Melbourne

7-Dec	Pacific War began
28-Dec	FSS Court of Inquiry first sitting
30-Dec	*Melbourne Bulletin*, final issue published by Warwick Hockley

1942

January	Currawong published its first SF novel by J W Hemming
4-Jan	Third Sydney SF Conference
February	*Futurian Digest*, sole issue published by Vol Molesworth for FSS
3-Feb	Soldier's Relief Fund established by FSS
July	*Futuruan Spotlight*, first issue published by Vol Molesworth and Graham Stone
September	*Ultra*, final issue published
September	FAA Bulletin, sole issue published by Colin Roden for the FFA
20-Sep	FFA abandoned and Sydney fans created and joined the Southern Cross Futurian Association (SCFA)
5-Nov	FSS Third Anniversary meeting, J W Hemming Guest of Honour
24-Nov	FSS dissolved, most Sydney fans joined the SCFA

1943

Hemming took control of the SCFA and changed it so several fans subsequently resigned. Stone attempted to establish a SF Section without success.

1944

FSS revived by a small group. After dissenting ideas it was resolved to postpone further activity until after the war.

1947

9-Aug	FSS, first meeting on revival
September	*The Sydney Futurian*, first issue published
late	Contact established with Ken Slater in Britain who became a first source of British and American SF
December	FSS renamed 'Futurian Society' to admit members outside Sydney

1948

March	FSS reverted to original name
April	FSS experiments with meeting in a restaurant (may have been in May)
10-Jun	FSS first Thursday Night meeting, initially at the Quality Inn

November	FSS unable to participate in World SF League due to government restrictions on sending money overseas
7-Nov	FSS ninth anniversary party attended by eight

1949

	US Convention voted $100 be spent on books for the FSS Library
April	FSS, lack of interests, minutes of meetings no longer recorded
August	Thursday Night meetings moved to the Mariposa after the Quality Inn closed
October	FSS emphasized difference in roles between the Society and the Thursday Night Group

1950

March	*Thrills Incorporated*, first issue published
May	FSS virtually defunct, Director Nick Solntseff had most of the responsibilities
June	Meeting of Sydney fans recommends the FSS be wound up
June	FSS Library Trust established separately to look after the FSS library
August	*Woomera*, first issue published by Nick Solntseff
13-Aug	FSS meeting, had four full members but decided to maintain minimum operations
September	Vol Molesworth bought a printing press and registered the business name 'Futurian Press'
29-Oct	Futurian Press launched with Checklist of Australian Fantasy
November	*Star Rover*, sole issue published by Roger Dard

1951

February	Australian SF Society (ASFS) formed by Graham Stone
March	*Science Fiction Courier*, first issue published by Graham Stone for the ASFS
1-Jul	Fourth Sydney SF Conference, resolved to create a SF organization in Sydney and hold a convention
July	FSS revived, monthly meetings held separate from the Thursday Night Group
July	FSS Library Trust renamed the Australian Fantasy Foundation
October	*Stopgap*, first issue published by Graham Stone for the ASFS
December	*Telepath*, first issue published by Arthur Haddon

1952

22-Mar	First Australian SF Convention, organized in Sydney by the FSS
April	*Vertical Horizons*, first issue published by the Femme Fan Group
April	*Notes and Comments*, first issue published by Vol Molesworth and Ken Martin
1-Apr	North Shore Futurian Society (NSFS) established
9-May	Race Mathews organized the first meeting of Melbourne fans, Melbourne SF Group (MSFC) formed as a result
5-Jun	Thursday Night Group first gathering at the Sydney Bridge Club
19-Jun	Fifth Sydney SF Conference, began planning the Second convention
August	FSS disagreement about the future of the Australian Fantasy Foundation
14-Aug	MSFC held its first fortnightly meeting at Val's Coffee Lounge
September	*Forerunner*, first issue published by Doug Nicholson
October	*NSFS Notesheet*, first issue published by Michael Bos for the NSFS
October	*S-F Review*, first issue published by Rex Meyer
14-Nov	MSFC moved its meetings to the Oddfellows Hall basement
24-Nov	Brisbane fans met with a view to holding regular meetings
December	*Ugh*, first issue published by Bill Veney
17-Dec	Futurian Court of Inquiry, second sitting

1953

January	*Science Fiction News*, first issue published by Graham Stone
February	MSFC began meeting weekly on Thursday evenings
February	*Perhaps* first issue published by Lee Harding
14-Feb	Brisbane SF group decided to hold regular meetings
1-Mar	*Etherline*, first issue published by Ian Crozier
April	*Bacchanalia*, first issue published by Race Mathews
April	*Terrific*, sole issue published by D Kenyon for the NSFS
May	*Futurian Society News*, first issue published by Brian Finch for the FSS
1-3 May	Second Australian SF Convention, held in Sydney by the FSS
25-May	Wally Judd elected to organise third Australian convention

June	*Wastebasket*, first issue published by Lee Harding
June	*Future Science Fiction and Popular Science Fiction* launched
July	Joyce Joyce convened meeting of Adelaide fans to form a group
27-Jul	FSS, Molesworth elected Director at AGM
8-9 August	Albury fan get-together, called the Riverina Conference
August	Lee Harding expelled from AFPA
August	*Question Mark*, first issue published by AFPA
October	Science Fiction Drama Club (Arcturian Players) formed
19-Oct	FSS meeting resolved to rent property adjacent to Taylors Square for clubroom
8-Nov	Futurian Society of Canberra (FSC) first meeting
3-Dec	FSS Clubroom at Taylors Square opened
23-Dec	FSS elected Graham Stone as Clubroom Executive

1954

8-Feb	FSS meeting censured executive over management
25-Feb	Heinlein visited FSS clubroom
28-Feb	FSS debate attempted to resolve split in membership, unsuccessfully
March	Don Tuck's *A Handbook of Science Fiction and Fantasy* ready for distribution
1-Apr	Blue Centaur Books and some Futurians returned to the Sydney Bridge Club for Thursday group meetings
17-18 April	Third Australian SF Convention, held in Sydney by the FSS
14-May	FSC began holding film nights
19-May	Adelaide SF Group launched
July	AFPA took over publication of *Bacchanalia*
1-Jul	*Scansion*, first issue published by Doug Nicholson
5-Jul	FSS meeting, Graham Stone elected Director
July	'No Sydney Convention for 1955' published by Graham Stone
September	Brisbane SF Group began meeting in the home of Betty and George Tafe
4-Nov	FSS Fifteenth anniversary meeting
December	Mountain District SF Club formed
3-Dec	Inaugural meeting of the Western Suburbs branch of the FSS
11-Dec	Arcturian Players performance at the Bondi School of Arts
30-Dec	Arthur C Clarke spoke in the FSS Clubroom

1955

	Arthur C Clarke visited Australia between January and August
6-Feb	FSS meeting, Bluey Glick fails to heal the rift
13-Feb	FSS meeting to discuss the future of the clubrooms
18-20 March	Fourth Australian SF Convention, held in Sydney by the NSFS
4-Apr	Conference held to resolve the fracture in Sydney fandom
10-Apr	Albion Futurian Society, inaugural meeting
21-Apr	*Etherline* announced the death of organized Sydney fandom
2-Jun	FSS leaves its Taylor Square clubroom
May	*Australian Fantasy & Science Fiction* launched
July	*Future and Popular SF* stopped publication
September	*SF Monthly* launched
October	MSFC moved from the Oddfellows Hall to 168 Lennox Street, Richmond
October	Blue Centaur Books acquired the NSFS library
14-Dec	FSS, last meeting until 1959

1956

	A Bertram (Bert) Chandler relocated to Australia
	Antipodes, first issue published by Lee Harding
	MC² first issue published by Peter Jefferson and Roger Sebel
April	*Extant*, first issue published by Michael Bladwin and Bill Hubble
Easter	Canberra, fan gathering called Can-Con
8-9 December	Fifth Australian SF Convention, 'Olympicon', held in Melbourne by the MSFC

1957

February	*SF Monthly*, final issue
April	MSFC moved to St James Building in Little Collins Street

1958

5-6 April	Sixth Australian SF Convention, held in Melbourne by MSFC

1959

Australian SF Newsletter, first issue published by Merv Binns
Australian Government lifted restrictions on importing American books and magazines
Ballarat SF group formed

early	MSFC moved to 25 McKillop Street
September	101st and final issue of *Etherline* published
September	American prozines began appearing in Australian shops again
September	Stone announced the FSS would represent the International SF Society in Australia and the ASFS would be retired
5-Nov	FSS, Twentieth anniversary meeting attended by three
late	*Notes and Comments*, first issue published by Graham Stone

1960

April	Blue Centaur Books ceased the Thursday Night Group gatherings
3-May	Sydney Thursday Night Group began meeting on Tuesday
May	*Scansion* revived by Pat Burke
November	Australian Government introduced the 'Credit Squeeze'

1961

November	MSFC moved to 19 Somerset Place

1963

	FSS, first meeting since 1959, attended by three
August	Graham Stone moved to Canberra

1964

	Australian SF Association (ASFA) established by Graham Stone

1965

September	*The Journal of the Australian Science Fiction Association*, first issue published by Graham Stone for the ASFA

1968

April	Graham Stone and the ASFA mentioned in the *Australian Science Fiction Review*

1969

January	*Science Fiction News*, second series first issue published by Graham Stone for the ASFA
29-Nov	Informal FSS reunion

1975

Graham Stone returned to Sydney

SOURCES

The following list includes all the sources used in writing this history but not every source viewed while researching it. Consequently, not all issues of all the fanzines and other fannish sources consulted are listed here and other researchers might find it convenient to consult complete runs of fanzines of interest rather than only the ones listed here.

Monographs

Binns, Merv, 'Confessions of a science fiction fan' printed separately but perhaps reprinted from an issue of *Interstellar Ramjet Scoop*.

Harding, Lee, 'I Remember AFPA', *Boys Own Fanzine* 3, since reprinted in *iOTA* 13.

Jenssen, Dick, 'CSIRAC and Science Fiction', printed separately but probably reprinted from *Interstellar Ramjet Scoop*.

Jenssen, Dick, 'My Life in SF Fandom', printed separately but probably reprinted from *Interstellar Ramjet Scoop*. Reprinted in *iOTA* 13.

Jenssen, Dick,, 'What Science Fiction has Meant to Me of the specific generalized', printed separately but probably reprinted from *Interstellar Ramjet Scoop*.

Mathews, Race, 'Whirlaway to Thrilling Wonder Stories; Boyhood reading in wartime and postwar Melbourne', paper presented for the Nova Mob on 7 September 1994. Since reprinted several times including *iOTA* 13.

Molesworth, Vol, *A history of Australian science fiction Fandom 1935-1963*, first published in full in *The Mentor* and separately by Ron Clarke in 1980, reprinted in 1995-95 and reprinted by Graham Stone, 2009.

Fanzines

Antipodes, 2

ASFS Circular to Members, undated, 19 June 1953, 20 August 1953, September 1953, 21

Austra Fantasy, 1, 2, 3, 4, 6, 7, 8, 9

Australian Fan News, 1

Australian SF Newsletter, 1, 3 May 1959, December 1960, 7 July 1961, September 1961, January 1962, April 1962, April 1966

Australian Science Fiction Review, 15

Bacchanalia, 1

Contact, 4, 8

Cosmos, 1, 2, 3, 4, 5, 6, 7, 8, 9, 10 2/1, 2/2, 13

Etherline, 1, 5, 8, 10, 11, 12, 13, 15, 16, 17, 18, 19, 20, 21, 25, 26, 27, 28, 29, 30, 31, 32, 33, 34, 35, 36, 37. 39, 40, 41, 42, 43, 44, 45, 46, 47, 48, 49, 50, 51, 53, 54, 55, 56, 57, 59, 62, 63, 64, 66, 68, 69. 70, 72, 73, 74, 75, 76, 80, 84, 85, 92, 94, 99, 100, 101

Extant, 1, 2, 3, 4

Fantasy Times (Science Fiction Times), 132, 179, 216, 219, 221, 222, 223, 229, 236, 237, 239, 241, 243, 245, 246, 250, 251, 253, 256, 258, 261, 263, 265, 267, 269, 273, 274, 278, 279, 282, 293A, 294, 301, 305A, 317, 324, 326, 331, 335a, 341

Fanzine Year Book, 1943

Forerunner, 1, 2

Futurian Observer, 1, 3, 4, 5, 7, 8, 9, 10, 11, 12, 13, 14, 15, 16, 17, 18, 19, 20, 21, 21 Extra, 22, 23, 24, 25, 26, 29, 30, 31, 32, 33, 34, 35, 36, 37, 38, 40, 42, 43

Futurian Society News, 2, 3, 4, 5, 6, 7, 8, 9, 14, 15, 16, 17, 18 19, 22

Futurian War Digest, 3/5

Journal of the Australian SF Association, 1/1, 1/8, 1/5, 1/10

Le Zombie, 23, 24, 25, 27, 28 29, 30, 31, 33, 34, 35, 36, 37, 38, 45

Luna, 2, 3

MC², 1, 2

Melbourne Bulletin, 2, 3, 4, 5, 6, 6a, 7, 8, 9

Mumblings from Munchkinland, 1, 2, 12, 13. 14, 15, 16, 17, 22, 23, 24, 26, 27, 28, 29, 30, 31, 32, 33, 34

The New Millenial Harbinger, 5

North Shore Futurian Society Notesheet, 1, 3, 4, 6, 7

Notes & Comments, 1, 2

Operation Fantast, 12, 16, 17, 1/3, 1/4, 1/6, 1/10, 1/12

Perhaps, 1, 2

Profan, 1, 2, 3

Science Fantasy News, 15

Science Fiction News, 1, 2, 3, 4, 5, 6, 7, 8, 9, 10, 11, 12, 14, 19, 23, 24

Science Fiction News (second series), 1, 4, 13, 16, 23, 27, 31, 32, 38, 39, 41, 48, 50, March 1969, June 1969, July 1969, August 1969, September 1969, November 1969, September 1970, January 1971

Science Fiction Parade, 5

Science Fiction World, 2, 3

S-F Review, 4, 5, 6, 8, 9, 10, 11

Spaceways, 4, 9

Star Rover, 1

Stopgap, 2, 10, 11, May-June 1951, December 1951, January 1951, January 1952, February 1952, March-April 1952, May-June 1952, February 1953

The Sydney Futurian, 1, 2, 3, 4, 5, 6, 7, 8, 9, 10, 11, 12, 13, 14, 15

Sydney Futurian News, 1

Telefan, 1

Telepath, 1, 2

Terrific, 1

Trial and Error, 3

Scansion, 1, 2, 3, 4, 5, 6, 8, 9, 11. 12, 13. 14. 15, 18, 21, 22, 23, 24, 25, 26, 27, 27(B), 28, 32, 33, 34, 36, 37, 41, 3/1, 3/2

Science Fiction & Fantasy Reporter, 1, 2, 3, 4, 5, 6, 7, 8, 9, 10, 11, 12, 13, 14, 15, 16, 17, 18, 19, 20, 21, 22, 23, 24, 25, 26, 27, 28, 34

Ugh, c.1947, 1, 2, 3

Ultra, 1, 2, 3, 4, 5, 6, 2/1, 2/4, 2/5, 2/6 3/1, 3/2

Vertical Horizons, 1, 2, 3, 4, 5

Voice of the Imagi-Nation, 4, 5, 8, 9, 10, 15, 16, 16a, 19, 20, 23, 24, 27, 34, 44

Wastebasket, 1, 2 (first version), 2 (second version), 3

Woomera, 1 (August 1950), 1 (February 1951), 2, 3, 4

Zeus, 1, 2, 3, 4, 5, 6

(Pseudo) Zeus, 1, 3

Oral History Interviews

Mervyn Binns

Lee Harding

Dick Jenssen

Doug Nicholson

Bill Wright

Other Sources

ASFS Membership List, January 1954

Commonwealth of Australia Yearbook, 1955

Panel discussions recorded at Continuum 13 (2017) and Continuum 14 (2018) in Melbourne

INDEX

2001: A Space Odyssey (Kubrick) 191–2
5000 Fingers of Dr T (Rowland) 108

Abbott and Costello Go To Mars 128
Ackerman, Forry 20, 32, 46, 167, 178
Adams, John 157, 158
Adelaide 83, 84, 95, 97, 152, 196
Adelaide fans 94, 126
    1940 29
    1950s 155
    1953 84
    Futurian Society Constitution and 126
    traded magazines and 33
Adelaide Science Fiction Group 164, 166, 176
    fourth anniversary gathering 163
    report 1954 135
    success during 1950s 155–7
adolescents, Sydney Futurians as 27
aims, Sydney Futurians 1940 28, 34–5
Albion Futurian Society, launch and disappearance 1955 146, 188
Albury Conference 1953 127
Amateur Fantasy Publications of Australia (AFPA) 111, 119, 120, 164, 168, 183
    Crozier's plans 114
    display panel at Olympicon 175
    disputes about 166
    financial limitations 113
    Gregor and 157
    Harding and 114, 117, 118
    publications 133
    Roneo 500 duplicator 113, 119, 164, 165, 166, 168, 171, 185, 186
Amazing Stories 10, 11, 14, 15, 16, 29, 33, 48, 64, 104, 106, 168
    letter column 12, 13
American conventions, Australian fans and 96
American culture, Australia and 7
American fanzines
    Harding and 117
    Australia fanzines and 36
American prozines 68
    availability in Australia after 1959 184

Futurian Society library and 66, 138
 Melbourne fans and 168
 Slater as supplier 104
American reprints, Australian SF magazines 1950s 122
American Science Fiction 152
Anderson, John 90
Angus and Robertson, science fiction titles on sale 88
anti-communism 1950s 122–3
anti-discrimination motion, Futurian Society 1952 92
Antipodes 119–20, 163
ANZUS Pact 1951 122–3
Arcturian Players 128, 135, 141, 145
Artists Ball 1953 126–7
artwork, *Etherline* 167
assistant librarians, Melbourne Science Fiction Group 169
Associate Members, Sydney Futurians 188, 190
Astounding 12, 14, 19, 64, 104, 119, 153, 161, 162, 184
Astounding (BRE edition) 33, 76
Astronomical society, Ballarat 184
atomic bomb testing, Australia 1953 121
attendance
 First Sydney (Austalian) SF Convention 1952 78
 Melbourne Science Fiction Group 1952 107
 North Shore Futurian Society 1954 139
 Sixth Australian SF Convention 182
auctions
 First Australian Science Fiction Convention 79
 Fourth Australian (Sydney) convention 1955 145
 Melbourne meetings 169
 Olympicon 174, 176
 Second Australian (Sydney) SF Convention 1953 96
 Third Australian (Sydney) SF Convention 133
Aussiecon 4 2010 3
Aussiecon 1975 3, 4, 7
Aussie Fans: Uniquely placed in Global Popular Culture (Lamd & Raphael) 9
Austra Fantasy 21, 42, 44, 46, 47
Australia: A Cultural History (Rickard) 7
Australasian Post 164, 168
Australia
 Korean War and 121
 story telling and 5–8
Australian Army, fans and 59, 105, 158, 170
Australian Atomic Energy Commission 121
Australian cultural history 7
Australian Fan Directory 1950 66
Australian Fan News 17, 18
Australian fandom 1941–1945 40–60

end of 1950s 184
membership 1953 152
membership 1940 29
proposed World Science Fiction League and 68
Australian Fantasy Foundation (AFF) 75, 77, 85
disputes about 1952–53 92
Australian Labor Party (ALP), anti-communism and 123
Australian National Library, Stone at 190
Australian politics early 1950s 100
Australian press, science fiction stories published in 63
Australian Science Fiction Association (ASFA) 191
Stone and 194, 196, 198
Australian Science Fiction Book Reviews 1969-1972 (Stone) 196
Australian Science Fiction Index 1939–1962 (Stone) 196
'Australian Science Fiction News Limited' 51
Australian Science Fiction Newsletter (Binns) 177, 183
Australian science fiction writers 160
Australian Security Intelligence Organisation (ASIO) 123
Australian Science Fiction News (ASFN) 185
Australian Science Fiction News (ASFN) (Second Series) 196–8
Australian science fiction publishers 63, 152
Australian Science Fiction Review (ASFR) 120. 193, 194
Australian Science Fiction Society (ASFS) 75, 83, 90, 128, 141, 142, 154, 189–90
Bangsund and 193–4
beginnings 1951 74–5
directory 110
future directions 1954 135
Melbourne agency 105
membership analysis by state 1954 126
membership increase 1952 77
policy 96
report 1954 135–6
S-F Review and 127
Stone and 191
Australian War Memorial 148
Australian Women's Weekly 94
Authentic 110
'Author Listings' (Tuck) 167

Bacchanalia 111, 114, 117, 118
'Balance of Power' (Hemming), production 1956 175–6
Baldwin, Mike 139, 146, 147, 149, 151, 167, 176
fiction writing 149
Ballarat 88, 184
Bangsund, John, Stone and 193–4
banned members' lists 1954 143–4
Banning, Lex (John Hilbery) 63, 76, 78, 79, 92, 128, 151

personality 89
verse 88
barbecues, Melbourne fans' 170
Barnett Street 106
Barrett, Mervyn 184
Bathurst expedition 1953 85
Baxter, John 151, 188, 195
Beginning of the End 133
BEMs (Bug Eyed Monsters) 164–5
Bennet, Betty 147
Bennet, Geoff 121, 126, 147, 153, 154, 155, 170
bibliographical work
    Stone's 189, 194, 195
    Tuck's 162–3, 191
Bicknell, Dan 108, 170, 171
Binns, Merv 8, 9, 101, 127, 108, 114, 118, 134, 147, 148, 153, 158, 164, 168, 169, 170, 171, 173, 174, 178
    Australian Fantasy Press Association and 114, 120
    Ballarat group and 184
    personality and career 103, 165, 183
    McGills and 106, 107, 185
    McKillop Street notice to quit and 186
    Melbourne SF Club and 182–3
    science fiction collection 104
    twenty-first birthday party 1955 170
'Biology in Science Fiction' (Meyer) 95
'Bizzyabody, Emma' 51
Blainey, Geoffrey 6
Blanks, Harvey 174
Blatt, John 129, 145
'Blinded They Fly' (Molesworth) 63, 64
Blue Centaur Books 124, 131, 133, 139, 149, 151, 153, 166, 167
Blue Mountains 86
Boggs, Redd 68
Bohman, Sherry 149
Bolte Government (Victoria) 1950s 100
Bondi School of Arts 141
Bonestell, Chesley 102
book-binding service, Latimer 167
book collectors 1950s 29, 64, 153
Book Collectors' Society 62
'Book of Futurian Law, The' (Molesworth) 57
book reviews
    Journal of the Australian Science Fiction Association 191
    Perhaps 2 114
    Science Fiction News 194
    Stone's 195–6

    Sydney 1953 81
        Wastebasket and 117
book sales, reduction during 1961 recession 185
book scarcity 1950s 31–2, 64
Booklist Of Australian Science Fiction (Stone) 191
bookshops, science fiction promotions 1950s 122
Boomerang 70
Borneo 61, 62
Bos, Michael 80, 126, 127, 134, 143, 144
Boyd, Raeburn 126
boys' magazines, British 11
Boys Own 11
Boys Own Fanzine 109, 118
Brick Bradford 101
Brick Moon, The 188
Brighton 38, 55, 81, 89, 96, 102, 107, 136, 152
Brisbane Courier-Mail 161
Brisbane fans 29, 57, 84, 94, 141
Brisbane Science Fiction Group 142, 157, 164, 166
    Arthur C Clarke visit 1954 158, 160
    monthly meetings 1950s 163
    report 1954 126
    report 1956 176
    report 1958 182
Brissenden, Bob 122
Bristow, Jack, Sixth Australian SF Convention and 180–1
Britain 160, 183
British book dealers, access 1952 68, 104
British boys' magazines 102
British fandom, Australian fandom and 14, 30, 46–7, 61, 68
British Fantasy Library 68
British postal links 66
British Reprint Edition (BRE) prozines 33, 56, 63, 104, 165
    Astounding 94, 153
    Binns and 169
    Dynamic 144
    US prozines and 153
    Sydney outlet 137
British science fiction 110, 153
Brook, Harry 84, 85, 94, 95, 96, 157, 158, 170
    Korean War and 121–2
Brown, Valma 9
Brunen, Harry 63, 76, 89, 129, 137, 141, 146
Bryning, Frank 84, 122, 157, 159, 160, 170, 176, 188
    fiction writer 88
    Guest of Honour, Olympicon 1956 174
Buck Rogers comic strips, science fiction as 101, 103

'bughouse books' 12
Bulletin for the Futurian Federation of Australia 55
Burke, Pat 97, 125, 129, 139, 141, 143, 144, 147, 148, 149, 151
Burlington Hotel 142
business acumen, Crozier 113, 166
business session
    Albury Conference 1953 127
    First Australian (Sydney) Science Fiction Convention 79
    Fourth Australian (Sydney) Convention 1955 145–6, 149
    Olympicon 1956 176
    Second Australian (Sydney) SF Convention 1953 96–7
    Sixth Australian SF Convention 182
    Third Australian (Sydney) SF Convention 135
Butt, Ted 96, 97, 146, 161, 170

Campbell, Bert 110
Campbell, John W 99, 158
Canada 89, 183
Canadian fans, Australian fans and 68
Canberra 152, 170, 190
    Australian Capital Territory, ASFS members 1954 126
Canberra Conference (Can-Con) 1956 147, 149, 166
Canberra fans 125, 126, 153–4
Canberra Futurian Society 155, 156
Canberra road system 147
Carnell, E J (Ted) 68, 104
Carter, Lin 196
Castellari, Bert 8, 20, 12, 16, 17, 18, 21, 22, 25, 33, 34, 35, 37, 38, 39, 40, 41, 43, 46, 47, 48, 49, 50, 51, 53, 55, 57, 59, 61, 62, 64, 109, 195
    socialism and 26, 27
Castellari, Roma 21, 28
Cat Creeps, The 127
censorship
    booksellers and 153
    film imports and 1953 108–9
    Melbourne 1950s 99
    pulp magazine imports and 12 101
    World War 2 30
censure motion, Sydney (Australian) SF Convention 1954 committee and 130
Chandler, A Bertram (Bert) 14, 77, 84, 101, 108, 126, 170
    career and relocation to Sydney 160–1
Chapman, Ken 68, 104
Checklist of Anthologies, A (Tuck 1959) 163
Checklist of Australian Fantasy (Lanarch) 63, 64, 73
chess matches
    Futurian Society 1954 138, 170
    Melbourne SF Club 169, 180

Chevron Night Club 100
Chicago worldcon 1940 23, 35, 46
Chicon II 163
China, Communist government 121
Christmas Party 1955 149
Chums 11
Cincinnati convention 1949, Australian fandom and 68
cinema, Melburnians during 1950s 99, 100
City and the Stars, The (Clarke) 160
Clarke, Arthur C, visit to Australia 1954 138, 145, 158–60, 161
clubrooms
    Melbourne SF Group 164, 183
    Sydney Futurians 128
club reports, Third Sydney (Australian) SF Convention 135
club fanzines 35, 36, 127
Cockcroft, Tom 74, 84, 142, 162
Cohen, Dave 66, 95, 96, 97, 110, 112, 116, 124, 131, 133, 139, 143, 149, 151, 153, 168, 184
    Thursday Night Group finances and 140
Cold War 1950s, science fiction fans and 121–2
colour duplicating 44, 45, 114
Comedy Theatre 100
comic strips and books, science fiction 102, 103
Commonwealth government and public service jobs, Canberra 154
Commonwealth of Australia Yearbook 1955 152
Commune 2000 AD (Reynolds), Stone review of 197
Communist Party Dissolution Act referendum 123
Communist Party of Australia 100
Connell, Alan 12, 14, 24, 30, 40, 56
conservatives governments, Australia 1950s 100, 123
conservative values, Melbourne early 1950s 99
constitution 1953, FSS 123
    Adelaide SF Society 1954 156
    Futurian Society disputes and 50, 65, 125
Convention Dinner (Mayfair), First Australian Science Fiction Convention 79
Convention proposal 1951 75
Convention report, Olympicon 178
Coogee 36, 37, 73
Coolangatta 29, 38, 127, 157, 158, 160
    Arthur C. Clarke visit 159
copyright restrictions, American books and Australia 184
Cordner, Alan 39, 47, 48, 49–50
corflu 110, 114
Cosmos 12, 20–1, 23, 36–7, 43, 44, 45
cost, prozines 1940 33, 34
'Court of Inquiry' (Molesworth) 52–3, 57, 93

Court-appointed lawyer 1952 93
Crane, Lyell 83, 84, 89, 95, 97, 109, 121, 124, 125, 127, 128, 129, 133, 135, 136
    unification aims 90, 96
Creature from the Black Lagoon 143
Crozier, Ian 94, 95, 97, 116, 126, 127, 133, 135, 144, 147, 158, 163, 164, 168, 169, 170, 171, 172, 173, 174, 180, 182
    attempt to resolve Sydney disputes and 146
    Etherline and 114, 118, 120, 166–7, 178
    personality and career 113, 117, 166, 182
    Stone's pamphlet 1954 and 137
CSIRAC, Jenssen and 119, 121
Cudden, R 48, 49
cultural life, Melbourne early 1950s 99
Cultural cringe 117
cultural studies, fandom studies and 6
Currawong Press 55–7
currency restrictions, international publications and 68
Customs seizures, overseas books and magazines 12, 87, 158, 162, 169

Dandenong Ranges 180
Dard, Roger 14, 66, 71, 73, 74, 77, 83, 84, 105, 110, 112, 113, 114, 142, 162, 166
    AFPA and 111
    censorship difficulties 100, 162
    fan activity 1950s 161
    prozine letter columns and 105
    Harding and 109
dartboard, Melbourne SF Club 183–4
Davison, Christine 97, 128
Day the Earth Stood Still, The 145
Day, Rick 157, 173
debate, Sydney Futurians 1954 129
Denver World Convention 32, 46
Deverne, John, *see* Gregor, John
Devore, Howard 162
Dianetics, science fiction and 122, 157
Dick, 'Moby' 70
Dillon, Kevin 80, 84, 88, 109, 125, 129, 130, 139, 142, 147, 190
disputes
    Business Session Fourth Australian (Sydney) Convention 1955 146
    Sydney Futurians 28, 69, 130–1, 140–3
distribution difficulties, *Forerunner* 88
Dovaston, George 76, 126
Driscoll, Ian 77, 79
Duggan, Michael 134, 139, 142
Dunbar House 144
Duncan, Arthur (Arthur Haddon) 41, 44, 52, 53, 55, 58, 58, 59, 60
    See also Haddon, Arthur

Dunk, Sid 76, 78, 97
Dunstan, Keith, report on Brisbane fandom 161
duplicators
    beginnings 19–20
    difficulties 1941 52
    types of 42
Dwyer, Noel 14, 21, 22, 27, 37, 40, 43, 50, 54, 58, 62

Earls, John 129, 134, 136, 139
    career 149
early fiction, Lee Harding 103
earth orbiting satellite, Clarke and 145
Eastern Market 103
Edmonds, Leigh
    as historian 4–6
    Stone and 188
electrostencils. fanzines and 113, 114, 167
Elizabeth Street 11, 103, 153, 165, 186
Ellison, Harlan, Crozier's defence of 166
Etherline 94, 108, 116, 117, 118, 120, 122, 125, 126, 135, 137, 139, 140, 143, 145, 146, 147, 149, 153, 154, 155, 156, 157, 158, 159, 161, 162, 163, 170, 172, 173, 174, 176, 183
    Convention issue 1954 133
    final issue 1957 178–9
    Harding and 114, 115–16
    last issues 182
    planning for 114
    production values 166–7
    Stone and 193
    success 167–8
Evans, David 14, 21, 22, 24, 27, 30, 34–5, 36, 43, 45, 46, 48, 49, 55, 56, 59, 62
    Futurian Society Director 37–8
    reported suicide and departure from fandom 51
Extant 147, 149, 167

factions, Sydney Futurians 36, 58
Famous Fantastic Mysteries 68, 83, 105
fan correspondence 1939–1940, USA and 23
fan desertions, Sydney 1954 136
fancy dress balls, Australian conventions 126, 144
Fancyclopedia III 9
fandom
    beginnings 14
    Stone's attitudes to 81, 85, 128, 189, 192
    post World War 2 61
fandom studies 6, 12
fanmags 12
fannish fanzines
    Burke rejection of 151

sercon fanzines and 116–17, 187
Fanscient 111
Fantasia (Disney) 108
Fantast Medway 153
Fantasy and Science Fiction, The Magazine of 184
    Australian edition 152
Fantasy Book Service 68
Fantasy Impromptu 81
Fantasy News (Taurasi) 15
Fantasy Times 152, 168, 188
    Dard and 162
    Stone and 189
Fantasy War Bulletin 30
fanzines 12
    artwork 19, 42
    as primary sources 8
    as traded currency 1940 33
    factionalism and 1940 39
    improvements during 1941 42
    Melbourne attitudes to 166
    post-war Sydney fans and 73
    production difficulties 42, 44–5, 81
    New Zealand 184
    restrictions during World War 2 55
    statistics 1939–1950 23
    Stone's attitudes to 192–3
    Sydney 1941 50–1
    Sydney 1953 127
    Sydney 1954 141
    Sydney Futurians and 28, 36
    trading 1940 23
Federation Hall 133
Femme Fan Group 80, 85, 96
Ferntree Gully North High School 182
fiction content, Australian fanzines 1940 24, 168
fiction markets
    lack of during 1940s 24
    Zeus 43
Fifth Sydney Conference 1952 93–4
Film Collection and Services, National Library of Australia 196
Film Exhibitors' Association 172
film programs
    Australian SF Association 191
    Canberra Futurian Society 1955 155
    First Sydney (Australian) Science Fiction Convention 79
    Futurian Society 1954 137–8
    Fourth Sydney (Australian) convention 145
    Melbourne SF Club at Somerset Place 178, 186
    Melbourne SF Group 1953 108, 171

Olympicon 1956 176–7
Second Sydney (Australian) SF Convention 1953 96
Sixth Australian SF Convention 182
Third Sydney (Australian) SF Convention 133
film-watching groups 143
financial arrangements, Thursday Night group 139–40
financial difficulties
    Olympicon 176
    Perhaps 113
    Sydney Futurians 1954 138, 143
    wartime fanzine publishing and 42
Finch, Brian 97, 125, 127, 129
Finch, Margaret 156
fire trap, Melbourne SF Clubrooms as 186
First Australian Science Fiction Convention (First Sydney SF Convention) 1952 76–9
first Moon landing 1969 195
First Staple War 19
Fisher, Lloyd 97, 139, 147, 148
Fitzroy 103, 106
Five Thousand Fingers of Dr T, The 176
Forbidden Planet 122
Forerunner 87–8, 96, 110
'Forerunner People, The' 131
formal Melbourne group, decision to establish 107
formal organisation, Stone's and Nicholson's belief in 140
formal program, Fourth Australian convention 1955 145
formality of meetings, Sydney Futurians 71
fortieth anniversary reunion, Sydney Futrians 1969 195
Fourth Australian Science Fiction Convention 1955 (Fourth Sydney Science Fiction Convention) 165
    Arthur C Clarke as Guest of Honour 158, 160
    preliminary plans 143
    success of 144–5
Fourth Sydney Science Fiction Conference 75
Foyster, John 150
Frankenstein meets the Wolf Man 127
Franklin's Lending Library 103, 104, 105, 169
Frederickson, Fred 97, 139, 147
Freedlander, Neville 27, 29, 35
FSS Circular (Stone) 190
Fullers Bridge barbecue 1953 126
fund raising
    Sydney convention 1954 and 124
    Olympicon and 173
Future 44, 50, 63
'Future of Man, The' 133
'Future of the Machine, The' 133

Future Science Fiction 122, 152, 188
future stories, science and 11
Futurian Fan Reporter (FFR) 43–4, 53, 55
Futurian Digest 55
Futurian Federation of Australia 44, 48, 49, 52
    mass resignations from 1942 58
Futurian News 128
Futurian Observer 20, 22–4, 28, 30, 31, 36, 37, 40, 43, 46, 48, 51, 112
    ceased publication 1942 55
    'print anything' policy 43
Futurian Press 63, 64, 73, 77, 93
Futurian Society of Australia proposal 35, 154, 187
Futurian Society of Canberra 125–6, 154, 176
    report 1954 135
Futurian Society News (FSN) 70, 125, 126, 127, 129, 137, 138, 142
Futurian Society New York 25
Futurian Society of Sydney (FSS) 8, 50–1, 53, 73, 90, 91, 195, 142, 169, 176
    1939–1940 25–39
    1941 47–8
    1948 69
    aims and new constitution 1946 64–5
    Annual General Meeting 1954 137
    Arthur C Clarke visit 1954 158
    Australian SF Association and 191
    Canberra and 154
    change of name 1947 69
    clubroom plans 1953 128
    collapse 1949 71, 72, 74, 190
    convention organising and 135
    disputes within 1954 91, 123
    dissolution 1942 58–9
    factions 1942 58
    Fantasy Foundation and 1953 93
    Fourth Australian convention and 144
    fortieth anniversary reunion 1969 195
    hoaxes 1941 51
    interest level 1940 34
    leadership 188
    library 72, 88, 96, 123–4, 153.
    library 1958 182
    Library Trust 72, 75
    meetings 1953 84
    meetings degeneration 1942 57–8
    Melbourne fans and 107, 172
    Melbourne fans and 1954 137
    membership 1940 25–6, 27
    membership survey 1952 89
    Molesworth and 57, 125
    name resumption 1943 60
    ninth anniversary 1948 70

North Shore Futurian Society and 80
organisational difficulties 1954 130–1
parties 1952 85
plans 1954 129
police investigation of 57
post-Convention meeting 1952 79
post World War 2 61
reorganisation proposal 92
report 1954 135
revival 1951 75, 77
science fiction and 86, 192
serious attitudes to science fiction 1952 85
social life 1954 142
suspension 1940 38
Sydney Bridge Club room ban and 144
tape recording and 121
third birthday celebration 58
Thursday Night Group and 139, 141
twentieth anniversary 190
western suburbs plan 1954 138–9
See also Vol Molesworth; Graham Stone
Futurian Spotlight 55, 58
Futurian War Digest 55

Galaxy 87, 89, 119, 153, 184
Garie Beach barbecue 1952 85
Geppen, Bob 44, 54, 65, 83, 84
Gernsback, Hugo 11, 15
Gerrand, Rob 9
gifted prozines, import prohibitions and 1940 32
Gilbert, C, fiction 88
Giles, Loralie 126, 127, 128, 129, 136, 170
    Glick and 90
    wedding 1955 170
Gillespie, Bruce 9
Gillings, Walter 14
Girvan, Iris 157, 158
Glick, Phinneas ('Bluey') 66, 69, 70, 72, 76, 95, 97, 125, 129, 136, 139, 144, 170
    Lorelie Giles and 90
    Sydney fandom feud and 1954 143
    wedding 1955 170
global fan organisation, aim to establish 68
'God in the Marijuana Patch' (Baldwin) 149
Gordon, Speed ('Flash') 11
Gordon and Gotch 165
Graham, Ron 14
Grand View Hotel 86
Great Barrier Reef, Arthur Clarke visit 1954 138, 155, 158, 160
Great Depression, Futurian aims and 25–6

Gregor, John (John Deverne) 14, 17, 18, 84, 157
Grigg, David 9
Grimwade House 105
GUOOF Building 75, 77, 95, 128
Gurney, John 157, 158, 170

Haddon, Arthur (Arthur Duncan) 12, 41, 65, 66, 68, 73–4, 75, 76, 86, 92, 98, 125, 134, 139, 142, 143, 144, 146, 173
    business session 1954 and 135
    career 149
    Diana Wilkes and 90
    dispute with Stone 1952 93
    fund-raising social activities and 142
    Second Sydney Science Fiction Convention 1953 and 94, 95
Handbook of Science Fiction and Fantasy, A (Tuck 1954) 84, 145, 162–3
hand typesetting, early Sydney professional publishing and 64
Hanley's 104, 106
Hannan, Jack 48, 53
hard-cover books, scarcity 1950s 63
Harding, Lee (Leo) 8, 9, 74, 101, 106, 108, 112, 113, 119, 149, 161, 163, 166, 168, 169, 172, 183
    Crozier and 120
    departure from Australian Fantasy Publishing Association 118, 166
    fanzine publishing 109–10, 116–17
    interstate and international connections 109
    Mathews and 105
    Operation Fantast and 104–5
    Perhaps production difficulties and 110–12, 114
    personality and career 102–3, 106, 117, 119
    science fiction collecting 1950s 104
    Stone and 105, 116
Harding, Ralph 29, 66, 83, 161
haven of safety and peace, MSFC meetings as 183
Hawthorn Football Club Supporters Club. 182
hectography 74, 142
Heinlein, Robert 121
    Sydney visit 1954 129, 138, 160
Hemming, J W 56, 58
Hemming, Norma 59, 63, 85, 89, 80, 81, 92, 122, 135, 144, 145, 146, 160, 174, 175–6, 188
    fancy dress ball and 126
    fiction writing 88
    playwright 128, 141, 176
Her Majesty's Theatre 100
Hermes 22
Heron, Bruce 118, 168, 172
Hewitt, William E 15, 16
Hilbery, John (Lex Banning) 63

Hiroshima bombing 62
history of technology, definition 4
History of Australian Science Fiction Fandom, A (Molesworth) 28, 63, 71, 130, 192
'History of Culture, The' 133
hoaxes, Sydney fans 1941 51
Hobart 44, 54, 152, 173
    Tuck and 83
Hockley, Pam 60
Hockley, Warwick ('Wog') 14, 21, 22, 29, 30, 40, 41, 42, 43, 44, 45–6, 50, 51, 52, 55, 60, 61, 62, 65, 105, 106, 164
    Tuck visit to Melbourne and 54
Hooper, Keith 21, 22, 27, 37
Horwitz, science fiction publishing 195–6
hospitality providers, fandom and 106, 107, 161
Hubble, Bill 94, 97, 127, 134, 135, 139, 141, 143, 144, 146, 147, 148, 149
Hubble, Tom 139
Hunter River Futurian Society 1954 126, 161
hydraulic lift, Somerset Place 186
Hyphen 83, 109

If 184
ill health, fans affected by 38–9
Imaginative Stories 29
immigration program, beginnings 1950s 100
import restrictions
    American science fiction publications 12, 62, 86–7, 152, 169, 183
    Australian fandom and 31
    lifted 1959 151, 184, 185
inclusiveness, Melbourne fandom 1950s 106
Index to British Science Fiction Magazines 1934–1953 (Stone) 190, 196
individual fannish action, belief in 140
informal structure
    Melbourne Science Fiction Group 107
    Thursday Night Group 71
Intelligence Department (Army) 41
international air mail service beginning 1947 66
international contacts, disappearance late 1950s 184
international distributor contacts, Binns and 183
international fandom
    Australia as third branch 46
    MC^2 and 149
    Melbourne fans and 109, 110
international reception
    Perhaps 1 113
    Etherline 168
International Reply Coupons or Money Orders 87
international science fiction, Baxter and 151

International SF Society, Sydney Futurians and 189–90
Interstate Advisory Committee, Olympicon 173
interstate visitors, Melbourne SF Group and 170
Iron Curtain, Australia and 121
isolation, science fiction fandom and 6–7

Japan 68, 105, 108, 158, 170
J C Williamson Company 100
Jefferys, Ken 18, 28, 55
Jenssen, Dick (Ditmar) 1, 8, 9, 101, 105, 106, 107, 108, 112, 113, 114, 118, 149, 166, 167, 169, 170, 172, 183
    as writer 110
    fanzine publishing and illustration skills 109–11, 119
    Harding and 106
    Perhaps production difficulties and 111
    personality and career 102, 118–19
Jones, Larry 175, 181
Journal of the Australian Science Fiction Association (Stone) 191–2, 193, 194
Joyce, Joyce 94, 95, 97, 126, 155, 156–7, 163
Judd, Wally 125, 129, 130, 136
    organiser of Sydney conventions 96, 97, 98, 124
Junior Australian Science Fiction Correspondence Club (JASFCC) 17–18
Junior Science Club 18

Katinka Library 77, 79, 91
Keating, Jack 106, 147, 158, 170, 173, 174, 175
Kemp, Norm 156
King, Terry 97, 139
'King's Cross Ludo, Science Fiction and Glee Club' 95
Kirby, Gordon 106, 107
Korean War 1950 121, 174
Krakatit: An Atomic Fantasy (Capek) 96
Kruger National Park 155

La Costa, Charles 15, 16, 27, 34, 35, 39, 40, 48, 49, 50, 97
Ladies Committee, Thursday Night Group 124
La Motte, Eric 172, 173
Lanarch, Stan 63, 65, 66, 72, 73, 93
Latimer, Don 147, 148, 158, 170, 172, 183, 186
    bookbinding service 167
Launceston 81, 89
Lawson, Don 76, 78, 96, 97, 125, 127, 128, 129
    as film projectionist 91, 124
Leggett, Jack 96, 97, 124, 125, 126, 128, 129, 146
Lennon, Harold 66, 70
Lennox Street clubrooms 1955 171

lesbian and gay community, Val's Coffee Lounge and 107
'Let There Be Monsters' (Molesworth) 63
letter columns
    letterzines and 20
    Perhaps 1 112
    pulp magazines 12, 14
Levy, Ron 21, 25, 27, 29, 33, 34, 35, 38, 39, 43, 46, 47, 48, 50, 49, 51, 58, 59, 62
    Court of Inquiry and 53
Le Zombie (Tucker) 19, 20, 23, 46
libraries
    Futurian Society of Sydney 65, 93
    Melbourne SF Club 169
    North Shore Futurians versus Futurian Society 131
Lincoln Coffee Lounge 90, 149
live theatre, Melbourne 1950s 100
Living Dead, The (Hemming) 56
location difficulties, Taylor Square clubrooms 129
Lovecraft, H P 114
Lucian Books 188
Luna 20, 23
Lyell, Graham 147, 148, 175, 181

McCarthyist movement (US) 123
Macoboy, Sterling 59–60, 65, 66, 70, 71, 72, 92, 129, 136
    arrival of television and 121
McCubbin, Bob 84, 101, 108, 110, 114, 120, 127, 134, 136, 147, 149, 158, 164, 168, 169, 171, 172, 173, 178, 180, 181, 183, 184
    final address Olympicon 1956 176
    first meeting room of Melbourne SF Group and 107
    informal leader Melbouren SF Group 108
    Perhaps and 111
    personality and career 105, 164, 182
    Val's Coffee Lounge and 107–8
McCubbin, Molly 147
McGills Newagency, Melbourne 11, 45, 106, 117, 153, 165, 166, 167, 169, 182
    Binns at 103, 106, 107, 120
    Etherline and 111, 168
    Melbourne SF Club clubrooms and 186
    Rex-Rotary duplicator 110, 113, 114, 119–20
    science fiction source 183–5
McGuinness, Judith 86, 94, 129
McGuinness, Michael 66, 72, 73, 76, 97, 108, 125, 127, 129, 191
McGuinness, Padraic 97, 139
McKenna, Jock 65, 66, 129, 137
McKeown, Geraldine 118, 127, 170
McKillop Street clubrooms, Melbourne SF Club 183, 186
McLelland, Keith 107, 108, 118, 147, 167, 170, 174, 184
McLennan, Marshall 14, 17, 29, 35, 45, 54, 55, 105, 106, 164

magazines and books, post-War scarcity 73
mail order services, books and magazines 168
Malian Press 63, 64, 122
Man Magazine 24, 101
Mandrake the Magician 101
Manly 85, 160
Mariposa Coffee Inn 71
Martin, Ken 81, 94, 125, 129, 144
Mathews, Race 1, 8, 9, 84, 101, 105, 106, 107, 108, 113, 114, 119, 127, 166, 169, 170
    centre of Melbourne fan contacts 1950s 106
    fanzine publishing plans 111
    interstate contacts 105
    McCubbin and 105–6
    personality and career 102, 106, 118
    science fiction collecting 1950s 104
    sole interstate visitor to First Australian SF Convention 77
    visits to First and Second Sydney Conventions 109
Meanjin 122
meetings
    Melbourne Science Fiction Club 178, 180
    Sydney Futurian disagreements and 37, 70
    Sydney venues 68–9
Melbourne SF Group 1953 108
Melbourne 38, 61, 83, 96, 97, 152, 162, 163, 184
    introduction of television 178
    Melbourne, science fiction collecting 104, 153
    Stone and 136–7
    Sydney visitors to 1943 60
Melbourne Bulletin 22, 40, 41, 44, 47, 54–5
Melbourne Convention Centre 3
Melbourne fans 29, 30, 45, 94, 126, 149, 154
    1950–1953 99–119
    1953–56 84, 164–86
    Albury conference and 127
    new generation 1950s 101
    proposal for 1956 convention 135
    publication sources and 104
    rivalry with Sydney fans 22
    Stone and 193
    Sydney disputes and 136, 137, 143
    World War 2 and 54
Melbourne Fantasy Film Group. 172
Melbourne Grammar School 102, 105, 106
Melbourne Science Fiction Club (MSFC) 184
    activities spectrum 187
    club rooms 1966 3
    relocation to Somerset Place 186
    renaming of Melbourne SF Group 178
    recession 1961 and 185
    report 1958 182

Stone and 193
Melbourne Science Fiction Conference 1968 193
Melbourne Science Fiction Group (MSFG) 113, 118, 153, 167
    Arthur C Clarke visit 1954 158
    Binns and 120, 168
    Etherline and 117
    first meeting 1952 106, 107
    Harding and 119
    Hemming play and 174
    meetings 1955 170
    newsletters 114
    Oddfellows Hall meetings 169
    renamed as Melbourne Science Fiction Club 178
    report 1954 135
    report 1956 176
    strengths 164, 165
Melbourne University 119, 168
Mellor, Clive 125, 126, 128, 129, 141
Melody Hall 138
membership
    Australian fandom 1953 152
    Australian SF Society 126, 192
    Melbourne SF Club late 1950s 182
    Melbourne SF Group 1953 108
    Sixth Australian SF Convention (Olympicon) 173–4, 176–7, 180–2
    Sydney fandom 1940 39
    Sydney Futurians surveys 89, 129
    Third Australian Science Fiction Convention 134, 135
Mentor, The (Clarke) 8
Metal Monster, The 1
Metropolis (Lang) 128, 138, 145, 155
Meyer, Rex 14, 81, 86, 95, 97, 108, 114, 124, 125, 127, 129, 142
migrant hostels, Canberra 154
Milcross Book Service 68
military service, Australian fans and 40
Mirka's, Melbourne SF Group and 108
Mirror, The (Sydney) 24
'Miss Denton's Dilemma' (Hemming) 145
Moccadore Café 72, 75, 76
Modern Boy 11
Molesworth, Laura 65, 70, 77, 80, 81, 85, 90, 97, 124, 125, 129, 138, 146, 147, 191
Molesworth, Vol (Voltaire) 14, 16, 18, 22, 23, 24, 25, 30, 34, 40, 43–4, 45, 46, 47, 48, 49–50, 51, 55, 56, 58, 59, 60, 66, 68, 69, 70, 71, 72, 75, 76, 77, 79, 81, 83, 94, 95, 96,

97, 98, 103, 109, 121, 124, 125, 129, 130, 131, 137, 138, 139, 140–1, 144, 146, 147, 149, 154, 156, 167, 188, 190, 192
    academic achievements 86
    Court of Inquiry and 53
    death 1964 190
    fanzines 20–1, 36
    fiction writing 73, 88
    Futurian Society and 26–7, 125, 130
    health problems 1941 38, 39, 52
    Laura Molesworth and 65, 93
    History of Australian Science Fiction Fandom, 1935–1963, A 8
    letter to fandom 1947 61–2
    overseas contacts 105
    parties 1952 85
    personality and career 50, 90–1, 149
    professional publishing and 56–7, 63
    Rosemary Simmons and 90
    Sydney disputes and 1954 109, 143
    tape recordings 136, 147
    Women's Auxiliary proposal and 92
Monash University, Rare Books Collection 9
Monterey Café 72
Morojo 20, 46
Morton, Val 147, 169, 170, 178
Moskowitz, Sam 14
Mount Stromlo astronomical observatory visit 1954 147, 154–5
Mountain District Science Fiction Club 180
Moxon, Keith 17, 22, 29, 30, 38
Moyes, Ian 84, 94, 95, 97, 155
Mumblings from Munchkinland (Nelson) 3–4, 12, 14, 128, 131, 135, 136, 168, 190, 193
Murdoch University, Special Collections 9
Mustchin, Charles 14, 17, 22, 29, 35, 38, 64, 65, 66, 84, 157, 158, 159
    Arthur Clarke visit to 1954 160
Mutschin family 159

Nash, George, bookshop 12, 41
National Fantasy Fan Federation (NFFF) 66, 83, 157
National Library of Australia 155
    Stone and 196
    Special Collection 9
National Service Act 1951, Australian fans and 122
Navy Reserve 182
Nebula 145
Nekromantikon 111
Nelson, Chris 3–4, 9, 12, 14
Neofan Party 58
New Guard 26
New Guinea 55, 60

New Idea 103
new members, Melbourne SF Group 170
New Millennial Harbinger (Bangsund) 194
New South Wales 127, 173, 176
    centre of Australian fandom 1950 66
New Worlds 80, 105, 145, 153, 165, 174
    covers 176
New York 110, 136
New Zealand fans 77, 84, 135, 161, 162
    international links 184
    Sydney fans and 83
    postal links 66
    Australian SF Society members 1954 126
Newcastle and Hunter Valley Science Fiction Society 96, 126, 135
newspaper comic strips, science fiction 101
newspapers
    science fiction stories in 122
    Sydney science fiction conventions and 122
Niagara, RMS, sinking of 30
Nicholson, Doug 8, 9, 76, 84, 86, 94, 95, 108, 110, 112, 116, 128, 129, 130, 131, 134, 139, 140, 144, 146, 147, 149, 151, 167, 170, 172
    story sale to *Galaxy* 87
    Sydney fans reconciliation move 1954 136
Nicholson, Valerie Pauline 90
Nicholson, Hal 97, 156
night life, Melbourne 1950s 100
'No Convention in 55' report (Stone) 142, 166, 172
North American fandom, Australian fandom and 46, 66, 68
North Shore Futurian Society (NSFS) 80, 124, 126, 128, 133
    bid for 1955 Australian Convention 135
    library 1955 149
    Stone and 130, 131, 136–7
    Sydney Convention 1955 and 173
    Thursday Night Group and 140, 143
North Shore Futurian Society Notesheet (*Sonic*) 80, 126, 127, 155
northern suburbs, Sydney 80
Notes and Comments (Stone) 81, 190, 192

Occidental Hotel 149
Oddfellows Hall clubrooms, Melbourne SF Group 108, 169, 173
    difficulties 1954 171
    film showings at 108
Olympic Games, Melbourne 1956 135, 174, 178
Olympicon (Sixth Australian SF Convention) 1956
    Melbourne SF Club and 178
    program book 173
    planning 147, 172, 173
    proceedings 174–6

Operation Fantast 71, 83, 95, 96, 109, 113, 117, 135, 135, 153, 166, 167
    Australian agency 124
    book donation to Adelaide fans 155
    Melbourne fans and 104–5
    publications supplier to Australian fans 68
organisational difficulties, Second Sydney SF Convention 1953 94
O'Shaugnessy, John 127, 170
Outline History of Australian Fandom, Part 1, 1935-1940 (Molesworth) 93
overseas connections
    Antipodes and 120
    Australian fans during World War 2 55
    Australian publications 1950s and 64
    Australian SF Society members and 126
    Crane and 89
    Crozier and 167
    Dard and 162
    Olympicon and 176
Oxford Street 128, 138

paperbacks (pocketbooks), first appearance 63
Park, John 66, 83, 161
pass-on convention funds 174
Pauline, Valerie, and Doug Nicholson 90
peacemakers, early 1950s 90
Peon 109
Perhaps 113, 114, 119, 149, 157
    joint publication with *Bacchanalia* 111
    opinions about 112–13
    production difficulties 110–12
personality-based history 8
Perth 71, 77, 84, 99, 152
    customs authorities and fans 83
Perth Fan News 161
Perth Science Fiction Group 29, 45, 83, 161
Philadelphia world convention 1953 96
photolithography 113
Pitt, Stan 103
plagiarism of American science fiction stories 63
Planet Stories 104
Pohl, Frederik 23
political deviance, Melbourne 1950s 100
Pollard, Howard 29, 45
Popular Science Fiction 122, 152, 188
Porter, Andrew 7–8
Porter, Arthur 147, 154, 155
Portland convention 1949 72
postage delivery time restrictions, international 14

post-war military service, fans and 61
pre-printed covers, *Etherline* 167
Preston Library 103
Preston, unsuitability for clubrooms 169, 171
Preview 110
production difficulties
    Forerunner 88
    Perhaps 110
Profan 44, 54
professional publications 1942 56
professional writer aspirations, Australian 45, 109, 170
program book, Sixth Australian SF Convention 182
promotion aims, Futurian Society 1946 66
prozine editors, Olympicon and 174
prozines 12
    as ship's ballast 33
    Franklin's Lending Library and 104
    import embargo 1940 32, 62
    Harding and 103
    letter columns 14
    Thursday Night Group and 71
    trading of 75
Pseudo Futurian 30
Pseudo Zeus 21
Psychos 21
pulp magazines 7, 11–12
    absence during 1950s 101
Purdey, Bruce 12, 124, 125, 129, 137, 141
    Betty Such and 90

Qantas display, First Australian SF Convention 77
'Quaine' 104
Quality Inn, Sydney Futurians venue 69, 71
Quarterly Associate Member's ticket, Futurian Society 1954 137
Queensland 84, 127, 170, 173
    Australian SF Society members 126
    censorship 153
Queensland Spear Fisherman's Club 160
Question Mark 117, 118, 157, 168
Quiz 24

radio, science fiction on 122
Raethel, Les 76, 91, 124, 125, 129, 136, 137
Rambler 43
Randwick 12, 36, 41
Randwick Intermediate High School 16–17
Rayner, Eric 162, 170

recession 1961, Melbourne Science Fiction Club and 185
regular schedule, *Etherline* 167
relationships and marriages, Sydney Futurians early 1950s 90
Remington typewriter purchase 1954 126
respectability ideal, Stone and 125
Rex Rotary duplicator 111, 119–20
Richmond 166, 171, 173
Richmond Town Hall, Olympicon and 173, 180
Rickard, John 7
right-hand justification 20, 114, 116
    Crozier and 167
Roberts, Alan 12, 23, 24, 38, 46, 55, 57, 61, 62, 84
Roden, Colin 22, 24, 27, 39, 43, 45, 48, 49, 50, 52, 53, 55, 56, 57, 58, 59, 60, 62, 65
Rogers, Buck 11
Rome, David, science fiction writer 196
Roneo 500 duplicator, Australian Fantasy Press Assocation's 113, 120, 160, 164, 166, 168, 171
Rosenblum, Michael 25, 30, 46, 47
Roth, Len 90, 129
Roth, Pauline 80, 90
Rover, The 11
Royal Arcade 33, 63, 89
rural New South Wales, Australian SF Society members 1954 126
Russell, Eric 12, 14, 16, 17–1921, 23, 24, 25, 35, 36, 38, 39, 40, 42, 43, 48, 49, 51, 52, 53, 54, 55, 56, 57, 58, 59, 60, 61, 62, 64, 65, 66, 68, 70, 72, 73, 76, 93
Russell, Joan 128
Russell, Ted 17, 18, 19, 21, 25, 27, 38, 39, 42, 44, 48, 52, 53, 55, 57, 58, 60, 62
Rutherford military camp 55

St James Building clubroom, MSFC and 180
St Kilda 171
Salgram, Barry 147, 174, 175, 176, 181, 183, 184
Santos, Tony 158, 170, 172, 174, 183
'Satellite Series' 152, 193
Sawyer, Bruce 21, 22, 27, 39, 40, 41, 42, 43, 48, 49, 55, 59, 62, 66
Scansion 130, 139, 140–1, 142, 149, 151, 157, 168, 172
'Scansion drunks' 139
science, fans and 25, 121
'science-adventure' label, publishers and 56
Science and Fantasy Fan Reporter 43, 54, 55, 58
Science Fantasy 105, 153, 165
Science Fantasy Club proposal 38
Science Fiction 63
'Science Fiction and Science' (Glick) 95
'Science Fiction and the Development of Modern Literature' (Stone) 95

'Science Fiction as a Specialist Literature' (Nicholson) 95
science fiction collection, Mathews' sale of 118
Science Fiction Courier 73, 74
science fiction discussion objective, Sydney Futurians 35–6, 53–4, 151
Science Fiction Drama Club (Arcturian Players) 128
science fiction fandom
    definition 1
    historians and 6
    See also fandom; fannish and associated entries
science fiction films 1950s 108, 122
Science Fiction League, Australia 15, 16
science fiction libraries 152
    Adelaide group 155–6, 163
    Australian SF Association 191
    Binns and 120
    Brisbane fans 157, 158, 163
    Canberra fans and 154
    Futurian Society 138, 149, 188, 190
    importance of 64
    Melbourne Science Fiction Club late 1950s 183, 186
    Melbourne Science Fiction Group 108, 165–6, 169, 171
    Mountain District Science Fiction Club 180
    North Shore Futurian Society 139
Science Fiction Monthly 122, 152, 170, 188–9
Science Fiction News 81–3, 95, 112, 113, 114, 116, 122, 127–8, 135, 142, 149, 152, 183, 189, 193
Science Fiction News (Second Series) 194–5
Science Fiction Parade 184
science fiction promotion, Stone and 189
science fiction publishing, Sydney 1950s 122, 195–6
Science Fiction Review 18
Science Fiction Times 152, 190, 193, 182, 193
science fiction
    abundance in Brisbane 158
    Australian SF Assocation and 191
    beginnings in *Amazing Stories* 11
    characteristics for readers 103–4
    fan attitudes to 84–5, 140
    history and 5
    import restrictions 1950s and 122
    Jenssen and 102
    McGills Newagency and 165
    Melbourne attitudes to 1950s 100–1
    public acceptability 1950s 62, 92
    public morality campaigns versus 12
    pulp magazines and 12
    Race Mathews' discovery of 102
    scarcity 1950s 101, 152, 184
    Stone's attitudes to 192–4, 196-8
    Sydney's sources 1950s 63

'science fiction' label, negative connotation to publishers 56
'Science in Science Fiction' (Blatt) 145
scientific films, availability 155
Scientifiction 14
scuba diving, Arthur C Clarke and 158
Sebel, Roger 139, 149
second anniversary party, Futurian Society 1941 52
Second Sydney Conference 51
Second Pacific Book of Australian SF, The (ed. Baxter) 195
Second Sydney Science Fiction Convention 1953 93–5
    Crozier's criticism of 166
second-hand book shops, as sources of science fiction 102, 104, 105
    McGills Newsagency 165
Secret Master of Sydney fandom 1950s, Molesworth as 91
sercon fandom
    Stone and 187
    Wastebasket 2 and 116–17
S-F Review 81, 83, 93, 105, 112, 114, 127
SFR War Bulletin 30
Shalders, N J 173
Shanghai 69, 102
Shapiro, Hal 114
Shaw Savil Line 160
ship's ballast, prozines as 33
Silver Starr 103
Silverberg, Bob 109, 110, 111
Simmons, Rosemary 76, 80, 81, 86, 89, 91, 97, 124, 125, 127, 129, 134
    Vol Molesworth and 90
    application to join Futurians 92
Sixth Australian Convention Easter 1958 (Melcon) 149, 176, 180–2
Slant 109
Slater, Ken 65, 69, 104, 105, 110
    offer to Australian fans 68
Smith, Bob 158, 170
Smith, E E, prize competition 89
Smith, Kevin 97
Smith, Ralph 19, 21, 22, 24, 27, 28, 35, 37, 40, 42, 43, 55, 62, 65, 68
Sneary, Rick 184
social activities
    Adelaide fans 156
    Brisbane fans 1950s 158
    early 1950s 85–6
    Futurian Society 1952 86
    Melbourne fans 170
    Sydney fans 40–1, 126, 142
social isolation
    Australian fan groups late 1950s 163

Mervyn Binns 103
　　　science fiction readers 1950s 103
social activities, Adelaide fans 156
socialist ideals, Sydney Futurians 26, 27
Soldiers' Relief Fund 59
Solensteff, Nick 66, 69, 71, 72, 73, 75, 76, 90, 93, 97, 125, 127, 136, 139
　　　academic achievements and career 86, 149
Somerset Place clubrooms, Melbourne SF Club relocation 1961 186
Sonic (North Shore Futurian Society Notesheet) 80, 126, 127
sound recording, Sydney fans 1949 72
South African films 155
South Australia 126, 173
South, Alan 97, 146, 149, 190
Southern Cross Futurian Association 58, 59
Southern Cross Hotel 3, 103
space-adjusting technologies 7
space science movies, Melbourne Group and 172
'Spacehounds' 16–17
Spaceship 109, 111
Spaceward 44, 52, 53
Spaceward Ho! (Molesworth) 56, 103
Spaceways 18, 20, 23
Special Branch, Victorian Police 100
Speed Gordon 101
Sporting Globe 101
Sputnik 1 189
Stanborough, Doug 127
Star Rover 83, 162
Startling Stories 12, 51, 104
State Film Library, Victoria 171
State Library of Victoria, Rare Books Collection 9
stencil-drawn art 110, 116, 120
Stewart, Alan 9
Stone, Graham 8, 12,, 33, 39, 41, 43, 48, 49, 51, 52, 53, 54, 55, 57, 58, 59, 60, 62, 63, 64, 65, 66, 70, 72, 73, 74, 75, 76, 77, 79, 80, 81, 85, 92, 94, 95, 97, 105, 109, 111, 121, 122, 124, 125, 126, 127, 135, 140–1, 143, 144, 149, 152, 161, 162, 166, 173, 182, 187–98
　　　as controversalist 90, 91
　　　Australian Science Fiction Society (ASFS) and 74
　　　disputes with Futurian Society members 1954 129–31
　　　Futurian Society Director 1954 137, 138
　　　group within Sydney fandom 109
　　　Haddon and 1952 93
　　　Melbourne fans and 172
　　　Nicholson and 146
　　　'No Sydney Convention in 1955' 136–7
　　　opposition to North Shore Futurians convention win 136–7
　　　Perhaps and 112, 113

Perhaps 2 and 114–15
S-F Review and 142
Sydney Futurians survey and 1952 89
Veney and 1953 96
Stopgap 74, 76, 77, 83, 84, 85, 105
story telling, Indigenous and Western 5–6
Stratosphere Patrol Stories (Molesworth) 56–7
Stubbs, Len 27
Subterranean City (Hemming) 56
Such, Betty 129
    Bruce Purdy and 90
Sun, The (Sydney) 24, 40
Sun Si Gai Chinese restaurant 73, 142
swear box, Futurian Society meetings 131
Sydcon, failure to hold 47, 51
Sydney 54, 89, 91, 92, 94, 101, 103, 110, 152, 154, 161, 166, 170, 173, 182, 184, 190, 192
    centre of Australian fandom 1953 84
    fandom's disappearance 1958 182
    Melbourne compared with 1950s 100
    sources of science fiction 153
Sydney Bridge Club meetings 91, 92, 95, 124, 125, 128, 131, 135, 138, 139, 142, 143, 149, 151, 184
    Futurian Society members banned from 144
Sydney fandom
    1939–1940 25–39
    1946–1952 61–79
    1952–1953 80–98
    1953–1954 121–32
    1954–1960 133–51
    Albury conference and 127
    Brisbane fandom and 157
    disputes 92, 109, 140
    Melbourne fandom and 22, 105, 109, 172, 180
    new members 1941 41
    other Australian fans and 45
    pronounced dead 1955 149
    prozine parcels 1940 and 32
    Stone and 89, 90, 91, 93, 109, 129–31, 137, 138, 193, 196
    Sydney Push and 149
    World War 2 and 55, 62
Sydney fanzines
    early 1950s 81, 105
    Harding and 116
    Melbourne fanzines and 1953 114
Sydney Futurian 65, 66, 67, 68, 70, 73, 85
Sydney Harbour 80, 144
Sydney Imaginative Film Society 1953 128
Sydney Push 90, 100, 149
Sydney Science Fantasy Society 60

Sydney Science Fiction Association 48
Sydney Science Fiction Conference 1940 39, 41, 43, 44
Sydney Science Fiction Conference 1941 47, 48–9, 50
Sydney Science Fiction Conference 1943, 59–60
Sydney Science Fiction Conference 1955 147
Sydney Science Fiction League 15–16, 27
Sydney Sun 18
Sydney University 72, 86, 90, 145, 149
Sydney University Rare Books Collection 9
Symmons, John 44, 83

table tennis, Melbourne SF Club at Somerset Place 186
Tafe, Betty 157, 161
Tafe, George 157
Tafe, Tom 157
Tafe family 158, 160, 163
Tai Ping Café 142, 149
tape recorders
    American convention links by 66
    science fiction fans and 121
Tasmania 81, 84, 95, 170, 173
Tasmanian fandom 29, 30
    1946 65
    1952–53 83
    1956 report 176
    ASFS members 1954 126
    Tuck and 162
Taurasi, James 15
Taylor Square FSS clubroom 128, 131–2, 140, 158, 188
    McIlraith's Chambers clubrooms 1953 128–9
    abandonment 1955 149
    members banned from 144
    move to 1953 128–9
Taylor, Keith 21, 22, 29, 30, 41, 42, 44, 45–6
Technical Book Shop 184
Telefan 44
Telepath 73–4, 142
television, arrival in Australia 1956 121, 178
Terrific 80
'That's the Way it Goes' (Hemming) 135
thematic history, chronological history versus 9
third anniversary party, Adelaide Society 1956 157
third birthday celebration meeting, Futurian Society 58
Third Sydney Conference 1942 53
Third Sydney SF Convention Easter 1954, organisation 124, 133–5
Thrilling Wonder Stories 102, 104, 105

Thrills Incorporated 63, 64, 79, 80
Thring, Frank 100
Thursday Night Group meetings 73, 74, 75, 76, 77, 80, 85, 88, 91, 92, 96, 110, 124–5, 126, 139, 139, 140, 142, 149, 153, 172, 176, 182, 184
    absorption of North Shore Futurian Society 143
    Can-Con and 147
    commencement 1948 69
    convention victory 137
    decline and commercialisation 1955 149
    Etherline and 168
    Futurian Society and 141, 143, 149, 187
    late 1950s 151
    library and 93
    Melbourne fans and 173
    popularity 1949 71
    premises change 1953 128
    Second Sydney Science Fiction Convention 1953 and 95
    Stone and 130
    see also Sydney Science Fiction Group
Thurston, Bob 127, 137, 146
time-space compression 7
Tolkien, J R R 104
Tomorrow (never published) 119
Toorak Teachers' College 118
Toronto Worldcon 1948 (Torcon), Sydney Futurians and 66, 68
total war footing, Australia 1942 54
Trading Bureau, *Etherline* 167
tram travel, Melbourne fans and 102
'Transportation in the Future' 145
travel difficulties 1953 152
Trial & Error 127
Tuck, Don 14, 17, 22, 29, 30, 33, 40, 43, 44, 55, 64, 65, 66, 74, 83–4, 105, 108, 112, 120, 142, 145, 164–5, 167, 173, 191
    arrival in Melbourne 1942 54
    collecting career 162–3
    Handbook process 163
    see also *Handbook of Science Fiction and Fantasy* (Tuck)
Tucke, Henry 139
Tucker, Bob 19, 20, 22, 23, 41, 46, 51
Tudor Hotel 149
Tuesday Night Group 1960 151
Turnbull, Bill 137, 146
Turner, E R 102
Turner, George 14, 40
    attraction to science fiction 11
    letter in *Amazing Stories* 1932 13
typewriter purchase dispute, Sydney fandom 1953 123
Tyranny of Distance, The (Blainey) 6

Tyrrell, Bill 158

Ugh 61, 81, 84, 85, 108, 112
Ultra 19, 20, 22, 23, 29, 30, 35, 36, 42, 43, 46, 49, 50, 54, 55
underground and illegal night life, Melbourne 1950s 100
Underwater Research Group, Arthur Clarke visit 1954 160
Unidentified Flying Object craze, science fiction and 122
Union Steamship Company of New Zealand 161
United Australia Party 26
University of New South Wales 149
University of Sydney 9, 72, 129,
university students, Sydney fans as 72
Unknown (BRE edition) 33
unsolicited magazine parcels 68
Upwey 180, 181, 183
USA 158, 174
US fandom, Australian fandom and 18, 19, 23
US science fiction, Australian currency restrictions and 31
US Information Service 155

Val's Coffee Lounge 107, 108, 109
van Vogt, A E 89
Veney, Bill 8, 14, 15, 16, 18–19, 20, 21, 22, 23, 25, 26, 27, 28, 35, 36, 37–8, 39, 40, 43, 44, 45, 47, 48, 49, 51, 55, 59, 61, 65, 66, 69, 70, 72, 73, 75, 76, 79, 81, 84, 92, 93, 94, 95, 96, 97, 107, 108, 109, 110, 130, 136, 139, 144, 146, 157, 167, 195
    Court of Inquiry and 53
    Futurian aims and 26, 58
    personality 89
    review of *Perhaps* 112
    versus Stone 1953 96
venue planning, Olympicon 173
Venus 41
Vertical Horizons 81, 83, 86, 93, 127, 128, 155
Vice Squad, Victorian Police 100
Victoria 127, 176, 180
    Australian SF Society members 1954 126
Korean War 1954 121
Vision of Tomorrow 1969–70 195
Voice of the Imagi-Nation 20, 23, 46, 51, 55, 62

Walsh, Dennis 156
War of the Worlds (film) 122, 128, 141, 143
Warner Jnr, Harry 14, 18, 19, 20, 23
'Warrigo' 161
wartime defence industries, fans and 55
wartime restrictions, fanzine publishing and 41, 54

Wastebasket 116–18, 120, 161
Watson's Bay 144
wedding, Giels and Glick 1955 170
Weinbaum, Stanley 28
Weird Tales 12, 100, 101
Wellington (New Zealand) fandom 120, 184
Wells, H G 11
Wentworth Falls outing 85, 86
Westercon 8, support for Olympicon 173
Western Australia 87, 95, 176
    Australian Science Fiction Society members 1954 126
    censorship 153
Western culture, Australia and 7, 24
'What is Fandom' (Stone) 77, 79
Wheelahan, Kevin 113, 117, 118, 167, 168, 170
White, Bill 57
Whiteford, Wynne 170, 174
'Who Goes There' (Campbell) 99
Wilkes, Alan 76
Wilkes, Diana 76, 80
    Arthur Haddon and 90
Williams, Ken 22, 27, 40, 70
Williams, Norma 14, 15, 80, 85, 88, 139, 146
    personality 89–90
Williams, Royce 63, 66, 68, 88, 97, 149, 151
Wilson, Mike 158, 159
Windsor Theatre 108
Wollheim, Don 23, 25
women attendees, Sydney Science Fiction Convention 1952 80
women, Futurians membership and 28, 92
Wonder Stories 12, 14, 15, 19, 33, 48
Wonder Stories Annual 105
Woolhara Golf Club cocktail party 1953 95
Woomera 12, 66, 73, 77, 93
World of Tomorrow Symposium, The' 133
World science fiction conventions, Australia and 7, 65
World Science Fiction League, proposed 68
World War 2 38, 55
    Australian fandom and 30, 40, 54, 55
    British fandom and 30
Worldcon award 1962, Don Tuck 163
Wright, Bill 9, 183

YMCA Building, Sydney, 53, 160
Youd, Sam 30

Young, Brig 175
younger Sydney fans 1954, conventions and 135

'Zero Equals Nothing' (Stone and Williams) 63–4
Zeus 21–2, 36, 42, 43, 55

www.ingramcontent.com/pod-product-compliance
Lightning Source LLC
Chambersburg PA
CBHW031241290426
44109CB00012B/387